DISC

`D1175006`

HARRY TRUMAN'S CHINA POLICY

HARRY TRUMAN'S CHINA POLICY

McCARTHYISM AND THE DIPLOMACY OF HYSTERIA, 1947-1951

Lewis McCarroll Purifoy

New Viewpoints
A Division of Franklin Watts
New York / London / 1976

New Viewpoints
A Division of Franklin Watts
730 Fifth Avenue
New York, New York 10019

Library of Congress Cataloging in Publication Data

Purifoy, Lewis McCarroll.
  Harry Truman's China policy.

  Includes bibliographical references and index.
    1. United States—Foreign relations—China.
2. China—Foreign relations—United States.   3. United
States—Foreign relations—1945—   4. Internal
security—United States.   I. Title.
E183.8.C5P87 ·   327.73′051   76–16060
ISBN 0–531–05386–5
ISBN 0–531–05593–0 pbk.

For Betty Lou

CONTENTS

INTRODUCTION

A curious thing about the cold war is that the greatest tension has been sustained in the Far East, and it is only there that violence has erupted. In the center of Europe, where Russia and the United States squared off for so long in angry confrontation, very little of consequence ever happened. And, in view of the fact that American fears reached their peak during the very period when the nation's preponderance of power over the Soviet Union (including a monopoly of nuclear weapons) was also at its peak, one wonders if there was ever the likelihood that anything would happen. The balance of power established by the two superpowers at the end of World War II remains intact, and, in retrospect, one notes that no serious effort has been made by either side to upset it. That much of the cold war rhetoric has been false and cynical was noted by General Douglas MacArthur in 1957 when he observed: "Our government has kept us in a perpetual state of fear—kept us in a continuous stampede of patriotic fervor—with the cry of grave national emergency. . . . yet, in retrospect, these disasters seem never to have happened, seem never to have been quite real."

Moral-ideological slogans have been used to cover the aggressive acts of the superpowers or to distract attention from them or to generate heat among the masses on behalf of them. But the slogans usually had not the slightest relationship to the particular nation's reasons for acting and served only to confuse the people as to the real object of their nation's foreign policy and, further, to inject so much passion into its discussion as to reduce the real object to a position of secondary importance. In spite of all the moral breast-beating and ideological posturing, the United States and Russia have achieved a fairly satisfactory relationship. Spheres of interest, levels of restraint, and rituals of protocol have been worked out with some precision; and all the talk is of détente.

It has been quite otherwise with America's Far Eastern policy, for on that subject emotion has been sustained at such a level of intensity as to preclude any possibility of dealing with Far Eastern problems in a calm and rational manner. Both the United States and China have been reckless of speech and behavior, but since it is the power of the United States that has encircled China, rather than the other way around, the major responsibility for the tension and violence that have convulsed China's periphery for the past twenty years must be borne by the United States.

When China fell to the Communists in 1949, the United States chose to feel itself insulted and threatened, although, as it turned out, China was not even so aggressive as to reconquer all of its own territory—Outer Mongolia, Formosa, Kowloon, Macao, Hong Kong. Nonetheless, America's China-obsessed politicians have engaged in some very strange activities: the incredible phenomenon of "McCarthyism," driving able and dedicated men from the foreign service, while elevating Chiang Kai-shek to the very top of the hagiography of American heroes; political leaders furiously denouncing Red China and, in all seriousness, demanding the "unleashing of Chiang"; a secretary of state actually threatening China with "the bomb" in defense of small islands within spitting distance of the China mainland; another secretary raising the specter of the "yellow peril"; and the United States contriving to get itself involved in two sizable wars, which were the result, more than the cause, of America's "China madness."

The strangest thing of all is that the United States has spent its fury in Korea, Vietnam, Laos, and Cambodia. All of these little states are huddled around the fringes of that great enigma Communist China, which is the common factor in all of America's involvements on the Asian continent. And since all matters having to do with continental Asia must ultimately take China into account, it is with China that the United States must finally negotiate an end to its bloody confrontations with that country's small neighbors. That China has long been willing to negotiate seriously with the United States on these matters is indicated in the fact that discussions between the two nations have been going on intermittently, in either Warsaw or Geneva, and more recently in Washington and Peking, for the past twenty years. Kenneth Young pointed out as early as 1968, in his book *Negotiating With the Chinese Communists,* that the Chinese had always indicated an eagerness to regularize diplomatic and commercial relations with the United States. But he also noted that they had made it abundantly clear that a precondition for fruitful negotiations was *America's acceptance of China as a great power.*

Acceptance of China as a great power requires the withdrawal of American power from those positions that encroach upon China's traditional "sphere of interest" and that constitute a threat to Chinese security. Included in this sphere of interest are all of those nations—Korea, Vietnam, Laos, Cambodia, Thailand, Burma, and Formosa—whose proximity to China and whose ancient associations with that land create a natural economic and cultural relationship. This is indeed China's natural sphere of interest, and it is not a more extensive one than that claimed by the United States in the Western Hemisphere or by Russia in Eastern Europe. Neither Russia nor the United States, nor any other Western power, has a moral warrant for intervening in China's relationship with its small neighbors, for their own activities in the Orient have never been conducted in any manner other than under the gun.

Indeed, it is the shift in the "balance of guns" that provides the ultimate argument for America's disengagement from the Asian continent: China is rapidly approaching the time when it will have the nuclear capability for attacking the United States. Since it has always been the nuclear threat held over the head of China that has made possible America's military encirclement of that nation from island and beachhead positions around its periphery, once China has acquired the nuclear capacity with which to neutralize that threat, the American position on the Asian continent will become untenable. Thus, to avoid confrontation with a nuclear-armed nation of 800 million people on its own doorsteps, the United States must remove its power from the Asian continent within the next few years. The great irony of it is that the United States is asked to do no more than to return to that offshore position toward which it had been moving during the period 1947–1950 and which it embraced as official policy in January 1950.

The necessary policy reversal was begun, albeit grudgingly, by the first administration of Richard Milhouse Nixon (1969–1972) through his policy of the "lowered profile in Asia." This involved a reduction of the American military commitment to Korea and Formosa, withdrawal of American troops from the fighting in Vietnam, and the beginning of the normalization of relations with Communist China. Doubtless the process will continue, and when American power has finally been returned to that offshore position set for it by

Secretary of State Dean Acheson on January 12, 1950, the "cycle of madness" will have been completed.

It will be the purpose of this study to show that the tragic cycle the nation is in the process of completing was totally *unnecessary*. The "wisdom of hindsight," purchased at the horrendous cost of twenty years of violence and bloodshed around the periphery of China, was already available to the nation in 1950 as the "wisdom of foresight," for the Truman Administration knew at that time that it should not, under any circumstances, become involved in a land war in Asia. This is not theory or conjecture but plain historical fact, demonstrated by the administration's stern refusal to become involved in China's civil war during the period 1947–1950 and by its policy statements of January 5 and 12, 1950, indicating that it would not, in the future, involve itself militarily on the continent of Asia. America's leaders knew how to defend the nation and how to secure its economic interests, and they knew that a military adventure in Asia was not the way to do either.

The desperate American lunge at the Asian continent in 1950 cannot be explained in terms of national interests, for there simply were none on that continent that justified military intervention. Certainly the ever-popular economic interest cannot explain it, for, if China, with its vast potential for serving American economic interests, had not been worth a fight, then those pathetic little appendages of China—Korea, Formosa, Indochina—most assuredly were not. Neither can orthodox "containmentism" explain it, for the offshore line of January 12, 1950 (Aleutians, Japan, Ryukyus, Philippines), was laid down by Secretary of State Acheson precisely for "containment" purposes. In fact, the more validity there may have been in the theory that a "world Communist conspiracy" was stalking America, the greater the necessity for the United

States to stand back from Asian beachheads—untenable in that case—and to base its defense upon an easily defensible offshore line. Even America's "imperialist tradition" in the Far East argued strongly against continental involvement rather than in favor of it. Neither the "carving up of China" by the great powers during the 1890s, nor the Japanese attacks on China in 1931 and 1937, nor the Communist threat to China in the 1940s had lured the United States into such a foolhardy course.

And so one must look for the explanation of the calamitous policy decisions of the 1950s not within the context of a calm analysis of national interests, but within the context of the unbridled hysteria of the time. It was the frenzied McCarthyite attacks upon the government for its alleged "softness on Communism"—and only this—that brought about the reversal of America's policy of disengagement from the Asian continent and frightened policy-makers into a military-ideological crusade against Communist China. This was a crusade that few people dared oppose, despite its blatant hypocrisy and its essentially irrational character. That it was hypocritical is demonstrated in its willingness to support any non-Communist government, no matter how reactionary and oppressive; and that it was irrational is revealed in its careful avoidance of any direct confrontation with the very Communist powers it was ostensibly designed to contain.

It is one of the greatest of paradoxes that the national leaders who offered the most determined resistance to the McCarthy attacks should themselves have become the most determined "McCarthyites" in foreign affairs. This is not to say that the nation's leaders and opinion-makers embraced "external McCarthyism" in any fully conscious or deliberate sense, but it is to say that they allowed themselves to be panicked by McCarthyism's extreme anti-Communism into equating America's real interests with an ill-conceived ideological crusade. In an atmosphere heavy with suspicion and hate, they so completely lost their bearings, or were so overborne by fear, that they could no longer keep the realities in proper perspective. They came to speak of Communism abroad as McCarthy spoke of it at home; and the rhetoric of McCarthyism, only slightly refined, became the official government language for speaking of that nebulous menace known as "the Communists."

Whether America's policy-planners began speaking the rhetoric of anti-Communist extremism because they had actually convinced themselves that Communist China was a threat to the United States or, what is more likely, because this was the only way they knew to combat the McCarthyites, they had no choice but to suit their policies to their rhetoric, which meant that they must lunge blindly at any movement on the Asian continent that smacked of Communism, so long as it was a small movement that could be "contained" by what came to be defined as a "limited war." It was only a token containment, for nothing of consequence was ever contained —or could be—from those tenuous Asian beachheads. In fact, they were never intended to contain anything but the fury of the McCarthyites in America.

L. M. P.

HARRY TRUMAN'S CHINA POLICY

CHAPTER ONE

America's "Chiang Kai-shek Problem": How to Disengage from the Asian Continent (1947)

The American people, caught up in the euphoria of a victorious peace, were not prepared in 1945 for the painful knowledge that "Victory Day" of history's greatest holocaust was but the first day of a strange new kind of conflict, which opened up the possibility of even greater horrors. Neither were they prepared to see their erstwhile allies, the Russian and Chinese Communists, cast so soon in the villainous role of the Nazis. While not many people shared the opinion of General Patrick Hurley (America's wartime ambassador to China) that their Red Chinese allies were little different from "Oklahoma Republicans," perhaps too many Americans were misled by the fact that Communists had celebrated as loudly as anyone the coming of the "democratic millennium" with the war's end. But if it turned out that China's Reds had in mind something entirely different from the "American dream" when they spoke of "democracy," then so much the worse for them. America's "man in China," with American help, would build it without them; for surely Chiang Kai-shek was, as

wartime propaganda affirmed and as Americans generally believed, one of the world's great democratic spirits.

In an effort to save Chiang Kai-shek from the wrath of the
Communists, which in American opinion meant saving China,
President Harry Truman commissioned one of the nation's
most distinguished citizens, General George Catlett Marshall,
to go to China in December 1945 to try to head off the civil
war that was threatening between Mao Tse-tung's Communist
Party and Chiang Kai-shek's Kuomintang (Nationalist) Party.
It was hoped that America's great soldier-statesman could
perform the miracle of "mixing oil and water" (as General
Douglas MacArthur would later put it), that he could actually
establish a pro-American government in China with the acquiescence of the Communist Party. This would have been a
happy consummation indeed, for America's entire Far Eastern
policy was built upon the premise that stability in China, and
thus in the Far East, could be achieved through an American-
sponsored Chinese government under the leadership of Chiang
Kai-shek and his Kuomintang Party.

As it turned out, the problem could not be solved at the
negotiating table, for the Communists would not place their
armies under Chiang's control, and Chiang would not accept
an armed Communist Party within his government. When
negotiations broke down, at least Chiang's course was clear:
If he would have China, he must fight for it. But from that
moment, American policy began to fall into a state of confusion. The agonizing question confronting the United States
was this: Would it be willing to go to war to establish Chiang
Kai-shek's dominance in China and, with it, a "pax Ameri-
cana" in the Far East? Unhappily, the nation was no better
able to resolve this question in the 1940s than it had been in
the years before World War II. It simply did not know, and
never would discover, what it wanted in the Far East.

Before World War II the only serious concern of the United

States in China had been the Open Door policy; and keeping that door and all other doors open to American economic enterprise would continue to be a major object of the nation's foreign policy. This requires no special proof; American statesmen plainly stated it, without embarrassment or apology. Dean Acheson told the House Subcommittee on Postwar Economic Planning in 1944, "The United States has unlimited creative energy. The important thing is markets. We have got to see that what the country produces is used and is sold under financial arrangements which make its production possible."[1]

The soldier George C. Marshall saw this matter just as clearly and warned that the failure of America's policy of economic rehabilitation of war-torn areas of the world would result in "the cumulative loss of foreign markets and sources of supply [which] would unquestionably have a depressing influence on our domestic economy and would drive us to increased measures of government control."[2] Other government and business leaders, including President Harry Truman, shared this view. After all, it was a traditional American policy and it did have the merit of being concerned with a *real* national interest, if not a *vital* one.

But the Open Door had never been a matter over which the United States would go to war; the most the nation could muster by way of protest to the Japanese invasion of Manchuria in 1931 had been the ineffectual policy of "non-recognition." The American people were no more willing in 1945 than they had been in 1931 to fight real battles on behalf of

1. Quoted in William Appleman Williams, *The Tragedy of American Diplomacy* (New York: Dell, revised and enlarged, 1962), p. 235. In this brilliant and provocative work, Williams shows that probably the strongest force moving the United States toward its expansive postwar foreign policy was not so much reaction to Russian aggressiveness as it was the almost neurotic fear of American leaders that depression would result from the failure to find expanding markets for America's expanding economy.

2. *Ibid.*, p. 271.

an economic principle such as the Open Door. Neither would they be inclined, without years of indoctrination, to intervene in the domestic strife of other nations, nor to build massive defenses against developing nations that *might* become powerful and that *might* conceive aggressive designs against the United States in some vague and distant future. Thus, when General Marshall returned from China to assume the duties of secretary of state in January 1947, he found very little disagreement with his own strongly held view that the nation should not get itself bogged down in the morass of China's civil war. There were no outcries about "loss of credibility" or "leaving America defenseless" when all but 10,000 of 113,000 American troops were withdrawn from China in 1946–1947. No one dared suggest a military adventure on any part of the Asian mainland.[3]

Actually, there was no reason why the United States should have entertained for an instant the thought of intervening directly in China's civil war. The nation's vital interests were more than adequately protected by the military situation resulting from World War II. The massive air and naval power of the United States, operating from the numerous island positions occupied during the war, guaranteed that the United States would, for the foreseeable future, control the Pacific Ocean right up to the shores of the Asian continent. Thus, American security on its Pacific side—the only *vital* interest in the region—was provided for in much greater depth than was necessary, without even taking into account the ultimate defense of nuclear weapons.

The nation's secondary interests were also safeguarded, for the United States was assured an important voice in all inter-

3. Edith Nourse Rogers complained in the House of Representatives that the removal of troops from China endangered the safety of the United States, but she found no support for this astonishing view. See *Congressional Record,* XCIII, 80th Cong., 1st Sess. (1947), p. 693.

national affairs of the Far East as well as secure access to every friendly port in the Orient. And all of those ports were likely to remain friendly (that is, open to trade) so long as the United States adhered to its traditional policy of not interfering in the internal affairs of other nations and so long as it did not threaten them by pressing too closely with its military power. Even Communist states, and others that might socialize their instruments of production, would be eager to trade with the United States, for they too would need the capital goods that only the United States could supply in abundance. They would, of course, insist upon trade between equals, carried on at the water's edge; but, under these conditions, there was every reason to believe that the Open Door would remain intact, whoever governed particular nations.[4]

Given such a position of impregnable strength, the wisest course for the United States would have been one of "splendid neutrality," of setting its face sternly against all meddling in other people's affairs, particularly on the mainland of Asia. But the United States was no more willing to let well enough

4. Ironically, America's Open Door policy came nearer to fulfillment than it ever had during its fifty-year history when the Reds came to power in China in 1949. The "territorial and administrative integrity of the Chinese government," one of the stated purposes of the Open Door, was achieved for the first time in over a century, and a *Chinese* government was able to impose its effective jurisdiction over all of China, except for Formosa and Outer Mongolia where the intervention of the United States and the Soviet Union, respectively, prevented China's national unification. The other major principle of the Open Door, "equality of commercial opportunity" in China, could have been achieved if the United States had remained true to its traditional policy of non-intervention in China's internal affairs, as it had vowed it would. And the latter continues to be an objective that can be achieved at any time the United States is willing to quit its intervention in China's internal affairs (Formosa) and remove its military threat from China's borders. This is borne out in the fact that trade with the United States has always been a major aim of the Chinese Communists, as shown in a study by Kenneth P. Young, *Negotiating With the Chinese Communists: The American Experience, 1953–1967* (New York: McGraw-Hill, 1968).

alone than it was to go to the opposite extreme of direct intervention in China's civil war. The only alternative then would
be to work for the establishment of a friendly—and presumably
democratic—government through assistance to Chiang Kai-
shek and his Kuomintang Party and to hope against hope that
this would not lead to deeper involvement.

This was a desperate gamble from the start, for the Kuomintang was a poor thing upon which to build a foreign policy. Secretary of State Marshall had little faith in its fighting
qualities and even less in its ability to administer a government or inspire a nation. This he had made quite clear when
he reported on his China mission in January 1947. While re-
serving his severest castigations for the Communists, Marshall
stated some plain truths about the Kuomintang. He deplored
"the dominating influence of the military" in the party and of
the reactionaries who "counted on substantial American support regardless of their actions." [5] Gloomily, he concluded
that the salvation of the situation "would be the assumption
of leadership by the liberals in the Government and in the
minority parties, a splendid group of men, but who as yet lack
the political power to exercise a controlling influence." [6] Marshall did not say under what circumstances this miracle should
be contemplated, but on the off chance that it might occur, he
continued the policy of supplying limited aid to the Chiang
government.

Substantial help had already been given that government,
more than $1 billion in military and economic assistance hav-
ing been provided in the year after V-J day. Shipments of war
matériels to the Chiang government had been suspended in

5. *The China White Paper* (Stanford: Stanford University Press, 1967);
originally published as *United States Relations With China,* Department of
State Publication 3573, Far Eastern Series 30, p. 292; cited hereinafter as
China White Paper.

6. *Ibid.*

August 1946 in an effort to convince the Communists that the Marshall mission was mediating in good faith and not showing partiality to the other side, which, in fact, it was. But on May 26, 1947, four months after mediation efforts ended, the prohibition on arms shipments was lifted and war goods began to flow again.[7] Marshall was unhappy about continuing aid, which some congressmen were beginning to characterize as "operation rathole," and on July 6, 1947, he warned Chiang Kai-shek that the United States was "perturbed over the economic deterioration resulting from the spread of hostilities . . . and could only assist as conditions develop which give some beneficial results."[8]

But Marshall was not free to thus summarily cut off aid to the Chiang government, his freedom of action being limited by the strong psychic involvement of the American people with China. A number of myths about that land, created or greatly enhanced by World War II propaganda, would make it very difficult for the United States to break loose from its entanglement with Kuomintang China. The oldest and most tenacious of these myths held that the traditional American involvement in China was an idealistic one and that there existed an old and deep friendship between the American and Chinese peoples.[9]

7. American marines in China did not wait for the lifting of the ban before they began turning over their artillery and small arms ammunition to the Kuomintang armies in April 1947; by September they had delivered 5,600 tons of such matériel to Chiang's forces. Moreover, during the period when the embargo was in effect, as Secretary Marshall later told the House Committee on Foreign Affairs, "there was a great deal [non-military goods] that was coming in through the surplus property transactions." *Ibid.,* pp. 356, 692.

8. *Ibid.,* pp. 251–252.

9. Dean Acheson, in reviewing the nation's historic China policy in 1949, spoke glowingly of this alleged ancient friendship; and the distinguished China scholar Tang Tsou marred somewhat an excellent work on America's China policy when he concluded on a sentimental note, be-

Actually, the American concern with China had never been disinterested. No nation had moved with more alacrity to take advantage of the "unequal treaties" that China had been forced to concede to the great powers after Great Britain's brutal assault upon that helpless nation in the mid-nineteenth century.[10] And the United States had joined with other powers in sending troops to China in 1900 to beat back the attempts of the Chinese Boxers to expel the unwanted foreigners from their soil. The vaunted Open Door principle, which sought to uphold the "territorial integrity" of China, was designed for no other purpose than to prevent the foreclosure of American commercial interests by the great powers, which were carving "spheres of interest" for themselves out of the body of China.

Neither material assistance nor moral encouragement was given to Sun Yat-sen in his efforts to create a parliamentary democracy in China after the fall of the Ch'ing dynasty in 1911; and when Dr. Sun was forging his Kuomintang Party into an instrument for democratizing China in the 1920s, it was the Russian Bolsheviks—not Americans—who gave him assistance. The United States did not recognize the Kuomintang as the government of China until 1928, after it had fought its way to a predominant position and taken a sharp political turn to the right. Neither did the United States aid China against Japanese aggression until it began to feel itself threatened by Japan; nor did it give up its special privileges

---

moaning the failure of American ideals in China. See Dean Acheson's "Letter of Transmittal," *China White Paper* and Tang Tsou, *America's Failure in China, 1941–1950* (Chicago: University of Chicago Press, 1963), pp. 590–591.

10. The term "unequal treaties" has reference to those treaties extorted from China during the nineteenth century and enjoyed by most of the great powers, including the United States. Among their infamous provisions were: the principle of "extraterritoriality," the "treaty tariffs" (limiting the right of the Chinese government to set its own tariffs in its own ports), and special protection for Christian missionaries in China.

under the "unequal treaties" until 1942 when World War II, not friendship, made America the ally of China.

If idealism is to be found in America's historic relations with China, one must look to the missionary movement for it. Undoubtedly many ordinary Americans conceived strong feelings of friendliness toward the Chinese people—at least, the Christian Chinese—as they contributed their nickels and dimes to the China missions; and they probably felt a warm glow when they heard returned missionaries, of whom there was a constant stream, tell wondrous tales of the conversion of the heathen. But even this philanthropical enterprise was tainted by the fact that it was protected by provisions of the "unequal treaties" and diminished by the fact that Americans in China, other than the missionaries, generally treated their "hosts" as second-class citizens in their own country and referred to them derisively as "Chinks" or "Slopes." The "friendship and idealism" myth, as a fact, rested on no more firm a foundation than that of Chinese impotence and American sentimentality. Nonetheless, as enhanced by World War II, it became a living presence to muddle all American thinking about China.

Then there was the "Great China" myth, which assumed that China, if not already a great power, could easily be made one by American proclamation. Thus it was, as the *China White Paper* solemnly records, that "American recognition of China as one of the Great Powers was demonstrated in the fall of 1943." [11] As it turned out, the Kuomintang government

11. The process of conferring "great power" status upon China began in October 1942 when the United States and Great Britain, by treaty, relinquished their "extraterritorial and related rights in China." This was followed by congressional repeal, in December 1943, of the Chinese Exclusion Acts, and by the inclusion of China, in October 1943, as a signatory of the Declaration of Four Nations on General Security, "which recognized the right and responsibility of China to participate jointly with the other great powers [the United States, Great Britain, and Russia] in the prosecu-

could not even fill the power vacuum left in China by the departure of the Japanese, which explains why it was necessary, in the Yalta Agreement of 1945, to concede to the Russians the right to partially fill that vacuum in Manchuria. But how stubbornly Americans clung to the view that the claims of power by others (Russia's attempt to fill the Manchurian power vacuum) should give way to their own worthy objective (filling that power vacuum with idealistic proclamations) was revealed in the angry outcries that would later be raised against the Yalta concessions.

Closely associated with the "Great China" myth was one that held that the United States was somehow responsible for the fate of China. This was a proposition of exceptional arrogance, and when the nation to be molded was as large, as turbulent, and as far removed, culturally and spatially, as China from the United States, it was quite unrealistic. Of course, no American statesman has ever confessed that this was a part of official thinking, let alone official policy. But it should be carefully noted that in the "China debate," which rocked America during the 1950s and in which the government participated directly, it was precisely this point that was debated in the astonishing question: "How did *we* lose China?"

Beyond the realm of myth, the United States was playing a very practical game in the Far East in which it expected the Kuomintang Party and China to play a crucial role. And that "game" was emphatically an "American game," as Congressman Mike Mansfield candidly revealed, when he explained the policy on February 2, 1947, to his colleagues in the House of Representatives: "Our policy in China is one based on national welfare. We want expanding opportunities for trade, we want to prevent China from becoming a satellite of

---

tion of the war, the organization of the peace, and the establishment of machinery for postwar international cooperation." *China White Paper,* pp. 36–37.

Russia, and we want to see China become the bastion for peace in the Far East." [12] The congressman expected China to do a great deal for America: to maintain the peace in the Far East—an American peace, be it noted, not a Russian one—and to provide expanding markets for the American economy.

That the Kuomintang might actually be able to accomplish the Herculean task assigned it had not seemed beyond the realm of possibility in 1941 when it became America's World War II ally. This political party, with its own military arm, had been fashioned in the 1920s by Dr. Sun Yat-sen, with Russian Bolshevik help, as an instrument for transforming China into a parliamentary democracy. After Dr. Sun's death in 1925, the Kuomintang gave every indication that it was the power to be reckoned with in China when it moved vigorously, under Chiang Kai-shek's leadership, to unite China and, apparently, attained that objective by 1928. Then, having broken with the Communists of its own left-wing in 1927, the Kuomintang set out upon a relentless campaign to destroy this last dissident element and, apparently, succeeded in that undertaking by 1935.

But appearances were deceiving. China's unity turned out to be illusory, having been brought about, in large measure, by a patchwork of agreements with regional warlords. Moreover, the Communists had not really been defeated, only driven into interior bases from which they steadily built and expanded their strength. Thus, the Japanese invasion of China in 1937 put Chiang on the horns of a cruel dilemma, from which he escaped by entering into an uneasy truce—and nominal United Front—with his old Communist enemies. Adversity seemed to revitalize the Kuomintang, and it manifested a degree of heroic idealism in the early days of the struggle against the Japanese from its interior capital of Chungking.

12. *Congressional Record, op. cit.,* p. 767.

But this heroic phase did not last, and the party's decline was swift during the 1940s. It moved along a disastrous course of militarism and reaction, while the Communists, with increasing success, usurped its role as champion of the peasant masses and leader in the cause of Chinese nationalism.

Little noticing these developments, Americans built their own heroic image of Chiang Kai-shek. They would listen to no evil spoken of a man believed to be a great democrat and Christian, one who had stood up for years, in lonely isolation, against totalitarian aggressors—whether Chinese Communists or Japanese militarists. How strong America's infatuation with Chiang had grown by the war's end is reflected somewhat in the following statement, again quoting the words of Congressman Mike Mansfield:

> Chiang is the one man who can make Chinese unity and independence a reality. His faults can be understood when the complexities of the Chinese puzzle are studied and they are no more uncommon than the faults of other leaders of the United Nations. We are committed to Chiang and we will help him to the best of our ability. He and he alone can untangle the present situation because in spite of the things he has done, *he is China*. [Italics supplied.] [13]

Since these words were spoken by an American congressman of some sophistication, it is not difficult to imagine how much grander was the average citizen's view of Chiang. And so it is little wonder that, even after the Kuomintang had registered one of history's most spectacular failures, Americans refused to blame the debacle on the Generalissimo or to speak any ill of him.

Very little of the truth about Chiang Kai-shek and his regime was ever spoken in the United States. "Owing partly to censorship but more to voluntary reticence," Barbara Tuch-

13. *Time*, January 22, 1945.

man has written, "the press up to 1943 published nothing realistic about the brave and favorite ally [China]. Probably never before had the people of one country viewed the government of another with misapprehension so complete." [14] Of the role of the American church press in building up the image of Chiang, Mrs. Tuchman commented, "They overpraised Chiang Kai-shek, and once committed to his perfection regarded any suggestion of blemish as inadmissible." [15] Indeed, how could one criticize American Protestantism's favorite convert, especially after he had been apotheosized on the cover of *Time* magazine as the "man of the year" for 1937.[16]

Few Americans knew anything of the dark side of the Chiang character, for example, that Chiang's conversion to Christianity had been a part of the price he paid for the hand in marriage of Mei-ling Soong, through whom he gained important connections with international banking circles, a foot in the door of the powerful Protestant establishment of the United States (he converted to the Soongs' Methodist faith at the time), and an added claim to the mantle of Sun Yat-sen (who, through this marriage, became his posthumous brother-in-law). And not many people were aware that Chiang had

14. Barbara W. Tuchman, *Stilwell and the American Experience in China, 1911–1945* (New York: Macmillan, 1970), p. 355.

15. *Ibid.*, p. 188.

16. The Generalissimo and Madame Chiang appeared on the cover of *Time* magazine as the "man and wife of the year" for 1937 (*Time,* January 3, 1938). An interesting example of the tendency of the churches to "overpraise" Chiang Kai-shek, as Barbara Tuchman put it, is a little volume (120 pp.) published by the Methodist Church press during World War II, thus serving the "war effort" as well as the "missionary movement." It is an unrelieved paean to the Chiangs and Soongs, celebrating their "heroic deeds," with "scarcely a suggestion of blemish." See Elmer T. Clark, *The Chiangs of China* (Nashville, Tenn.: Abingdon-Cokesbury Press, c. 1943). Somewhat more substantial, but hardly less adulatory, are the works of Emily Hahn, *The Soong Sisters* (New York: Doubleday, Doran, 1941), and *Chiang Kai-shek, an Unauthorized Biography* (New York: Doubleday, Doran, 1955).

not been able to marry Miss Soong until he had first arranged to divorce the wife of his youth who had borne him two sons.[17]

Little was known of Chiang's stock-jobbing days in Shanghai or of his associations with that city's unsavory secret societies. Nor was very much ever made of the fact that when Chiang decided in 1927 to break with the Communists of his party, after they had delivered the city of Shanghai to him, he did it in the most treacherous and murderous fashion, taking several hundred thousand lives in the process.[18] And certainly Americans were not told, in the midst of World War II, that the "bold" Generalissimo had never had any taste for fighting Japanese and that he had agreed in 1937 to fight them rather than the Communists of his own country only after he had been kidnapped and threatened with death by the troops of the Manchurian warlord Chang Hsueh-liang. Actually, Chiang never did acquire a taste for fighting Japanese. And why should he, when he could persuade American "barbarians" to do it for him? [19]

Never was a more unheroic figure raised to the hagiography of "American heroes" than this Chiang Kai-shek whose career was marked at every important turn by the tawdry and opportunistic. In the final analysis, he was no more than another Chinese warlord with a larger ambition, a keener sense for

17. Henry McAleavy, *The History of Modern China* (New York: Praeger, 1967), p. 251. Chiang apparently made the most of his Soong connections: "After his marriage in 1927 to Soong Mei-ling, a Wellesly graduate and sister of Sun Yat-sen's widow, Chiang became a confirmed Methodist and maintained contact with the West through his wife, her brother T. V. Soong (a Harvard graduate) and her brother-in-law H. H. Kung (Oberlin). He used these relatives with American background in top financial posts. . . ." John K. Fairbank, Edwin O. Reischauer, and Albert M. Craig, *East Asia, the Modern Transformation* (Boston: Houghton Mifflin, 1965), p. 693.

18. *China White Paper,* pp. 43–44.

19. Barbara W. Tuchman has shown that Chiang never had a feasible strategy for defeating the Japanese other than that of persuading the Americans to do the job for him. See her *Stilwell in China.*

the main chance, and, above all, a genius for the modern techniques of public relations. This he demonstrated by his constant parroting of the clichés Americans loved so well, whether in the style of evangelical Protestantism, democratic snobbery, or anti-Communist fanaticism. But he was suspect on all counts, for the time had been when he just as readily mouthed Red slogans when it suited his purposes.[20] All of which is not to say that the man was a Communist any more than it is to say that he was a democrat. Insofar as he had any definite political principles, they were probably nearer to those of his idol, Tsêng Kuo-fan, the suppressor of the Taipings, whose only ideal had been to restore to China a centralized Confucian despotism.[21]

Being aware of all these things, General Marshall knew how utterly remote the piously held sentiments of the American people about Chiang and China were from the harsh realities of the postwar period. He also knew that the very fact that such sentiments were held constituted the harshest reality of all for the nation's policy-makers, who were thereby condemned to consider no other policy for the Far East than one that was synonymous with China's Kuomintang. They would

20. On July 9, 1926, Chiang issued a proclamation to the troops setting forth on the Northern Expedition (for the unification of China) in which he expressed these interesting sentiments: "What does 'red' mean? It means the Red Party and The Red Army of Soviet Russia, who use the Red Flag as a symbol of the red blood of the revolutionary masses, shed as the price of their national independence and freedom. It means the release of mankind from misery, the guarantee of human rights, opposition to international imperialism, the abrogation of unequal treaties and the liberation of two thousand and fifty million people over the whole earth. If a government is a government of the masses, and its army is an army of the masses why should it fear to be called 'red'!" Quoted in McAleavy, *op. cit.,* p. 243.

21. The retrograde movement of Chiang's thought, from revolutionary, democratic ideals back to the reactionary, Confucian ideals of Tsêng Kuo-fan and the T'ung-chi Restoration, has been delineated by Mary C. Wright in "From Revolution to Restoration: The Transformation of Kuomintang Ideology," *Far Eastern Quarterly,* XVI, August 1955, pp. 515–532.

have to build America's Far Eastern policy upon the back of this collapsing political party, knowing full well that it was beyond saving and that Chiang Kai-shek, far from being the likely agency for its redemption, was in actual fact its supreme failure.

This latter story was one that had been tragically unfolding since the World War II days when General Joseph Stilwell commanded American forces in the China-Burma-India Theater and, unhappily, doubled as chief-of-staff to Chiang. Stilwell had been driven half mad by the political chicanery that frustrated all his efforts to field a first-rate Chinese army against the Japanese, but from the time of his appointment in December 1941 until he was relieved of his command in late 1944 he never ceased trying to fight his way through the maze of "war politics" that characterized China in the 1940s. Relations between him and Chiang had steadily deteriorated until they finally became intolerable, as was bound to happen where two strong-willed men were trying to direct the same military operation. There could be no common ground between these two, the one a devious Oriental despot, whose main concern was to hold on to his power, and the other an American general, aptly called "Vinegar Joe," whose main concern was to get on with the war.

Much of what Stilwell had to say about the China situation is usually discounted because of the bad relations between him and Chiang, and it is possible that the hard-bitten American general was not as sympathetic as he might have been toward Chiang's problems, particularly his biggest problem— the Communists. But Stilwell probably understood the political situation as well as anyone. He attempted, for example, to convince Chiang that a powerful and efficient army under Central Government command would be his best protection against all dissidents, whether of his own or of the Communist Party. Stilwell confided this to his diary, revealing therein somewhat more than his desire to build a strong Chinese army: "His [Chiang's] best cards are the air force, the artillery, and the ten armies whose training is under the Central Government. Why doesn't the little dummy realize that his only hope is the 30-division plan, and the creation of a separate, efficient, well-equipped and well-trained force." [22]

In his last report to the War Department, Stilwell made the following appraisal of Chiang Kai-shek and his party:

> The Kuomintang party, of which he is the leader, was once the expression of genuine nationalistic feeling, but is now an uncertain equilibrium of decadent, competing factions, with neither dynamic principles nor a popular base. Chiang controls by manipulating these functions with an adroit political sense. His reluctance to expand military strength, his preoccupation with the security of domestic supremacy, his suspicion of everyone around him, and his increasing emotional instability betrayed a realization of this. He became a hostage of the forces he manipulated.[23]

This single paragraph summarized the situation as well as it could be done, and, except for filling in details, no later report would alter it in any significant way.

Some of the details of the war period were filled in by foreign service officers John Stewart Service and John Paton Davies; and for the integrity of their reporting, particularly about the Communists, they would one day be rewarded by aspersions upon their loyalty, which would lead to their dismissal from the foreign service.[24] Undoubtedly, Service was

22. Joseph Stilwell, *The Stilwell Papers* (New York: William Sloane, 1948), p. 152.

23. *China White Paper,* p. 70.

24. It was Major General Patrick J. Hurley (President Franklin Roosevelt's personal representative to Chiang, August–November 1944, and Ambassador to China, November 1944–November 26, 1945) who was responsible for charges of disloyalty against senior foreign service officers in China. But if anyone ever served the United States poorly in China it was Patrick Hurley. Ironically, no other American representative was ever on such close personal terms with Chou En-lai and other Communist leaders, and no one

naïve in believing that the Chinese Communists were sincere in their professed devotion to democracy and to America, and clearly Davies was off the mark in thinking that China's Reds were "Marxist backsliders," but neither of these men were tools of the Reds, neither ever put out the propaganda line that China's Communists were "mere agrarian reformers," and certainly there was no reason for believing that either was disloyal. Both of them saw the Communist Party of China as a tough, well-disciplined party, single-mindedly pursuing its own ends. But, what is more important, they saw that the Communists were likely to win in China, and so they urged their government to keep a foot in the Red camp, if for no other reason than to keep the Russian foot out. They never advocated abandonment of the Kuomintang; rather they saw it as the only available agency for the creation of a pro-American China, assuming it could be kept on its feet. How this could be done they were not sure.[25]

Service thought the United States should press hard for a United Front government, which might democratize China through a multi-party arrangement, including the Communists but dominated by the Kuomintang. Davies' assessment was less naïve; he saw a coalition government between the Kuomintang and the Communists as an acceptable course for the United States only because it offered a bare possibility of saving the Kuomintang. But three weeks after making this appraisal, he commented that Chiang would never consent to a genuine coalition government because he realized that, under such an arrangement, the Reds would dispossess him. Service and Davies were excellent reporters, depicting with

---

else ever affirmed as emphatically as Hurley that "the Communists are not in fact Communists, they are striving for democratic principles. . . ." *Ibid.*, pp. 86, 581–584.

25. For extensive excerpts from the reports of Service and Davies, see *ibid.*, pp. 564–576.

astonishing accuracy the steady rise of the Communists and the equally steady disintegration of the Kuomintang. But at finding "American solutions" to China's problems, they were no better than anyone else and, for that matter, no worse.

If any good word was ever going to come out of China, it would surely have come from Ambassador John Leighton Stuart. This kindly Christian gentleman had been born in China of missionary parents and had spent most of his life there serving the Chinese people. In view of his long service in China (he had been president of Yenching University, an American missionary enterprise, from the time of its founding in 1919) and of his wide acquaintance with Chinese leaders, he was appointed American ambassador to China in 1946. He was a close and devoted friend of Chiang Kai-shek's, having been impressed from the time of their first meeting by the Generalissimo's "masterful personality and magnetic charm." Moreover, as Stuart further commented, "I had been widely known for my educational activities and my strong sympathy with the Chinese nationalistic aspirations. In fact, the Chinese constantly said that they regarded me as one of themselves." [26] Chiang himself could not have chosen an American ambassador who would have pleased him more, but the association was not destined to be a happy one. Stuart would be forced to witness at close hand the slow but sure disintegration of a movement that he had seen accomplish much for the regeneration of China and give promise of so much more but which, having lost touch with the people, was now falling apart. It would thus be the ambassador's task to chronicle for the State Department the tragic denouement of that movement.

Stuart seldom found anything good to report from Nation-

26. John Leighton Stuart, *Fifty Years in China* (New York: Random House, 1954), p. 175.

alist China, and it seemed that even when there was good news, it was always vitiated by the bad, as when he reported on April 17 that the reorganization of the Kuomintang State Council gave promise of improvement because of the high caliber of appointees but felt it necessary to add that "the C-C-clique, while at the moment not in the forefront, is still substantially in control of the Kuomintang party machinery." [27] Stuart had earlier observed that the reactionary C-C-clique, headed by the two Chen brothers (thus the double C), was becoming so firmly entrenched in its hold on the party and the country that Chiang would not be able to dispense with it and that this could "only serve to aggravate those social conditions basically giving rise and strength to the Communist movement." [28] The only hope Stuart ever held out for Nationalist China was nothing more than that—groundless hope—and it was in this spirit that he implored Chiang in October 1947 "to lead wholeheartedly in a new revolutionary movement with the adventurous and unselfish zeal of the Kuomintang when he first joined it, rallying present-day youth as it had done when he was one of them." But Stuart sadly confessed that this, the only practical solution, was visionary.[29]

For one brief moment it had seemed that Chiang might be able to master China's chaos. He had launched an all-out offensive against the Communists in May 1946, in violation of the truce established by General Marshall, and succeeded in capturing the Manchurian cities of Changchun, Harbin, and Kirin, which the Reds had occupied the previous month, also

27. *China White Paper*, p. 746.

28. *Ibid.*, p. 735. It is of some interest that *Time* magazine, about a month after Stuart's devastating commentary on the C-C-clique, featured Chen Li-fu, the head of the "notorious" clique, on the cover of its magazine and presented him as an excellent example of those splendid Chinese leaders who were laboring to build a new China within the old Confucianist framework. See *Time,* May 26, 1947, pp. 33–36.

29. *China White Paper*, p. 833.

in violation of the truce. Although Chiang knew that his offensive would probably destroy all possibility of a negotiated
settlement with the Communists (as it did), the success of
the campaign encouraged him to extend the fight northwest-
ward, where his armies took Kalgan on October 14, 1946. He
then moved against the Red capital of Yenan in Shensi prov-
ince and entered that city in March of the following year,
boasting loudly of the routing of thousands of enemy troops.

The only trouble with these victories was that they were
not victories but Communist traps. Chiang had been warned
in the fall of 1945 by his American chief-of-staff, General
Albert C. Wedemeyer, against attempting to take Manchuria
until he was considerably stronger. Such an ambitious undertaking, thought Wedemeyer, would spread the Kuomintang's
best troops too thinly and overextend its lines of supply. The
general thus urged Chiang to "concentrate his efforts on the
recovery of north China and the consolidation of his military
and political position there prior to any attempt to occupy
Manchuria." [30]

Ambassador Stuart knew how sound this advice had been
—and how empty Chiang's victories. He cautioned Washington
in March 1947 not to credit the Kuomintang's claims of a
glorious victory and of the routing of 100,000 men at Yenan.
The city had been evacuated before Chiang's troops entered
it, and Stuart did not believe that the Communists had ever
intended to defend it. "Rather it is more in keeping with their
long developed tactics to evacuate any given point in the face
of enemy pressure, draw him into a pocket, and thereafter
gradually sap his strength with guerilla tactics." [31]

Two months later Mao Tse-tung, writing from the other
side, confirmed Stuart's view:

30. *Ibid.*, p. 131.
31. *Ibid.*, pp. 237–238.

Chiang Kai-shek and Chen Cheng made a wrong appraisal of the strength and fighting methods of the People's Liberation Army. Mistaking our retreats for cowardice and our abandonment of a number of cities for defeats, they had fondly hoped to finish us off south of the Great Wall in three months or at most six, and then proceed to finish us off in the Northeast. But after ten months, all Chiang Kai-shek's invading troops are in desperate straits; they are completely besieged by the people of the Liberated Areas and the People's Liberation Army and find it very difficult to escape.[32]

This analysis reflects Mao's understanding of the close relationship between the military and political aspects of a revolutionary struggle, a lesson Chiang had steadfastly refused to learn, despite the best efforts of Generals Marshall and Wedemeyer and other Americans to teach him. It also reflects the hopelessness of the situation that confronted American policy-makers.

The news from China continued to be only bad, as in Stuart's report of July on the steadily worsening conditions in Manchuria. It told a sorry tale of corruption, incompetence, and defeatism:

The recent Communist drive has met with little Nationalist resistance. Northeast Combat Command sources and military observers admit that many Nationalist withdrawals were premature and without military necessity. The words "strategic retreat" have lost all significance. As a result the Communists possess almost complete initiative and are able to maneuver practically at will. . . .

Nationalist southern military forces and civil administrators [Kuomintang] conduct themselves in Manchuria as conquerors, not as fellow countrymen, and have imposed a "carpetbag" regime of unbridled exploitation upon areas under their control.[33]

Chiang had scarcely left off gloating over his supposed victory

32. *Selected Works of Mao Tse-tung,* 4 vols. (Peking: Foreign Languages Press, 1967), Vol. IV, p. 167; cited hereinafter as *Selected Works of Mao.*

33. *China White Paper,* p. 733.

at Yenan, and already the Communists were beginning to tighten the noose they had prepared for him in Manchuria and into which he had so obligingly thrust his neck. These developments created pessimism in the United States but not yet despair.

It was concluded that a fact-finding mission would have to be sent to China to find out what, if anything, could be done to save the Kuomintang government. The obvious choice for the mission was General Wedemeyer who, as Stilwell's successor in China during the last year of the war, had acquired much painful experience of the country and its problems.[34] President Truman handed Wedemeyer this thankless task on July 9, asking him to study the China situation carefully and then "to state as concisely as possible your estimate of the character, extent, and probable consequences of assistance which you may recommend, and the probable consequences in the event that assistance is not given." [35]

Although known to be friendly to the Chiang regime, Wedemeyer did not whitewash the Kuomintang but excoriated that body in thoroughgoing fashion. In a speech to the leaders of the party, he detailed their faults in what must surely have been one of the most scathing rebukes ever administered by an individual to the heads of a foreign government. He noted general discrimination against poor peasants and in favor of the rich in matters of taxation and conscription; widespread corruption and incompetence in the government and in the army; and the rudeness and arrogance of the army toward the civilian population. Finally, he charged the use of police-state methods: "Secret police operate widely, very much as

34. In the last year of World War II, Wedemeyer had organized, trained, and partially equipped a Chinese Army of thirty-nine divisions. Against the advice of Wedemeyer, Marshall, and others, Chiang had promptly squandered this army by spreading it thinly over the vast, untenable area of Manchuria. See Tang Tsou, *op. cit.*, p. 86.

35. *China White Paper*, p. 256.

they do in Russia and as they did in Germany. People disappear. Students are thrown into jail. No trials and no sentences." [36]

His report of September 19 to the President was in the same vein, relentlessly pursuing Kuomintang corruption and incompetence into every nook and cranny of China. He concluded on this dispiriting note: "In China today I find apathy and lethargy in many quarters. Instead of seeking solutions to problems, much time and effort are spent in blaming outside influence and seeking outside assistance. It is discouraging to note the abject defeatism of many Chinese, who are normally competent and patriotic. . . ." [37] The report could only have created distress in the State Department; it offered no way out of the quandary but only deepened it. It said what all the reports from China had been saying, in effect, for five years past: Chiang cannot be helped, but he must be helped; he cannot be saved, but he must be saved.

In spite of the discouraging prospects, Wedemeyer recommended large-scale economic and military assistance to Nationalist China, to be given over a five-year period. In order to assure efficient use of military aid, he recommended that "military advice and supervision be extended to include field forces, training centers, and particularly logistical agencies" but cautioned that such advice "should be carried on outside operational areas to prevent the criticism that American personnel are actively engaged in fratricidal warfare." [38] Although

36. *Ibid.*, pp. 758–762.

37. *Ibid.*, p. 763. The most discouraging aspect of the Wedemeyer mission was that Kuomintang leaders made it very clear that they did not intend to pay the slightest heed to Wedemeyer's advice. On September 2, the American Consul General at Shanghai informed the State Department that "Premier Chang Chun in an exclusive interview with the United Press today declared there will be no change in either the domestic or foreign policy of the Chinese Government as a result of the Wedemeyer Mission. . . ." *Ibid.*, p. 815.

38. *Ibid.*, p. 261.

Wedemeyer's report was suppressed,[39] it undoubtedly had some influence—possibly decisive—in persuading the Truman Administration to try once again to rescue the Nationalist government of China. In any case, on November 10 Secretary Marshall informed the House and Senate committees dealing with foreign affairs that the administration was planning to embark upon a new program of economic assistance to China.

This critical step was taken when President Truman sent a special message to Congress on February 18, 1948, asking for renewed assistance to the Chinese government in the amount of $570 million.[40] The most striking thing about the message is that it made only a passing reference to China's civil war and was careful to avoid all mention of the "other side" in that war. One might have gotten the impression that the civil war was only incidental to China's economic deterioration (the main theme of the message) and that the "other side" was nobody in particular. This was a strange oversight for the President who, for more than a year, had been alerting the "free world" to the threat of the "world Communist conspiracy." [41] Clearly the President was now being guided by his good common sense, and he was determined that the United States should not be drawn into China's bloody civil war, whatever "world conspiracy" was allegedly operating there.

Still, the administration ran the risk of the direct involve-

39. Wedemeyer's report was suppressed because it was believed that his suggestion that Manchuria be placed under a five-nation guardianship, including the Soviet Union, or a United Nations trusteeship, would be highly offensive to Chinese susceptibilities. *Ibid.,* p. 260.

40. *Public Papers of the Presidents: Harry Truman, 1948* (Washington: United States Government Printing Office, 1963), pp. 144–146. Cited hereinafter as *Presidential Papers: Truman* (1947).

41. President Truman was still not prepared, or did not think it necessary, to explain this oversight when he came to write his memoirs. See his *Memoirs: Years of Trial and Hope* (New York: Doubleday, 1956), Vol. II; cited hereinafter as *Years of Trial and Hope.*

ment it so dreaded if it gave any assistance at all to China; and it took that risk in the reasonable assurance that it could not save Chiang's government, no matter what it did. In presenting the China Aid bill to the appropriate committees of Congress, Secretary of State Marshall admitted that the situation was very nearly hopeless and that the Chiang government would not be able to reduce the Communists "to a completely negligible factor in China" without massive American assistance: "The United States would have to be prepared virtually to take over the Chinese Government and administer its economic, military and governmental affairs." [42] Requesting money for China under these circumstances was very much like asking Congress to pour a half billion dollars down the drain.

42. *China White Paper,* p. 382.

CHAPTER TWO

Chiang Kai-shek's America Problem: Preventing American Disengagement from the Asian Continent (1947–1948)

There appeared to be no alternative to the foolish, wasteful policy of continuing aid to the Chiang government. According to Tang Tsou, a leading scholar of Sino-American relations, "The policy of granting limited assistance to China was entirely necessary to guarantee acceptance by Congress of the Administration's programs for Europe." [1] Perhaps expediency did require that this sop be given to Congress as the only way to lure men of a pro-China bias into supporting the administration's European policies. But this intercontinental linking of policies, in view of the administration's persistent haranguing of the people about the menace of "world Communism," threatened to make a shambles of the nation's Far East policy. For there was a danger that the people would be gripped by real terror once they realized that the measures being taken to halt that "menace" in China were having no effect whatsoever. The President sensed the danger, and while he reluctantly agreed to go on supporting Chiang Kai-shek's

1. Tang Tsou, *America's Failure in China, 1941–1950* (Chicago: University of Chicago Press, 1963), p. 463.

cause, he apparently hoped to neutralize the anti-Communist aspect of it by simply ignoring it.

But this sleight of hand would not work, for it flew in the face of the most elementary logic. If the "Communist conspiracy" was worldwide in scope, as the administration contended, then surely Asian Communism was a part of it, and a policy designed to "contain" this "commie-bogie" (world Communist conspiracy) in Europe would also have to "contain" it in Asia. In fact, it was the fear of Asian Communism that, in the end, would come to obsess the American people, thus forcing the administration to concern itself with "stopping the Communists" there—or seeming to—no matter what foolhardy or violent acts were required to do it. One needs, therefore, to take at least a cursory look at the origins of those complementary concepts—the "commie-bogie" and "containment of the bogie"—which were summoned forth to serve America's European interests but which, in the end, took complete possession of America's Far Eastern policy.

It is well to begin with the question as to whether the chicken or the egg came first: Did the Truman Administration create the "containment doctrine" out of a real need to contain the commie-bogie, or did it create the commie-bogie in order to justify a containment doctrine that would protect American economic interests in Europe? Of course, if a real "bogie" were stalking America, it would have to be "contained," but there was a distinct possibility that the need to rehabilitate the European economy and to integrate it with the American (economic "containmentism") was perceived long before the commie-bogie—that is, Russia—had become a threat that required a "containing wall" of global proportions. This is not to say that the administration created the bogie entirely out of whole cloth, but it is to say that if there had been no bogie, it would have been necessary to create one.

It is not surprising then that the man who probably did

the most to conjure up the commie-bogie was the same accomplished diplomat and Russia expert who created the nation's "bogie-containment" policy. His views on the subject were set forth in an article entitled "The Sources of Soviet Conduct," which appeared under the pseudonym X in the July 1947 issue of *Foreign Affairs*.[2] With the assistance of such reputable pundits as Arthur Krock of *The New York Times*, the world soon learned that the mysterious Mr. X was George Frost Kennan, chief of the State Department's Policy Planning Staff, and that the X article was to be the "sacred text" for the conduct of American foreign policy in the years to come. But, like other sacred texts, this one turned out to mean different things to different people, which was most distressing to its author.

What apparently did not distress Mr. Kennan, however, was the astonishing contradiction involved in arguing that, even though the dynamics for a sustained expansionism probably did not exist in the Soviet Union, "the main element of any U.S. policy toward the Soviet Union must be that of a long-term, patient but firm and vigilant containment of Russian expansive tendencies."[3] Neither was Mr. Kennan much disturbed, until too late, by the fact that his containment doctrine would require the United States to build a military wall around the Soviet Union and its satellites (and its alleged satellites), a task that was certain to prove so costly and so onerous that it was doubtful that the nation could muster the will for its accomplishment or, if it did, that it would not be morally and financially drained by the effort.[4]

2. "The Sources of Soviet Conduct," *Foreign Affairs*, XXV, July 1947, pp. 566–582.

3. *Ibid.*, p. 575.

4. Kennan would later argue that his containment theory had been misunderstood, that he had not meant it in a military sense. But one is at a loss to know what other conclusion was likely to have been drawn by a government and people when they were being urged, in the strongest

The creation of a foreign policy based upon an improbability,[5] which could be capsuled and marketed in the single word "containment" and at the same time could call forth the expenditure of fantastic sums of money and the passionate devotion of an entire nation, was an achievement that staggers the imagination. Actually, somewhat more than a seventeen-page, anonymous article was required to accomplish it. In a long telegram, dispatched to the State Department from his post in Moscow on February 22, 1946, Kennan had presented a more complete and forceful statement of his views. They merit quoting at some length:

> In summary, we have here a political force committed fanatically to the belief that with US there can be no permanent modus vivendi, that it is desirable and necessary that the internal harmony of our society be disrupted, our traditional way of life be destroyed, the international authority of our state be broken, if Soviet power is to be secure. This political force has complete power of disposition over energies of one of the world's greatest peoples and resources of the world's richest national territory, and is borne along by deep and powerful currents of Russian nationalism. In addition, it has an elaborate and far-flung apparatus for exertion of its in-

---

manner possible, to prepare measures for "containing" the "expansive tendencies" of one of the world's great military powers. Kennan had stated the Soviet threat in even stronger terms in a long telegraphic message from Moscow in February 1946 (see below). Possibly he became alarmed by Washington's overreaction (particularly in a military sense) to his telegraphic message, and perhaps this accounts for the fact that his later article (the X article of 1947) seemed contradictory in that it called for containment while playing down the Soviet threat. Probably the most significant commentary on the "containment doctrine" is the fact that Kennan himself was one of the first top policy-makers to draw back from its frightful implications. See George F. Kennan, *Memoirs, 1925–1950*, Vol. I (Boston: Little, Brown, 1967), p. 358, and Appendix C.

5. Russia's industry, puny at best by American standards, had been badly hurt by the war; much of its most productive land had been devastated; fifteen to twenty million of its people had been killed; and it had not a single atomic bomb to its name. That this nation should have conceived aggressive designs against the awesome power of the nuclear-armed United States, or any of its vital interests, was a patent absurdity.

fluence in other countries, an apparatus of amazing flexibility and versatility, managed by people whose experience and skill in underground methods are presumable [sic] without parallel in history.[6]

This, Kennan later confessed, "reads exactly like one of those primers put out by alarmed congressional committees or the Daughters of the American Revolution designed to arouse the citizenry to the dangers of the Communist conspiracy." [7] Indeed it does, but it would have been more accurate if Mr. Kennan had said that *they* sounded like *him,* for no one had been earlier in the field or worked harder at creating the commie-bogie than he.[8] After all, without that bogie, the containment doctrine would never have seen the light of day.

But the doctrine did indeed see the light of day. Never did a proposition in foreign policy get so much attention, and it opened up unlimited vistas.[9] Little wonder that it caused a stir in the Pentagon and, in fact, in all of official Washington.

6. Kennan, *op. cit.,* p. 557.

7. *Ibid.,* p. 294.

8. Winston Churchill's famous "iron curtain" speech was delivered at Fulton, Missouri, on March 5, 1946, two weeks *after* Kennan's "long telegram" and over a year *before* his X article. Key phrases from Churchill's momentous address, the worldwide unveiling of the "commie-bogie," were these: "From Stettin in the Baltic to Trieste in the Adriatic, an iron curtain has descended across the continent. . . . Nobody knows what Soviet Russia and its Communist international intends to do in the immediate future, or what are the limits, if any, to their expansive and proselyting tendencies. . . ." *The New York Times,* March 6, 1946.

9. The "doctrine" got wide exposure in the popular press as reflected in the titles of articles in popular magazines by Mr. Kennan (reprints in whole or in part of the X article) or about him, such as the following: "America's Global Planners," *The New York Times Magazine* (July 13, 1947); "Stop Russia Policy for U.S.," *U.S. News & World Report* (July 25, 1947); "Only Way to Deal With Russia," *Reader's Digest* (October 1947); "Brain Trust that Guides America's Stand Up to Russian Policy," *U.S. News & World Report* (October 1947); *Life* magazine ran the entire X article in its issue of August 28, 1947, explaining that it was the "official U.S. view of why the Russians act as they do," p. 53.

Kennan marveled at the effect of his "long telegram" on the nation's leaders:

> The President, I believe, read it. The Secretary of the Navy, Mr. James Forrestal, had it reproduced and evidently made required reading for hundreds, if not thousands, of higher officers in the armed services. The Department of State . . . responded with a message of commendation. With the receipt in Washington . . . of this telegraphic dissertation from Moscow, my official loneliness came in fact to an end—at least for a period of two or three years. My reputation was made. *My voice now carried.* [Italics supplied.] [10]

It is doubtful that Mr. Kennan's voice now carried because he had worked a miraculous conversion of the government's top policy-makers to a new point of view but, rather, because he had expressed so well their own deep-seated antipathy toward the Soviet Union. Kennan had simply provided an apparently objective analysis of alleged facts, which was in perfect accord with the "conditioned reflexes" of many government leaders.

When reflexes have had thirty years of conditioning, they are bound to have the feel of truth, of "folk wisdom," of "plain common sense." Ever since the Bolshevik Revolution of 1917, millions of Americans had been brooding over the dark plots of the Kremlin and the evil machinations of the Comintern. Little matter that Stalin had replaced the Marxist concept of "world revolution" with that of "socialism in one country," he could not fool hardheaded Americans possessed of "folk wisdom" and "good common sense." And there were many such hardheaded "realists" in the Truman Administration.

Had not Senator and President-to-be Harry Truman, the very personification of "folk wisdom," urged the United States in 1941 to pursue a policy that would encourage Germany and Russia to fight each other, "and that way let them kill as many

10. Kennan, *op cit.,* pp. 294–295.

as possible"; and had not Secretary of the Navy James Forrestal, bolstered by tough cables from Averell Harriman in
Moscow, started calling for a hard line with the Soviets well
before the end of World War II? [11] Indeed, folk wisdom and
intellectual analysis consummated a happy marriage in the
containment doctrine. The despised Bolsheviks were cast in
the role of arch-villains on a global scale, which provided an
excellent justification for maintaining an American "sphere
of influence" in Western Europe or in any other place where
an American interest might be served.

Obviously there was no real fear that Russia would attack
Western Europe, for during the very period when the commie-
bogie was being created, the administration was in the process

11. The strong anti-Russian feeling that had begun to manifest itself in
the nation's leaders well before the end of World War II is discussed at
length in Gar Alperovitz, *Atomic Diplomacy: Hiroshima and Potsdam*
(New York: Random House/Vintage Books, 1965), pp. 25–30. Anti-Russian
belligerance was revealed at its meanest and pettiest when Secretary of State
James F. Byrnes, at the first Conference of Foreign Ministers in London,
September 30, 1945, insisted upon the presence of the French and Nationalist Chinese delegates during the treaty-making for Eastern Europe, even
though their participation in these sessions had been barred by the Potsdam
Agreement. Byrnes' Republican adviser John Foster Dulles would later
boast, incredible as it may seem, that he had stiffened Byrnes' resolve in
this small matter and that "at that moment, our postwar policy of 'no
appeasement' was born. . . ." John Foster Dulles, *War or Peace* (New York:
Macmillan, 1950), p. 30; see also James F. Byrnes, *Speaking Frankly* (New
York: Harper, 1947), pp. 216–217. The same antipathetic emotions toward
the Soviet Union are fully and cogently revealed in a report to the
President, prepared in September 1946 by a Special Council under the
direction of Clark Clifford, in which the general views expressed by George
F. Kennan in his "long telegram" were given comprehensive form. The
report, suffused with preconceptions and generalizations, explains all Soviet
behavior in terms of a vast conspiratorial scheme of world domination.
Russia's building of air bases in Siberia (its own territory) and its attempts
to weaken American influence in China (which, after all, is a next-door
neighbor to Russia and thousands of miles from the United States), aston-
ishingly, are seen as threats to American security. This remarkable document was published for the first time in Arthur Krock, *Memoirs: Sixty
Years on the Firing Line* (New York: Popular Library Eagle Books, 1968),
Appendix A, pp. 389–453.

of dismantling the nation's military establishment and, except for air power and nuclear weapons, would not seriously begin to rebuild it until the outbreak of the Korean War in 1950. General George Marshall would later complain that when he was being urged in 1947 to "give the Russians hell," he had a total of one and a third divisions at his disposal.[12] The administration was thus dealing falsely with the people when, in Senator Arthur Vandenberg's approving words, it persuaded them to bear heavy burdens by "scaring hell out of them" about Communism.[13]

Under Secretary of State Dean Acheson undoubtedly "scared hell out of" congressional leaders when he lectured them on February 27, 1947, at a White House briefing on foreign policy. Noting that Secretary of State Marshall had not done a proper job of alarming congressmen about the alleged Russian threat to Greece and Turkey, Acheson took over and instructed them in the ways of this international conspiracy:

> In the past eighteen months . . . Soviet pressure on the Straits, on Iran, and on northern Greece had brought the Balkans to the point where a highly possible Soviet breakthrough might open three con-

12. Cited in Tang Tsou, *op. cit.*, p. 366.

13. Quoted in Eric F. Goldman, *The Crucial Decade and After: America, 1945–1960* (New York: Random House/Vintage Books, 1960), p. 59. Dean Acheson also noted Senator Vandenberg's "repeated request that the problems of the two small countries [Greece and Turkey] be put in the setting of the larger confrontation between the Soviet Union and ourselves." Dean Acheson, *Present at the Creation* (New York: Norton, 1969), p. 225. Further evidence that the nation's leaders were prepared to work upon popular fears of foreign nations in order to secure support for an expansive foreign policy (primarily to serve economic interests) has been provided by John Foster Dulles, a leading Republican architect of America's postwar bipartisan foreign policy. Dulles had noted as early as 1939 the need to arouse the masses to the support of a "vigorous" foreign policy: "Mass emotion on a substantial scale is a prerequisite. The willingness to sacrifice must be engendered. A sense of peril from abroad must be created." John Faster Dulles, *War, Peace and Change* (London: Macmillan, 1939), p. 90.

tinents to Soviet penetration. Like apples in a barrel infected by one rotten one, the corruption of Greece would infect Iran and all to the east. It would also carry infection to Africa through Asia Minor and Egypt, and to Europe through Italy and France, already threatened by the strongest domestic Communist parties in Western Europe. The Soviet Union was playing one of the greatest gambles in history at minimal cost.[14]

This was not a "domino theory," but it was the next best thing, a "rotten-apple-in-the-barrel theory." With it, Dean Acheson won congressional leaders, including the Republican majority, to the support of the Truman Doctrine and to a general program of "commie-fighting."

Only two weeks later, President Truman lectured Congress and the nation (to "scare hell out of them") on the same subject. The President's speech, moderate by comparison with later statements on the subject, was strong enough to alarm George F. Kennan, who was already beginning to draw back from the reckless uses to which his containment doctrine was being put.[15] With little modification, however, the speech was delivered. The people were solemnly told that Greece was "threatened by the terrorist activities of several thousand armed men, led by Communists . . . ," and that Turkey was also threatened, but by a different form of pressure.

It seemed that just about everybody was threatened, and the nations of the earth would have to "choose between al-

14. Acheson, *ibid.,* p. 219.

15. Kennan objected to the suggestions, in the President's message, "that what we were concerned to defend in Greece was the democratic quality of the country's institutions," since we would likely find it necessary to give aid to a number of regimes "which could hardly qualify for it on the basis of their democratic character." He also took exception to the tendency to divide the world neatly into Communist and "free world" components, a way of thinking which would lead both the American and foreign governments into the belief that "all another country had to do, in order to qualify for American aid, was to demonstrate the existence of a Communist threat. Since almost no country.was without a Communist minority, this assumption carried very far." Kennan, *op. cit.,* pp. 321–323.

ternative ways of life. One way of life is based on the will of
the majority, and is distinguished by free institutions. . . . The
other way of life is based upon the will of the minority, forci-
bly imposed upon the majority." [16] The role of the United
States in this global confrontation was explained as follows:

> I believe that it must be the policy of the United States to support
> free peoples who are resisting attempted subjugation by armed
> minorities or by outside pressures. Should we fail to aid Greece and
> Turkey in this fateful hour, the effect will be far reaching to the
> West as well as to the East.[17]

Who was responsible for these tragic developments? The
President did not say, but he gave a very "broad hint" when
he noted that a number of countries "have recently had totalitarian regimes forced upon them against their will. The Government of the United States has made frequent protests
against coercion and intimidation, in violation of the Yalta
Agreement, in Poland, Rumania, and Bulgaria." [18]

It was all very well to ask Congress for the means to defend
a legitimate American interest against the encroachments of
another power. But for the President to see a military-ideological campaign of far-reaching—possibly world—conquest in the
Soviet Union's attempt, if indeed it was such,[19] to gain a
strategic or economic advantage in an area near its own

16. *Presidential Papers: Truman* (1947), p. 178.

17. *Ibid.*, pp. 178–179.

18. *Ibid.*, p. 178.

19. Milovan Djilas, an important figure in the Yugoslav Communist
Party at the time of the Truman Doctrine, later wrote, after he had broken
with the party and had no reason to justify its acts, that Stalin had strongly
opposed encouragement of the Greek insurrection by Yugoslav and other
Communists. According to Djilas, Stalin had said, "What do you think, that
Great Britain and the United States—the United States, the most powerful
state in the world—will permit you to break their line of communication in
the Mediterranean? Nonsense. And we have no navy. The uprising in
Greece must be stopped, and as soon as possible." *Conversations with
Stalin* (New York: Harcourt Brace and World, 1962), p. 141.

borders (just as the United States sought such advantages far from its own borders) was to transform a great power confrontation over particular interests into a worldwide "struggle to the death" between contending ideologies.[20] Such reasoning was as fantastic as it was foolish.

Probably Congress and the people were thought incapable of grasping the realities of power politics, and perhaps this is what Dean Acheson had in mind when he said, "These Congressmen had no conception of what challenged them. It was my task to bring it home." [21] What they got was "rotten apples in a barrel," for "containmentism" was conducive to pat analogies, which swept continents full of nations into barrels. It foretold the exact nature and purpose of every conceivable future action of the Soviet Union, not on the basis of ascertainable facts but of a general theory.

Hardly pausing to catch its breath, in mid-1947 the administration began preparing its second major crisis of the year. It was launched by Secretary of State Marshall in a

20. President Harry Truman, many years after the event, spoke of three things that had impelled him to action with regard to Greece and Turkey. The one that he claimed had weighed most heavily was Russia's "callous disregard of the rights of a small nation." This, of course, was in line with the ideological aspects of his message to Congress; but, since the United States, contrary to popular belief, had never been known to rush to the rescue of a small state where no substantial American interest was involved, or thought to be, this can be dismissed as so much rhetoric. A second reason noted was the "security of Turkey," and this had to do with preventing Turkey from being outflanked by Russia and other Communist states. But obviously this consideration would have relevance only if Turkey's strategic position defended something of *real value* to the United States. And so the President came to the important point when he spoke of his concern about the oil reserves of Iran: "That Russia had an eye on these vast deposits seemed beyond question. If the Russians were to control Iran's oil, either directly of indirectly, the raw-material balance of the world would undergo a serious change, and it would be a serious loss for the economy of the Western world." *Years of Trial and Hope* (New York: Doubleday, 1956), p. 95.

21. Acheson, *op. cit.*, p. 219.

June 5 address at Harvard University, in which he proposed
to rescue Europe from the doldrums through a policy of massive economic assistance. This was undoubtedly a sound program, which would contribute immeasurably to world order,
and it was to Marshall's credit that he did not raise the specter
of the "Communist conspiracy" but called for a policy "directed not against any country or doctrine but against hunger,
poverty, desperation, and chaos." [22] But alas, such a high-
minded policy could not be, for expanding markets required
containment, and containment required a commie-bogie.

In this crisis there was no uprising "of several thousand
armed men, led by Communists," as there had been in Greece.
In fact, no armies were marching or even threatening to
march. This was an economic crisis, a part of the bitter legacy
of World War II, and it was not immediately apparent how
the Communists could be made the villain. The situation
briefly was this: the European economy had not recovered
from the war, and this was a serious drag on the American
economy. Secretary Marshall made no bones about it and
plainly said, as previously noted, that failure of Congress to
enact his proposals for bolstering up the economies of Europe
(the Marshall Plan) would result in a cumulative loss of
markets, which "would unquestionably have a depressing influence on our domestic economy and would drive us to increased measures of government control." [23] Marshall, the
tough economic realist, knew a thing or two about fluttering
the dovecotes of capitalist orthodoxy.

Such economic realism suited Harry Truman, the man of
"plain common sense," which doubtless explains his preference
for such tough-minded advisers as Marshall and Acheson. It
was precisely their hardheaded economic realism that per-

22. "European Unity," *Vital Speeches*, XIII, June 15, 1947, pp. 553–554.
23. See p. 5.

vaded his Marshall Plan message of December 19, in which he urged Congress to act on "these grave issues now before us":

> Considered in terms of our own economy, European recovery is essential. The last two decades have taught us the bitter lesson that no economy, not even one so strong as our own, can remain healthy and prosperous in a world of poverty and want.
>
> In the past, the flow of raw materials and manufactured goods between Western Europe, Latin America, Canada and the United States has integrated these areas in a great trading system. In the same manner, Far Eastern exports to the United States have helped pay for the goods shipped from Europe to the Far East. Europe is thus an essential part of a world trading network. The failure to revive fully this vast trading system, which has begun to function again since the end of the war, would result in economic deterioration throughout the world. The United States, in common with other nations, would suffer.[24]

Here was a statement of "economic imperialism" that was breathtaking in its vast sweep. And yet it was so ingenuously put that it is doubtful that the President, let alone the people, grasped the full implications of it. Hailed as yet another plan to "make the world safe for democracy," the Marshall Plan was preeminently a plan to make the world safe for a domineering American economy. Whether so intended or not, an economy "so strong as our own," in the President's term, was bound to dominate the "vast trading system" he spoke of.

Twice within a year now the Truman Administration had confronted the nation with world-shaking crises, and the President himself had alerted the people to the threat of a nameless menace. But if the President thought it impolitic to name the menace, the news media did not.[25] Generously sup-

---

24. *Presidential Papers: Truman* (1947), p. 516.

25. President Harry Truman was not reluctant to name the menace when he came to write his memoirs: "I think the world now realizes that without the Marshall Plan it would have been difficult for western Europe to remain

plied with press releases from the government, the media, almost without exception, assumed it as a patriotic duty to inform the public of the "true" nature of the "world Communist conspiracy." They did a thorough job of it, as Under Secretary of State Acheson discovered when he began lecturing around the country on behalf of the Marshall Plan. He noted that such a philanthropic purpose as combating "hunger, poverty, desperation, and chaos," which Marshall had emphasized in his Harvard address, would not move the American people to "so great an effort." What the people and Congress alike wanted to know, said Acheson, was how Marshall Plan aid would operate "to block the extension of Soviet power and the acceptance of Communist economic and political organization and alignment." [26]

The country was so edgy about the "Communist threat" that it seemed likely that a single overt act of the Soviet Union, no matter how trivial, might touch off a panic. And this is exactly what happened in February of the following year when the Communists of Czechoslovakia took over their country's government by *coup d'etat*. By March, Washington was gripped by a war scare of such proportions that the Central Intelligence Agency thought it necessary to inform the President that the "big war" would not come within sixty days; and two weeks later the armed forces upped the ante, the Army and Navy not being prepared to grant more than ten more days of peace, while the Air Force was less sanguine.[27]

---

free from the tyranny of Communism". The President was clearly under the spell of the "Munich analogy," which would always be a favorite, if facile and misused, cliché of commie-bogieism: "We had fought a long and costly war to crush the totalitarianism of Hitler, the insolence of Mussolini, and the arrogance of the warlords of Japan. Yet the new menace facing us seemed every bit as grave as Nazi Germany and her allies had been." *Years of Trial and Hope*, pp. 101, 119.

26. Acheson, *op. cit.*, p. 233.

27. James Forrestal, *The Forrestal Diaries*, ed. by Walter Millis with the collaboration of E. S. Duffield (New York: Viking, 1951), pp. 395–409.

Meanwhile, politicians rushed to fill the breach with rhetoric. Senator Arthur Vandenberg informed Congress on March 2 that "the exposed frontiers of hazard move almost hourly to the West"; on the following day Senator Joseph H. Ball of Minnesota solemnly told the nation that "all the governments and people in Europe are living in constant fear of tomorrow." [28] And on March 11, Congressman Richard Milhouse Nixon of California, already in the process of building a political career out of "commie-hunting" and patriotic sloganeering, introduced a resolution in the House calling upon Congress to defend America by "assisting free governments to resist aggression." [29]

Members of the popular press also recognized tragic drama on a grand scale when they saw it. *Newsweek* noted that military government officials in Europe had sharply reduced their estimate of the time margin left before Russia "forces the issue of war or peace. . . . In contrast to their former tactics, the Russians are playing for months rather than years of delay." [30] *Time* magazine, not intending to be outdone by anyone

28. *The New York Times,* March 2 and March 3, 1948.

29. Richard Nixon had early discovered the "commie-bogie" to be a potent political issue, having won his congressional seat in 1946 by casting aspersions upon the patriotism of his opponent and implying that the latter was "soft on Communism," and he would use the same tactics to win a Senate seat in 1950. A close perusal of the *Congressional Record* for the period of the late 1940s reveals that Congressman Nixon bestirred himself more often on this than on any other subject. And, by his own account, three of the six major crises of his life ("The Hiss Case," "Caracas," and "Khrushchev") had been almost wholly concerned with his confrontations with the "commie-bogie"; and the other three crises ("The Fund," "The Heart Attack," and "The Election of 1960") had to do with the perpetuation of the political career of Richard M. Nixon, which Richard M. Nixon appeared to believe was essential to America's struggle against Communism. For Mr. Nixon's congressional resolution, see *Congressional Record,* XCIV, 80th Cong., 2nd Sess. (1948), p. 2607; for the discussion of the six great crises of his career, see *Six Crises* (Garden City, New York: Doubleday, 1962).

30. *Newsweek,* March 8, 1948, p. 27.

on this subject, observed: "Every month brings a calamity graver than most major battles. Millions pass into slavery between one week and the next. The fate of whole continents swings with a day's news." [31] That the situation was indeed grim was confirmed on March 3 when the ultra-respectable *New York Times* added its shrill voice to the general cacophony, editorializing with abandon on the "Russo-Communist steamroller," which was "driving ruthlessly across Eastern and Central Europe and a large part of Asia, crushing beneath it the last vestiges of liberty. . . ." [32]

One is at a loss to know what all the shouting was about. In terms of great-power relationships, nothing of very great significance had occurred in Europe. The Czech Communists had simply perfected their control of a government they already dominated. This was bound to happen, given the fact that Czechoslovakia was within the "sphere of interest" that the West, however grudgingly, had conceded to Soviet Russia. It is doubtful that the Czech Communists needed either prompting or assistance from Moscow to carry out their coup. As for Russia, it had not so much as snapped a rifle. Its effective power remained where it had come to rest at the end of the war against Nazi Germany. In fact, Russian power was receding, as George Kennan had predicted would happen, from such positions of temporary (or attempted) hegemony as Trieste, northern Greece, Yugoslavia, and Finland. [33]

These exciting "events," which were allegedly concerned with hurling back encroaching Russian power in Europe and most assuredly were concerned with consolidating American economic interests there, distracted attention from the fast-approaching debacle of China. But the very frenzy that was

31. *Time,* March 8, 1948, p. 26.
32. *The New York Times,* March 3, 1948.
33. Kennan, *op. cit.,* p. 250.

building up over pseudo-events in Europe during 1947 would begin to shift its focus to the Far East by the end of 1948, and no very painful intellectual effort would be required to make the shift. The concern would be with the same "Communist conspiracy," operating from the same Russian base, only the direction of the attack being changed. The old clichés would serve well enough, as Chiang Kai-shek had already discovered in his efforts to attract attention to his own desperate plight.

In attempting to isolate China from the world struggle against Communism, the Truman Administration failed to take fully into account the exceptional gifts of this enigmatic Oriental politician. Although Chiang Kai-shek had no great talents as an inspirer of men or as a leader of armies, he was a master at myth-making and image-building, and he had a particular genius for projecting himself as a "man of destiny," standing always at the center of great world events. His keen appreciation for the public-relations value of the "grand gesture" had led him on more than one occasion to retire from public affairs, in self-effacing humility, only to reappear opportunely, wearing the mantle of Sun Yat-sen and posing as the savior of China.

Chiang also had "an adroit political sense," as General Stilwell had noted, for manipulating groups and individuals.[34] This special talent served him well enough in some matters, especially those involving intrigue, such as contracting an advantageous marriage or playing upon the needs and fears of foreign powers. But he had none of the larger political vision that would have shown him that the support of his own people would serve him far better than the support of the foreign governments he so assiduously courted. The fact was, however, that he had very little of the former and so would need all of

---

34. *China White Paper,* p. 70.

the latter he could get. Just as his strategy for defeating the Japanese had been to get the United States to do it for him, he would now try to persuade the United States to save him from his own people. And it was indeed his own people from whom he required rescuing. The masses of people going over to the other side were not de-nationalized by the fact of going Communist. *They were all Chinese,* notwithstanding the best efforts of Chiang and his American supporters to have it otherwise.

It would thus be Chiang's main task to convince the American people that their very survival hung upon the fate of the Kuomintang—surely one of the strangest suggestions ever made to the American people concerning their national destiny. An idea so bizarre would have been greeted with raucous laughter by Americans of an earlier generation, but there was every likelihood that Americans of the late 1940s would swallow it whole. They had already been confronted by this very proposition, solemnly stated by Congressman Walter Judd and ex-Ambassador to Russia William C. Bullitt, and no one had laughed. After all, the other side was Red, and that was no laughing matter. Chiang understood the power of this line, for he was aware of the almost neurotic fear with which Americans viewed the "commie-bogie." He also knew—or hoped—that a "prophet" might get along very well "without honor in his own country" if he were sufficiently honored by the world's richest and most powerful nation.

Some men perceived, early on, that Chiang would use the "Communist menace" to try to panic the United States into coming to his rescue. John Paton Davies had predicted it in January 1943:

> . . . we may anticipate that Chiang Kai-shek will exert every effort and resort to every stratagem to involve us in active support of the Central Government. We will probably be told that if fresh Ameri-

can aid is not forthcoming all of China and eventually all of Asia will be swept by communism.[35]

Although Davies' perspicacity was of a rare order, even he probably did not envisage Chiang and his American friends projecting this "domino theory" right around the globe. Actually, the latter would have no difficulty at all in seeing Communism, once it had gobbled up all of Asia, leap the Pacific at a single bound.

President Truman and his advisers were no better prepared than Davies for such globe-vaulting imagination as this. They were not yet fully adept at the "commie-fighting" game; at least, they were not yet willing to play it in Asia. Chiang Kai-shek, on the other hand, had every intention that the game should be played in Asia. And, in his struggle with the Truman Administration for possession of the American mind, he had been handed a very useful weapon in the administration's own containment doctrine. Applied to the Far East, the doctrine provided Chiang with a simple and powerful logic: if the "free world" was engaged in an all-out struggle with the "world Communist conspiracy," then it was the Chinese Nationalists who were carrying on the battle—only they were fighting real Communists with real guns; only they were manning actual battlements against the Communist hordes. And at their head stood the "man of destiny" Chiang Kai-shek, defending not only China, but also America and civilization.

One understands how Chiang, following this logic, was able to reach the startling conclusion that the United States—"the arsenal of anti-Communism," if no longer of democracy—was duty-bound to provide him unlimited assistance. And one may also come nearer to understanding how he could have had

35. *Ibid.,* p. 571.

the effrontery to tell junketing members of the Military Affairs Committee of the American House of Representatives, as he did on October 11, 1947, that his "predicament in Manchuria [where the Reds were closing in upon him] was an American responsibility" and that if his government were finally defeated it would not be because of the Russians or the Chinese Communists, "but because the United States had failed to give promised assistance at a time of desperate need." [36]

Chiang's gall knew no bounds, and neither did his appetite for American assistance. Although the Truman Administration's projected aid fell far short of what he wanted and expected, he could count it a sort of victory over the administration that the latter had been forced, against its better judgment, to formally renew its policy of assistance to China. Chiang doubtless saw this as a step in the right direction, and, once the China Aid bill discussions got going in Congress, he would be able to draw new courage from the manner in which his American friends rallied to his support.

36. *Ibid.*, p. 264. When Chiang Kai-shek wrote the second volume of his memoirs from his island refuge of Formosa in 1957, he was still complaining bitterly about the failure of the United States to save his regime from the Communists; but, still hoping to be rescued and restored to power on the mainland, he persisted in the myth that the Communist victory in China had been primarily a Russian operation and that a conspicuous feature of it was its "anti-Americanism." His dogged use of the "commie-bogie" line in an effort to goad the United States into coming to his rescue is graphically illustrated in the singular title he chose for this memoir: *Soviet Russia in China, A Summing Up at Seventy* (New York: Farrar, Straus and Cudahy, 1957).

CHAPTER THREE

"Asialationists" to the Rescue: Save Chiang for the Saving of America (1947–1948)

President Truman had no enthusiasm for a policy of renewed aid to the Chinese government—"operation rathole" as some discourteous persons called it. But he had to deal with a conservative Republican Congress in which he did not have a great deal more sway than the president of China. And looming menacingly within the ranks of that Republican Eightieth Congress was a host of unregenerate, "old isolationists" who were determined to play a large role in the making—or unmaking—of the nation's Far Eastern policy.

These angry, reactionary men had been envenomed in their isolationism but not cured of it by the cataclysm of World War II. The only thing they had learned was that they could no longer publicly admit to being isolationists without appearing ridiculous. While they believed devoutly in the menace of the "commie-bogie"—seemed even to treasure it—they would not readily accept President Truman's method of dealing with it through the grand strategy of "containment." This called for too much expenditure on far-flung adventures. What they would accept—even demand—was less attention to Europe and more attention to Asia, which was the traditional diplomatic preserve of Republicans. And they were prepared to turn the President's own "commie-fighting" doctrine against him if he did not fall in with their muddled schemes. Since they were nothing if not budget-balancers, however, they had no intention of spending much money or getting very deeply involved in Asia or anywhere else. This hypocritical stance with regard to Asia would earn them such derisive epithets as "new isolationists" and "Asialationists." [1]

In spite of the intemperance of these men and of the derision heaped upon them by the liberal press, there was a certain element of "old-fashioned republican virtue" in their isolationism. Their tragedy was that they failed the country at the point where they were uniquely equipped to render it a valuable service. With their strong antipathy to foreign entanglements, and with a properly scrupulous regard for the people's money, but also with a growing awareness of the irrelevance of isolation, they might have forced the nation to pursue a more moderate course in foreign affairs. But the strain of their contradictory desires—wanting to annihilate Communism everywhere and balance the budget at the same time—was too much. In the end, they gave way to a negative partisanship of the worst kind, using unfounded statements, reckless charges, and personal invective as their weapons.

1. That the Asialationists were actually pursuing a strategy of reducing the nation's European involvement by making a lot of noise about Asia was borne out by the fact that they generally opposed the Marshall Plan for Europe or, at least, insisted upon scaling it down. And in Asia, for all the noise they made, they (the 80th Congress) reduced the Truman Administration's China Aid bill of 1948 by $100 million. This interpretation of the phenomenon of Asialationism was suggested by Arthur Schlesinger, Jr., in "The New Isolationism," *Atlantic Monthly* (May 1952), pp. 34–38. A fuller exposition of the same theme is to be found in Norman Graebner, *The New Isolationism: A Study in Politics and Foreign Policy Since 1950* (New York: Ronald Press, 1956).

It might have been thought that Senator Arthur H. Vandenberg of Michigan would provide a moderating influence. The ranking Republican member of the Senate Foreign Relations Committee, he was a man much admired for having changed his mind in public—from isolationist to internationalist in a dramatic turnabout. But there was little likelihood that he would create an alternative to the unrestrained globalism of the Truman Administration. Cured of his isolationism by the shock of World War II, Vandenberg had gone over completely and unreservedly to the "cult of internationalism" and become the leader of bipartisanship in foreign policy. The one Republican politician possessed of the qualities of leadership and intellect that might have enabled him to play a creative role in foreign policy was Senator Robert Alphonso Taft of Ohio, but his strong political partisanship and deep-seated isolationism led him into positions that were, as his admiring biographer William S. White commented, "inconsistent to the point of inconceivability." [2]

Failing then to create an intellectual basis for a moderate internationalism, conservative Republicans generally took their international bearing from a parochial view of domestic concerns—particularly economic ones. Seeking a less expensive alternative to deep European involvements, they turned their attention to the technologically backward Asian nations, which had always been easier to deal with than European nations and which, being undeveloped, offered as good opportunities for making money as for spending it. The depth of political and social ferment in Asia had not been fully recognized as yet, and so these schemes did not seem wholly illogical.

Indeed, the Asialationists were quite logical within certain narrow confines, for example, in the question that they con-

2. William S. White, *The Taft Story* (New York: Harper and Brothers, 1954), p. 142.

stantly put to President Harry Truman: If Communism, operating from its Russian base, is a menace, then will not Communism, with its base expanded to include the great land and population mass of China, be an infinitely greater menace? The only logical conclusion to be drawn from this question was that there was a need for greatly expanded international commitments, which was not a desirable position to be reached by men obsessed with reducing foreign involvements and balancing the budget. The budget balancers were undone by their Asia fixation. It drove them straight to "containment-ism," but without their having noticed that they had stumbled into the camp of their most hated enemies, the liberal eastern internationalists. This paradoxical turn of events probably explains their unswerving illogic and their perennial carping, as well as their desperate unhappiness with every kind of for-eign involvement, even when they were loudest in their de-mands for yet greater involvements.

The Asialationists hitched their cause to that of Chiang Kai-shek, apparently little noticing or caring that his was a dying cause. One of the first of them to challenge "the Com-munists" on Chiang's behalf was Congressman Walter Judd, a former medical missionary to China turned Republican politician.[3] Elected to Congress from Minnesota in 1942, he was hailed as one of the foremost experts on China (if not *the* foremost). Every popular journal and public rostrum was open to him, in fact, eagerly sought him. And Judd was no man to hide his light under a bushel.

In March 1945, while World War II rushed toward its finish in Europe but continued unabated in Asia, Judd made

3. Congressman Judd was not, strictly speaking, an Asialationist; his concern with China came from an obviously genuine belief that China was of extreme importance to the United States in the scheme of world politics. For a somewhat fuller explanation of the relationship between the budget-balancing Asialationists and Judd's so-called "China bloc," and of why it is not inappropriate to thus cavalierly lump them together, see p. 60.

his first major address to Congress on the subject of China. *Time* magazine, no more behind the times than Judd on matters having to do with Communism and Asia, saw to it that the speech was carried beyond the halls of Congress. Obviously convinced that in carrying such a speech it was doing a great public service, *Time* informed its readers: "Of all Americans occupying elective office, the man who knows most about the Far East is almost certainly Congressman Walter Judd of Minnesota." [4]

Congressman Judd developed two main theses in his speech. The first and most significant was that the revolutionary Communist movement in China was primarily concerned with the expansion of Soviet power in the Far East: "I am convinced now [that] the primary allegiance of the Chinese Communists is to Russia . . . and [that] their purpose is to make Russia overwhelmingly the strongest power in Asia as well as in Europe." [5] The second thesis was that American Communists and fellow travelers, "who were first Communists and second Americans," were working hard to undermine confidence in the government of Chiang Kai-shek and to sell the idea that the Communists were "agrarian reformers" seeking to democratize China.[6]

The first thesis was remarkable for its several glib and sweeping assumptions: that there exists a complete solidarity of interest among all Communists, that all Communists work only to further the power of the Soviet Union, and that a revolution, on the scale of that in China, could actually be manipulated by or on behalf of a foreign power. Absurd though these assumptions were, they were of the very essence of "Communist conspiracy" theories. So was the second Judd

---

4. *Time,* June 18, 1945.

5. *Congressional Record,* XCI, 79th Cong., 1st Sess. (1945), pp. 2294–2302.

6. *Ibid.*

thesis, which sought to brand, in advance, all critics of the Chiang regime as Communists or fellow travelers, a tactic that would be used increasingly by the more reckless of the conspiracists and by not a few reputed to be responsible.

Some degree of restraint was still being exercised in March 1945, however, and Congressman Judd was not yet prepared to make explicit charges against the Soviet Union. He was even so gracious as to report that he could find no evidence of direct Russian assistance to the Chinese Communists. Nonetheless, he was convinced that the latter were determined to make Russia the great power in the Far East, "whether Russia wants it that way or not." The idea that great power status in the Far East was literally being "thrust upon" the Russians was a bit too much, and obviously the congressman did not expect it to be believed. But it would not have been polite to label as the arch-aggressor of all time a nation that was still being called America's "gallant fighting ally." And so Judd left men free to decide for themselves about Russia, little doubting how they would decide. Although the speech had no great impact on public opinion, it did lay down the main lines of Asialationism. And there would be other speeches in more propitious circumstances.

These circumstances had been created when the enactment of the Truman Doctrine made "containment of Russia" the official policy of the United States government and, at the same time, made "crying with alarm" a major American preoccupation. It was thus with a considerable display of logic that Congressman Judd insisted that the Truman Administration treat China (that is, the Chiang government) at least as well as it treated Greece and Turkey.[7] Why, he asked in May

7. Under Secretary of State Dean Acheson, who had the task of defending the Truman Doctrine before the appropriate committees of Congress, commented on the Asialationist attack: "The China specialists, notably Representative Walter Judd of Minnesota, pressed me on what we should

1947, should we not have "some sense of regret that we have been assisting a Communist minority in China in its efforts to overthrow the Chinese government, which with all its weakness has steadfastly refused to yield to such internal and external pressure as today threaten Greece and Turkey." [8]

The same alarm was raised by ex-Ambassador to Russia William C. Bullitt, the one man perhaps as deserving of the title "the Paul Revere of Nationalist China" as Congressman Judd. No one came so near to a state of pure frenzy on the subject as he, and for that he was called "prophet" and "patriot." Congressman John Rankin, a race-baiting Democrat of Mississippi, paid tribute to the prophetic gifts of William C. Bullitt who had tipped off the House Un-American Activities Committee in May 1947 that "Communism's" object in China was "to overthrow democratic government in the interest of the domination of the democratic country by the Soviet Union and the world Communist movement." [9] By October Bullitt was telling the mass readership of *Life* magazine that the very existence of the United States as an independent nation hung upon the fate of Chiang Kai-shek, for, said he, "If China falls into the hands of Stalin, all Asia, including Japan, sooner or later will fall into his hands. The manpower and resources of Asia will be mobilized against us. The independence of the United States will not live a generation longer than the independence of China." [10]

The Judd-Bullitt view of the "Asian peril" was given weighty endorsement, albeit in gentler tones, by *Foreign Affairs,* the most scholarly and authoritative journal of opinion in the

---

do in China. We were doing a great deal under radically different circumstances. He thought not enough." Dean Acheson, *Present at the Creation,* (New York: Norton, 1969), p. 225.

8. *Congressional Record,* XCIII, 80th Cong., 1st Sess. (1947), pp. 1984–1985.

9. Quoted in *ibid.,* pp. A2032–2033.

10. *Life,* October 13, 1947.

field of international relations. In its issue of October 1947, Walter Mallory, a sometime diplomat and professional internationalist, particularly on matters Far Eastern, warned the government that it must not "reverse our traditional policy of the Open Door" by refusing to "support the government of China." [11]

Actually, it was Mallory who was proposing to reverse, or amend, the Open Door policy, for in his view that policy called for something more substantial than moral support, whereas the Open Door had never been more than the statement of a general principle to which the United States paid lip service through polite notes and empty treaties. Mallory was convinced that the people would not tolerate a reversal of *his view* of the Open Door (aid, but not "unstinting" aid) unless, he added with sinister overtones, "we are of the opinion that the Communists are preferable to Chiang, and that Chiang's government should be overthrown. . . ." [12]

Of far greater significance was the fact that moderate Republicans, recognizing a hot political issue when they saw it, were beginning to ask the same questions. Governor Thomas E. Dewey of New York, soon to be his party's candidate for President and no Asialationist, demanded to know why the government did not do something about China. "We have a whole struggle on our hands, world-wide in scope," said he. "We and all other nations which resist totalitarian dictatorship are being attacked by all means short of war." [13]

These men were determined that the United States should not "abandon" China—the Chiang government—which is exactly what the Truman Administration proposed to do for the excellent reason that continued aid, on an ever-increasing

11. "The Open Door in China: A Reappraisal," *Foreign Affairs*, XXVI, October 1947, p. 166.

12. *Ibid.*

13. Quoted in *Congressional Record, op. cit.*, p. A4452.

scale, was likely to drag the nation into China's bloody holocaust, whereas no vital American interest demanded it and
the American people almost unanimously opposed it. The
United States government was willing to incur the small risk
involved in granting limited assistance, but it wanted assurances that its aid would be used with a modicum of efficiency.
Knowing that such assurances would not be forthcoming, and
that they would be meaningless in any case, the Truman Administration was strongly disposed to "abandon" the policy of
pouring money into what was increasingly referred to as "operation rathole." [14]

Unfortunately, the government did not have the choice of
"abandoning" Chiang's government; that option was fore-
closed by the clamor of Asialationists. And it was clear, even
in 1947, that the Truman Administration would not be able
to stop these people or even to answer them convincingly. The
President could not very well rebut the arguments of men
who employed his own logic and mouthed his very own clichés. Had not the administration affirmed the existence of a
"world Communist conspiracy" and of the need to contain it?
Very well, then, said the Asialationists, Communism's main

14. Scholars and publicists made frequent use of the term "abandonment
of China," which was unfortunate. The term implied that the United States
was "deserting" an old and dear friend to whom it owed a sizable moral
obligation; but this simply was not the case. Any obligation to the Chiang
regime had been paid many times over. As for the reputed ancient friendship, it had been created out of the moralizing cant about the missionary
movement, the Open Door policy, and the wartime alliance (of convenience,
not of intent). The term "abandonment" also implied that the Chinese
people had little or nothing to do with their country's civil war, that the
carnage there was being done to them and not by them, and that it was
being done only because the United States allowed it to be done. It was
as though China, having turned Red, ceased to be China, for certainly no
one deplored the abandonment of *Red* China. Tang Tsou, for example,
entitled Chapter XI of his book on Sino-American relations, "Partial
Withdrawal, Limited Assistance, and the Decision to Abandon China." See
America's Failure in China, 1941–1950 (Chicago: University of Chicago
Press, 1963), pp. 441–493.

theater of action is China; why does the administration not contain it in China? Even so strong a figure as George Marshall dared not brush aside this most relevant question, for it was asked by men who wielded real political power. Thus, the administration did not dispute them; it joined them. This it did when the President asked Congress to vote another half billion dollars for Chiang's tottering regime.

Waiting to whoop this bill through Congress—in truncated form—were the dominant personalities of the Republican majority in Congress. In the House of Representatives, Speaker Joseph Martin of Massachusetts and Majority Leader Charles Halleck of Indiana, and in the Senate, "Mr. Republican" himself, Robert Taft of Ohio, would be faithful in the cause of Asialationism, so long as the budget-balancing aspect of it was not forgotten. Swelling the chorus in the Senate were the angry voices of Styles Bridges of New Hampshire, Owen Brewster of Maine, William Jenner of Indiana, Kenneth Wherry of Nebraska, and the redoubtable Joseph McCarthy of Wisconsin, not to mention the Democrat Pat McCarran of Nevada. And valuable assists could be counted on from such moderates as the highly regarded bipartisanist Senator Arthur Vandenberg [15] of Michigan and, outside Congress, from the perennial Republican presidential hopeful, Governor Thomas E. Dewey of New York.

The stalwarts who squeezed the most political fame and fortune out of the issue were a pair of Californians. One of

15. Senator Arthur Vandenberg was the leading Republican proponent of a bipartisan foreign policy, but he did not view his commitment to that policy as carrying over into China policy: "On previous occasions," he said in 1949, "I have categorically replied [on the question of a bipartisan policy for Asia] that there was no such liaison in respect to China policy. I wish to reiterate it, because I disassociate myself, as I have publicly done upon previous occasions, from the China policy which we have pursued." Arthur Vandenberg, *The Private Papers of Senator Vandenberg, 1944–1951,* ed. by Arthur H. Vandenberg, Jr. (Boston: Houghton Mifflin, 1952), p. 532.

them, Senator William F. Knowland, was facetiously but aptly dubbed the "Senator from Formosa," because of his single-minded devotion to the cause of Chiang Kai-shek after the latter had become an exile on the island of Formosa. The other, Congressman Richard Nixon, was a less specialized "commie-hunter" than Knowland but a no less dedicated one. And, ultimately, he would ride this issue, and the coattails of Dwight Eisenhower, into the White House.

The loudest and most persistent voice of all, however, was that of Congressman Walter Judd of Minnesota. As Asialationism's unofficial spokesman, Judd took a major part in the China Aid bill discussions and, as was his wont, spoke in spacious terms. If China goes Red, the congressman asked, "Who would hold the balance of power? Not we. The billion and a quarter people who live in Asia would have the balance of power. . . . Their immediate fate, especially China's, is in our hands; but in the long run, our fate is in their hands." And Judd had an explanation for why the United States failed to manipulate the fate of its own eventual fate-maker. Men in the American government, he asserted, had built up a favorable attitude toward the Chinese Communists by putting out the propaganda line that they were "merely agrarian reformers." [16]

In a manner characteristic of devotees of the "grand theory," Judd left many loose ends hanging. He did not explain why a billion and a quarter Asiatics turned anti-colonial would not just as well hold the balance of power against the West as a billion and a quarter Asiatics turned Red. Neither did he explain how or why this "balance of power" was to be mobilized against the United States and the West. And while Judd explained the Truman Administration's supposed hostility to Nationalist China by its alleged "softness on Communism,"

16. *Congressional Record*, XCIV, 80th Cong., 2nd Sess. (1948), p. 3329.

he did not explain why his own Republican Party failed by $107 million (as it did when it cut the China Aid bill) to come up even to the Truman Administration's level of support for Chiang.

Actually, there was no reason why Congressman Judd should have explained the latter action; it was none of his doing. He and his House colleague John Vorys, as well as Senators Styles Bridges and William F. Knowland and a few others, were not really Asialationists but rather members of what was sometimes designated the "China bloc"; their concern with China was genuine and not born of an obsession with economy in government. They consorted with Asialationists for the simple reason that these men of isolationist and budget-balancing proclivities gave them strong support in calling attention to China and in damning the Truman Administration for its alleged "softness on Communism." And, once the Asialationists had been led into a strong commitment to Asia—much stronger than they ever intended—"China bloc" and Asialationists would be very nearly indistinguishable. On the subject of China and the Communist menace, they were equally strident and relentless.[17]

They were in a position to work considerable mischief, for, although their party held a majority in Congress, it did not control the presidency and so had no responsibility for foreign policy. Thus they used their congressional majority to make

17. Of the interesting relationship between Asialationists and the "China bloc," Tang Tsou had this to say: ". . . the greater danger confronting the global policy of the administration, of which the Marshall Plan was the key, came not so much from the China bloc in Congress, of which Judd and Vorys in the House and Bridges in the Senate were the leading figures, as from the combined forces of the economy block and the unreconstructed isolationists [Asialationists] of which Representative John Taber in the House and Taft in the Senate were the spokesmen. Subsequent events show that by making limited concessions to the China bloc, the administration succeeded in averting serious opposition from that quarter to its European program." Tang Tsou, *op. cit.,* p. 470.

certain that the chief witnesses called to testify about China aid in the spring of 1948 were men who saw America's safety as being inextricably bound up with the security of a non-Communist China. It did not seem to disturb them that persons testifying from this perspective were bound to point up by implication the contradictions in the Asialationist position. For surely, if one took at face value these witnesses' dire predictions as to the terrible consequences of failing to sustain the Chiang government, the United States would have to enormously increase its aid to China, and the adored budget-balancing schemes of the Republican Party would have to go out the window. But the public was not very clever at sniffing out contradictions, particularly when the rancor of debate obscured them even from their perpetrators.[18]

Three of the men called to give testimony were generals, all having some kind of claim to expert knowledge of the Far East. The first of them to testify was General Douglas MacArthur who, without leaving his military governor's post in Tokyo, was undoubtedly the star witness. Even Congressman Judd deferred to MacArthur as an expert on the Far East, although the general himself was more modest, at least about China, for he denied any special knowledge of that country. But in the realm of global strategy, he was quite expansive, as in his telegram of March 4 to Charles A. Eaton of the House Committee on Foreign Affairs:

> The problem insofar as the United States is concerned is a global one and can only be resolved on the broadest possible global basis.

18. Senator Owen Brewster of Maine almost apologized for his party's contradictory stance when, upon being chided during the Truman Doctrine debates for the Republican promise to balance the budget while "getting tough with Communism," he said: "It embarrasses me a little when the President takes us at our own word and suggests that he is going to get tough with Communism, to note how quickly some would seem to want us to pull from under and say 'you should not have believed what we said.'" *Congressional Record*, XCIII, 80th Cong., 1st Sess. (1947), pp. 3698–3699.

... For if we embark upon a general policy to bulwark the frontiers of freedom against the assaults of political despotism, one major frontier is no less important than another, and a decisive breach of any will threaten to engulf all.[19]

What was more interesting in General MacArthur's testimony, however, was his warning against committing "our resources beyond what we can safely spare—the sapping of our national strength to the point of jeopardy to our own security." [20] Clearly MacArthur did not believe that American security was necessarily bound up with a policy of "bulwarking frontiers of freedom" or that such activity should be allowed to jeopardize the nation's security. Unfortunately, the general's global rhetoric tended to obscure this sound advice, but it should be carefully noted that his warning against an excessive commitment of American resources in Asia was entirely consistent with his later *reluctance to engage in military operations on the continent of Asia.*

General Albert Wedemeyer, of the China fact-finding mission, was somewhat more explicit than MacArthur. He told Congress that Chiang could not be saved by dollars alone but that military assistance would be necessary to stop the Communists. And the latter must be stopped, he thought, because "The Communist action in China is a definite part of the world Communist movement." [21] This was orthodox "containmentism," but other things the general said were more interesting, and probably more to the point, for example, "We must have military support and protection of our economic investments wherever forces threaten everything that we hold dear." [22] It is not clear whether General Wedemeyer was planning to defend all American investments or only those

19. Quoted in *ibid.,* XCIV, 80th Cong., 2nd Sess. (1948), p. A1377.
20. Quoted in *ibid.*
21. *The New York Times,* March 5, 1948.
22. *Ibid.*

where "forces threaten everything that we hold dear." In any case, Nationalist China apparently qualified, and Wedemeyer seemed prepared to go all the way to direct military intervention there in defense of whatever was "held dear." At least, this was implied in his statement that American "military participation" for the purpose of implementing military aid was not necessary "*at this point*." [23] (Italics added.)

The last of the generals to testify as a Far Eastern expert was Claire Lee Chennault, whose American "Flying Tigers" had fought the Japanese on Chiang's behalf even before the United States entered World War II. But since General Chennault had taken up residence in China, married a Chinese woman, and established a business in that country, it could be questioned whether he was, strictly speaking, testifying as an American concerned primarily with American interests. In his immodest demands for American money (he was the only one of the generals to specify an amount, $1.5 billion), he sounded like nothing so much as a foreign supplicant. However that may be, General Chennault thought the price should be paid because, in his opinion, China's civil war was a Russian operation in which the Russians, having carefully studied the mistakes of Germany, were securing their eastern flank before attacking Western Europe.[24] The general did not explain how he had discovered what the Russians were "carefully studying."

No hearings on the subject of China aid would have been complete without the testimony of ex-Ambassador William C. Bullitt, for here was a man who spoke with authority about world-conquering behemoths, puppeteers of nations, and "vulnerable global flanks." He began by announcing that General Marshall's statements on China aid were "contrary to fact,"

23. *Ibid.*

24. *Ibid.*, March 11, 1948.

which one supposes was the "diplomat's" way of calling the
general a liar. Shrewdly guessing that a man as moderate and
as sensible as Marshall was not for these times, Bullitt began
the process—which would take several years to complete—of
reducing this truly great and dedicated public servant to the
rank of "imbecile" or "traitor." The ambassador's main blast
was his flat assertion that if Marshall's plans for China had
succeeded, that "country would now be under the control of
Soviet Russia." [25]

Moving into the realm of global strategy, which was his
forte, Ambassador Bullitt projected what must have been one
of the first "domino theories." He contended that "a Communist victory in China would sweep through Indo-China,
Thailand, the Malay Peninsula and [the dominoes were a bit
out of line] into Japan." But this "magical mystery tour" of
the world ended in anticlimax; the ambassador asked for only
$100 million for Chiang and an American general ("the best
man that can be found") to show him how to use it.[26]

Like the politicians and the generals, the mass-circulation
press supported China aid on the grounds that it would contribute significantly to America's defense against the "world
Communist conspiracy." The Truman Administration had
not been able to neutralize the Communist issue in Asia, the
inexorable logic of its own "bogie-crying" having made that
impossible. Thus, the press quibbled over such details as how
much aid would be necessary to save Chiang's government;
should aid be primarily economic or military; and should aid
be contingent upon genuine reform of the Kuomintang? On
the basic issue of *whether or not* aid should be given, there
was virtually unanimous agreement: every effort, *short of
direct intervention,* should be made to save Chiang's govern-

25. *Ibid.*, March 3, 1948.
26. *Ibid.*

ment, reformed or not, as a bulwark against Communism in the Far East.

Among the first of the press pundits to call for China aid were the self-appointed global strategists Joseph and Stewart Alsop who boldly confronted Asia's Communist conspirators (the Soviets) in the columns of *The Saturday Evening Post*. They asked the question, "Must America save the world?" Of course, they thought it should but warned that, in doing so, "we must expect the Soviets to attack our vulnerable flank. . . . They are doing so already in Greece . . . and in China and Manchuria." [27] This vulnerable flank, whether it was in Greece or Turkey or China, caused a great deal of worry to pundits of the press and the military, and they ceaselessly called attention to it, wherever it was.

The *Reader's Digest* provided General Chennault with a forum for imparting to the nation his thoughts on "China as a vulnerable flank" (he thought it was Russia's). In an article, which was certain to make its way into the waiting room of every dentist's and doctor's office in the land, if not into every last middle-class household, Chennault warned that "Communism will not stop at international frontiers unless it is opposed." [28] But, as it turned out, the "Flying Tiger" was less concerned with making China an "invulnerable flank" of America's defense than with using it as an offensive "flank" against the Soviet Union. He told *Newsweek* that China could provide air bases from which the United States could reach eastern Russia.[29]

Of all the mass-circulation magazines, none was more devoted to the cause of Chiang Kai-shek or to "commie-fighting" than the publications of Henry Luce. This influential pub-

27. *The Saturday Evening Post*, February 21, 1948.
28. *Reader's Digest*, April 1948.
29. *Newsweek*, April 5, 1948.

lisher had been born in China of missionary parents, and his strong commitment to China and its supposedly democratic leader was reflected in the columns of his magazines. "It appears," said Luce biographer W. A. Swanberg,

> that Luce had largely closed his mind against any thought that China's problems would not now be solved by Chiang, with American help, and had shut himself off from information and opinions running counter to this theory. He was entering on a period of confusion and error which would be in some part responsible for China's and America's greatest postwar disaster.[30]

Time writers were sometimes a little annoyed by the poor military showing of the Kuomintang, but they never gave up on Chiang the "democrat," who was, they thought, trying to lead China away from one-man leadership.[31] But the real issue, as *Time* saw it, was that the "world Communist movement" threatened to take over the world in ten years' time; it was America's task to halt Communist aggression and prevent nations from "committing suicide by yielding to Communist pressures." [32]

This was mild stuff compared to *Life*'s angry attacks upon the Truman Administration. In a slashing editorial of April 5, 1948, entitled "China: Blunder and Bluster," the administration was castigated in the harshest terms for daring to blame Chiang's failures upon Chiang rather than upon itself. The sweeping statements of Generals MacArthur, Wedemeyer, and Chennault were taken at face value, *Life* not bothering to note that these men, like publisher Henry Luce, had strong personal or career involvements in the Far East that might

30. W. A. Swanberg, *Luce and His Empire* (New York: Scribner's, 1972), p. 237.

31. *Time*, April 12, 1948.

32. *Ibid.*, March 29, 1948.

have colored somewhat their judgment as to the importance of the area.

Only bad motives were imputed to the President and his secretary of state, the most vicious of these being that their policies were, for whatever reason, pro-Communist. In its global generalizations, however, *Life* was astute enough to note the seeming contradiction between the administration's vigorous "containmentism" in Europe and its restrained demeanor in Asia: "At the very moment the government recognizes the global nature of the world conflict, the Chinese front is virtually given up for lost." [33]

Time's chief competitor, *Newsweek,* worried a great deal about Communist encroachments in Asia, although it did not share its rival's enthusiasm for Chiang Kai-shek.[34] Probably the most sensible attitude of any of the newsweeklies was that of David Lawrence's *U.S. News & World Report,* which hoped to see Asian Communism checked but was not willing to pour unlimited quantities of cash down the China "rathole"; it was unsparing in its criticism of the Chiang government and insisted that the latter be held to strict accountability for the use it made of American aid.[35] The more sophisticated *Atlantic* was also gloomy about the misuse of American aid to China but fretted, at the same time, about whether enough was being given.[36]

The prestigious *New York Times* swallowed whole the simplistic notion that China's earth-shaking revolution and civil war was but a phase of Communist Russia's alleged drive for world domination. The *Times* was inspired by the congres-

33. *Life,* April 5, 1948; see also the issue of March 15, 1948.

34. *Newsweek, op. cit.*

35. *U.S. News & World Report,* March 5, 1948.

36. See the *Atlantic Monthly,* particularly the issues of January and April 1948.

sional testimony of Generals MacArthur and Wedemeyer to assert editorially that the "'cold war' declared by Russia against the democracies is a global struggle in which Russia, by virtue of its Eurasion position, takes the place of Germany and Japan as an exponent of totalitarian aggression." Girding the nation for the worst, the editorial concluded that in Greece and China the war had become hot and that "the situation in those countries is not primarily economic but military and must be met by military means." [37]

A general orthodoxy of opinion was clearly emerging. As there was one "world Communist conspiracy," so was there *one* "containment," and in Asia Chiang Kai-shek was its prophet. The idea that this Oriental despot manned the Eastern bulwark of American freedom was a little strange, but it was one for which the American mind had been prepared by World War II propaganda. Particularly well prepared to receive the Chiangian gospel was the nation's Protestant community—the most powerful single element of American opinion—which had been for two decades indoctrinated in the belief that Chiang was a great Christian leader. Hardly a pulpit or Sunday-school class in the land had not, at one time or another, rung with the praises of China's "man of destiny" who was fighting valiantly in defense of democracy and Christianity—and against the "world Communist conspiracy."

With a ground swell of favorable opinion among pundits, preachers, and politicians, the passage of the China Aid bill was assured from the beginning. It was passed on April 2, 1948. But, in view of the fact that the bill was enacted by an Asialationist-dominated Republican Congress, there are features of it that call for special comment: (1) Congress cut $107 million from the $570 million requested by the Truman Administration (provision was made, however, for using $125

37. *The New York Times,* March 5, 1948.

million of that amount for military purposes), and (2) the bill explicitly forbade the use of American troops in China.[38] Not only was the United States unwilling to send its own troops to save Chiang Kai-shek's government, it was not even prepared to spend its money unstintingly to that end. And so one must conclude that, for all the "crack-of-doom" rhetoric being thrown around, the nation was not yet wholly in the grip of the "commie-fear."

Nonetheless, the bill's enactment set the nation on a tragic course from which there would be no turning back. Secretary of State Marshall's dread of going that route and his conviction of its hopelessness were reflected in his anguished cry of the following August: "I wash my hands of the problem which has passed altogether beyond my comprehension and my power to make judgments." [39] But the secretary did not have the choice of "washing his hands"; his hands were tied. In this moment, so fateful for the nation, the President and his secretary of state were not free to choose a course of action.

The Asialationists and the China bloc had determined that the United States government should consider no other policy for the Far East than the least desirable one—continued aid to the Chiang government. Never had so many Americans of power and influence worked so hard to bend the nation's policy to the purposes of a foreign government. And these same Americans, apparently oblivious to the near-treasonable anomaly of their position, wrapped themselves virtuously, and no doubt sincerely, in the cloak of patriotism, biding their time until their own anomalous position—devotion to the cause of Chiang Kai-shek—should become a major test of "Americanism."

38. *China White Paper,* pp. 387–388.

39. Quoted in Robert Payne, *The Marshall Story* (New York: Prentice-Hall, 1941), p. 311.

CHAPTER FOUR

The "Asialationist" Frenzy: Disengagement from Chiang a Sellout of America! (1948)

While Congress debated the China Aid bill during the early months of 1948, the Nationalist position in North China had been steadily deteriorating. Mao Tse-tung described that winter's fighting for his party's press: "The Northeast Field Army led by Lin Piao . . . waged a winter offensive on an unprecedented scale . . . [and] wiped out 156,000 enemy troops. . . . After this, the area under enemy control in the Northeast [Manchuria] shrank to only one percent of the whole, and the enemy lairs in the cities along the Changchun-Shenyang-Chinchow line were isolated." [1] Speaking to the Chinese National Assembly on April 9, Chiang Kai-shek acknowledged the loss of seven divisions in Manchuria that winter as well as serious reverses of the previous summer in the Yellow River area of central China. But, full of bold words as always, Chiang promised to speedily recoup these losses and to press on to ultimate victory.[2]

1. *Selected Works of Mao,* IV, p. 216, fn. 5.
2. *The New York Times,* April 9, 1948.

If the Generalissimo did not make good on his promises—
and there was no reason to believe he could—America's Far
Eastern policy would be in serious difficulties. That policy, it
must be remembered, depended entirely upon the success of
Chiang's government but offered it only limited assistance and
no direct support by American troops under any circumstances. It was likely then that the American people would
soon find themselves acting in a manner that went directly
against the grain of the national character—sitting on their
hands in the face of events that they regarded as the most
tragic. How poorly Americans were prepared emotionally for
such a quiescent role would later be revealed in the bitter
complaints that would rise from all quarters against this "do-
nothing policy," once the Red tide had begun to engulf all of
China. And yet this is exactly what the nation had opted for.
Amid all the clamor for aid to China, no one had dared suggest that American troops be sent to fight on the Asian
continent.

This reluctance to assume any direct responsibility for the
security and stability of client governments, while at the same
time insisting that they be assured perfect success in all their
undertakings, created the most intense frustration among the
American people, who simply were not willing to believe that
any task to which their nation seriously turned its hand—even
one conducted by proxy—could not be accomplished. Consequently, when the China policy failed, the people were inclined to believe that there was mischief afoot and to demand
that conspiracies be uncovered and conspirators run to ground.
In their furious search for scapegoats, the people would be led
by angry politicians, including some from the administration's
own ranks, and overwrought journalists, including allegedly
responsible ones, who would wrench the facts of history gro-
tesquely out of context.

A pat explanation for America's "loss of China" was provided well in advance of the actual event by simply extending the theory of the "world Communist conspiracy" to Asia where, it was alleged, the same Moscow-directed movement that was supposedly terrorizing Europe was also manipulating China's civil war in the interests of Russia and "world Communism." But the theory did not stop here; it insisted that the Soviet apparatus for subversion had been thrust into the very bosom of the American government where high officials were presumably being manipulated, one way or another, into selling out Nationalist China. Such theories had already been suggested by Congressman Judd and Ambassador Bullitt, by *Life* and *Time,* and by that most erudite of mind-shapers, *Foreign Affairs.*[3] All of this was somewhat excessive, but America's dedicated anti-Communists were never willing to concede any limits whatsoever to the manipulative and conspiratorial talents of the Russians.

It is not altogether clear why a great many people were so devoted to this "devil theory" of history; thus, one must explain it by what seems obvious and plausible. It has already been pointed out that many conservative Republicans got themselves hung up on the China question as a result of their efforts to reduce the nation's European involvements. Their concern with the latter objective, while undoubtedly stemming partly from the traditional American mistrust of foreign entanglements, was motivated largely by their obsession with monetary policy. They were determined to force the Truman Administration to sharply reduce its expenditures and balance the budget.

3. Walter Mallory thought he saw a sinister influence in certain elements of the American press. The policy of allowing Chiang to lose in China, he said, was "being championed by a number of writers in American newspapers and periodicals. It is in accordance with the world-wide Communist Party line. . . ." "The Open Door in China: A Reappraisal," *Foreign Affairs,* XXVI, October 1947, p. 168.

Out of this strange amalgam had come the Asialationists, who where almost as devoted to "stopping the Communists" as to balancing the budget. But if they did both things—balance the budget and stop the Communists—they would have to find a cheap way to do the latter. This they found in the policy of fighting Communists by proxy: Let the United States simply provide money and weapons, "within prudent limits," to others who were fighting Communists. But if this policy of "cheap" failed, they might have to confess that they had been in error, and, worse yet, that there was a need for vastly increased overseas expenditures, neither of which were they likely to do. In that case, they could go on justifying the policy of "cheap" only if they could find an explanation for its failure within the government itself. They would thus charge that the government had bungled the policy because it was incompetent and corrupt, or, even better, because of its "softness on Communism," which could mean anything from a "fatuous liberal misunderstanding of Communism" to treason.

For many simple citizens—and some simple politicians—such explanations were probably unnecessary. It is likely that most of those who charged conspiracy, subversion, and the like were honestly convinced that the charges were true. It was not a wholly unreasonable belief, given the Truman Administration's own basic assumptions. The administration itself had set the stage for a theory of internal subversion on the grand scale when it built its foreign policy upon the assumption of a "Communist conspiracy" on the grand scale, insisting that the Soviet Union was bent upon world domination by external attack and internal subversion.

Indeed, the President's own special council, headed by his trusted adviser Clark Clifford, had concluded in 1946 that "Soviet leaders appear to be conducting their nation on a course of aggrandizement designed to lead to eventual world domination by the U.S.S.R." [4] And George Kennan, chief of the State Department's Policy Planning Staff, had affirmed in that same year that the Soviets possess "an elaborate and far-flung apparatus for exertion of its influence on other countries . . . managed by people whose experience and skill in underground methods are presumably without parallel in history." [5] Beginning then with the administration's basic premises, there was sound logic in the assumption by Asialationists and others that the Soviets would exert every effort to infiltrate and subvert the American government, just as there was sound logic in their contention that a "bogie" that could threaten America through the front door of Europe could also threaten it through the back door of Asia.

But to make palpable a "conspiracy theory" for use against an administration that was itself the creator of the original "conspiracy theory," it would be necessary to completely revise the history of America's relations with China since 1940, particularly the history of the Marshall mission and of General Marshall's attitude in 1946 toward a possible coalition government between the Kuomintang and Communist parties. Such a revision of history was, as the liberal pundit Elmer Davis called it, "history in double-think," and it operated to place the Marshall mission in the worst possible light. That mission, as had been well understood in 1946, had recommended a temporary suspension of arms shipments to the Chiang government in order to safeguard the integrity of General Marshall's role as impartial mediator and to convince the Communists that he was not resorting to trickery when he tried to persuade them to give up their independent armies in exchange for such political advantages as Chiang might be willing to grant them; but the revised version, put out by Asia-

4. Arthur Krock, *Memoirs: Sixty Years on the Firing Line* (New York: Popular Library Eagle Books, 1968), Appendix A, p. 396.

5. See p. 32.

tionists in 1948 and after, insisted that the suspension of
ms shipments had been for no other purpose than to *force*
hiang to take Communists into his government.

The original (1946) version realistically accepted the fact
at one could not peacefully disarm a dangerous adversary
ithout paying a price. The second (1948) version confused
rice with objective when it insisted that getting Communists
to the government of China had been the main objective of
merican policy and not merely the price offered in an effort
 secure the disarmament of the Reds. The only conclusion
 be drawn from the latter interpretation was that America's
p policy-makers had been influenced by underlings in the
tate Department who were dupes of the Communists or
aitors, or that the top policy-makers were themselves either
upes or traitors. Either way, it branded America's political
aders as muddleheaded or traitorous; and, in time, both
harges would be made, and, in some measure, one or both
ould be believed.

Already, by 1948, thought patterns had been so drastically
eoriented by the strident, emotional rhetoric of the cold war
hat probably not many Americans would have been able, even
f they had tried, to recall the different circumstances and at-
itudes of 1946. They were no longer disposed to remember
hat, in the former time, quite different objective conditions
ad prevailed, such as the following: (1) the Communists of
China had emerged from World War II as a political force
which, like it or not, had to be reckoned with, since it gov-
rned a substantial territorial base and commanded large
rmies of some potency; (2) the Communists had the same
mandate to govern the areas they held as Chiang had to govern
reas held by him—that is, acquiescence of the people secured
hrough political agitation and armed force (Chiang had
 never been given a mandate to rule through a free vote of the
people of China); and finally (3) China's Reds, having fought

against the Japanese in World War II, could claim a mora
right to participate in the setting up of a postwar government
and Americans of 1946 had not been of a mind to deny then
that right.

Such had been the circumstances of the Marshall mission
as informed persons knew quite well. And they surely under
stood—if they understood anything—that the very fact tha
General Marshall had been sent to help work out a politica
settlement in China had constituted a tacit acceptance by th
United States of the possibility of a Nationalist coalition witl
the Communists. Yet, knowing these things, American opin
ion-makers had not opposed the Marshall mission but gen
erally applauded it. Chiang himself had not been averse t
seeking a political accommodation with the Communists unde
an American mediator. This would seem to be indicated b
the fact that he had entered into the talks at all, the General
issimo never having been given to doing anything he did no
want to do. What the Chinese did with the opportunity, o
course, was up to them. As General Marshall later explained
"I remained aloof from the political discussions because tha
was a Chinese affair." [6]

What Marshall had concerned himself with primarily wa
the work of the military committee, in which he sought t
persuade the Communists to merge their military forces witl
those of Chiang at the short end of a five to one ratio.[7] Clearly
then, a major object of United States policy had been t
neutralize the armed power of the Communists, which, a
Marshall had known and as events later proved, offered th
only possibility of saving Chiang's government. If this ob

6. *Military Situation in the Far East,* Hearings Before the Committee
on Armed Services and the Committee on Foreign Relations, U.S. Senate
82nd Cong., 1st Sess. (1951), p. 549; cited hereinafter as *Military Situatior
in the Far East.*

7. *China White Paper,* pp. 140–142.

ective could have been attained, then granting the Commu-
ists a subsidiary role in China's government would not have
een too high a price to pay. And, from the American point
f view, a temporary suspension of arms assistance to Chiang
ad been an entirely logical and proper means toward that
nd.

How sensitive the question of a coalition government had
ecome by 1948, however, and how much mischief could be
vrought out of it by the insidious device of "double-think,"
vas revealed in the considerable furor that was kicked up
ver the matter that spring. Truman and Marshall sensed the
great danger lurking in this question and were extremely wary
vhen, in March, it was raised by a Pennsylvania Republican
congressman, James G. Fulton, of the House Foreign Affairs
Committee. Secretary Marshall, seeking to clarify the matter
at a press conference on March 10, affirmed that the United
States still held to the position of President Truman's policy
statement of December 15, 1945, which had called for "broadening the base" of the Chinese government.[8] But this did not
answer the crucial question of whether or not "broadening the
base" had meant that the United States had accepted the possible inclusion of Communists in the Chinese government. If
that is what it had meant (and, of course, it was), it could
not be admitted in 1948.

Under the drastically altered circumstances of the latter
year, the President and the secretary of state could not afford
to be entirely candid on the subject. They quickly discovered
this, if they had not known it before, when Marshall's forthright remarks at his press conference of March 10 created a
mild sensation. In a statement of March 11, presumably intended to clarify Marshall's clarification of the day before, the
alarmed State Department neatly obfuscated the issue once

8. *Ibid.,* pp. 130, 607–608.

again. It blithely ignored the only question being asked—ha
the "broadened base" statement of 1945 included Commu
nists?—and boldly, if irrelevantly, affirmed that the Commu
nists (of 1948) were in open rebellion and that the questio
of their inclusion in the government "was for the Chines
Government to decide and not for the United States Govern
ment to dictate." [9]

The President himself was drawn into this "clarificatio
game" at a press conference of the same day. When asked i
his December 1945 statement had included Communists, h
asserted emphatically, "It did not include Communists, a
all." [10] But the President's statement was misleading. Sinc
the Communists had been the only serious obstacle to Chiang'
government in late 1945 and early 1946, any proposed politi
cal settlement that failed to include them had surely bee
meaningless and, consequently, the Marshall mission point
less. Apparently "history in double-think" was working on th

9. *Ibid.,* p. 272.

10. In the same news conference, the question of "Communists in th
government of China" occasioned several interesting colloquies betwee
the President and newsmen, such as the following: "Q. You mean th
broadening does not include taking Communists into the National Govern
ment? THE PRESIDENT: It does not. It does not," and later, "Q. Mr
President, Secretary Marshall, just before he became Secretary of State, i
his report on China, did recommend the broadening of the base of the
Chinese Government, that Communists be included? THE PRESIDENT: I
don't think General Marshall intended to take any Communists into the
Chinese Government. We don't want a Communist government in China
or anywhere else, if we can help it," and finally, "Q. Mr. President, a grea
many people, I believe, thought that 'broadening the base' meant taking
in Communists, or at least liberals. THE PRESIDENT: Chinese liberals
There is a very great difference between the liberal element in China and
the Communists. The Chinese Communists are those people who believe
in government from the top—the totalitarian state. There are a great many
liberals in China. . . . They are the people in whom we are interested
principally. We would like to see them included in the broadening of the
base of the Chinese Government." *Presidential Papers: Truman* (1948),
pp. 180–181.

President, as on others, and he was unable to re-create the mood of two years earlier when he had most assuredly accepted the possibility that Communists might be taken into the Chinese government. This is demonstrated in the above-quoted statements of Marshall and other State Department officials to the effect that the makeup of the Chinese government was not the business of the United States. Certainly, these statements prove at least a tacit acceptance of the possibility of a Nationalist coalition government with the Communists.

But President Truman could not be convicted of having held such views; his controversial statement of 1945 had not specified the Communist Party, or any other, by name. Neither could the President be convicted of the altogether different charge—the vicious and irresponsible one—that he had actually wanted Communists in the government of China and had worked hard to bring it about. At least, the latter charge could not be made to stick until a mood of hysteria had been created to sustain it. Unhappily, some men would work hard to create just such a mood and, shrewdly guessing that its time would come, went on making their impudent slurs against the President.

That time had not yet arrived, however, and so the Administration remained virtually immune to damaging attacks on its foreign policy. After all, it had met every international challenge, real or imagined, with great firmness and, apparently, with invariable success. Even the wretched "China mess," so far as one could tell, was not yet hopeless. Chiang Kai-shek was still in nominal possession of most of China. He held every major city and port in the country, and, in spite of all his bungling in Manchuria, he still held that area's strategic gateway city of Mukden and its capital city of Chang-chun. There did not seem to be any cause for undue concern;

besides, the American people were beginning to lag in their enthusiasm for Chiang and his chronically ailing government.[11]

Further diverting the nation's attention from the gathering crisis in China were the momentous events in Europe, where one "earth-shaking crisis" seemed to follow hard upon the heels of another. The "Czech crisis" of March was followed by the "Berlin crisis" of June, when the Russians attempted to cut off the Western powers' access to Berlin. Instead of brushing aside this crude bluff as should have been done, the United States decided to meet it with the technological grandstanding of the Berlin airlift. This spectacular "air show" provided the world with a demonstration of American know-how and resourcefulness, but it also did much to convince the world that Soviet power was far more awesome than it actually was and that American nerve was far less steady than it should have been.[12] The terrifying image of "world Communism" was thus enormously enhanced, but it still wore only a European mask.

The Far East continued to be a secondary theater of Amer-

11. The percentage of the general public, according to the National Opinion Research Center, who held a "favorable opinion" of the Chiang government declined from 31 percent to 26 percent, and the "unfavorable" percentage rose from 25 percent to 33 percent, between 1947 and 1948. See A. T. Steele, *The American People and China* (New York: McGraw-Hill, 1966), pp. 46–47.

12. It must be remembered that at this time Russia was still suffering from grievous war wounds, that its industrial capacity for providing the sinews of war was vastly inferior to that of the United States, and that it had no nuclear weapons. There is not the remotest likelihood that such a nation, guided by the realist Stalin, a man wholly disinclined to reckless adventures, would have risked an act of war to prevent an armed American convoy from proceeding to Berlin in the exercise of a clear, legal right. By way of proving that the Russians "meant business," Dean Acheson notes in his memoirs that an American military train which attempted to reach Berlin was shunted onto a siding, but this only proves that the Russians were willing to engage in technological manipulation to block access to Berlin, not that they would overtly oppose it with armed force. See Dean Acheson, *Present at the Creation* (New York: Norton, 1969), pp. 261–263.

ican concern, just as it had been during World War II. Even congressional Asialationists were willing to forget it for a time, being quite pleased with themselves that they had forced President Truman to ask for more money for China and then had gleefully snatched back more than a hundred million dollars of it. Little matter that this action did not make a great deal of sense; Asialationists were more devoted to the politics of budget-balancing than to China, in any case. They were already girding themselves to take the rest of Harry Truman's scalp in the coming presidential election, and since it was obvious that the election was going to be fought on domestic issues, the China question would have to be put aside for a time.

But those men who were more concerned with China than with balanced budgets did not intend that the matter should be put aside for a moment. "Old China hands" Congressman Walter Judd, "Flying Tiger" Claire Lee Chennault, and publisher Henry Luce knew that prodigious and unceasing efforts would be required to arouse America to the "sacred task" of saving Chiang Kai-shek. It was these men who would devote themselves to rewriting the entire recent history of Sino-American relations so that the people would know with what "vindictiveness" their hero, the Generalissimo, had been pursued.

To carry forward this operation in "double-think," it would be necessary to call into question the credibility of everyone who had been involved with China in any important way and who had dared to write off the Generalissimo as "a loser." Conversely, those who had clung tenaciously to Chiang in the face of every calamity must have their credibility established as beyond all question. The "old China hands" doubtless saw themselves as plain, honest men who were setting the record straight, for they could not believe that those who had spoken ill of Chiang could have done so except out of villainy or stupidity.

Congressman Judd was surprisingly—or naïvely—frank about his method of establishing credibility:

> When a few American generals [presumably Stilwell and Marshall] are unsuccessful in dealing with Chinese leaders, but many others, including Generals Wedemeyer, Hurley, and Chennault, are remarkably successful in dealing with those same leaders, it must be clear to all that in the cases of failure the fault is not all with the Chinese. Any sensible person will give more credence to the reports and views of those who succeeded, than of those who failed. . . .[13]

Judd's only standard was whether these generals had succeeded in *getting along with Chiang,* not whether they had succeeded in getting Chiang to perform creditably. No one had ever succeeded in doing that.

Among those who had borne patiently with Chiang's manifold infirmities and who were thus credible witnesses in Judd's book were Generals Wedemeyer, Hurley, and Chennault and Ambassador Stuart. Of these, however, only Chennault had a record of whole-souled devotion to Chiang.[14] The others would have to be forgiven certain lapses before they could take their places in the circle of integrity. General Hurley, for example, would have to be forgiven his warm, personal regard for Communist Chou En-lai and his insistence that the Chinese Communists were democrats (or "Oklahoma Republicans"), not to mention the fact that he had once drawn up a plan for a coalition government. But forgiveness could be

13. *Congressional Record,* XCIV, 80th Cong., 2nd Sess. (1948), p. A4490.

14. Even Chennault had encountered difficulties with the Generalissimo during the war. He complained to the War Department that he could not train competent flyers unless he had full authority over the flying schools, but, as Barbara Tuchman notes, "Later when pressing the thesis that Stilwell's personal faults caused his clash with the Generalissimo, Chennault left his own difficulties unmentioned." *Stilwell in China* (New York: Macmillan, 1970), p. 310.

arranged, since Hurley had come home from China breathing patriotic fire and denouncing senior foreign service officers for having "sided with the Chinese Communist armed party and the imperialist bloc of nations whose policy it is to keep China divided against herself." [15] And it would not be difficult to forgive Wedemeyer and Stuart the fact that their reports on the Chiang regime had been as damning as any that ever came out of China.[16] These reports would probably never see the light of day; besides, both men had held fast to their "bright and shining image" of Chiang.[17]

While certain reputations were built up, others must be cast down, but it would be no easy matter to diminish the monumental prestige of George C. Marshall. Certainly he could not be dismissed as fool, incompetent, or traitor, having so recently led his country's military forces to victory in history's greatest war. It would be necessary to get at him by indirection, the main attack being centered upon President Harry Truman who was always "fair game" for the most unrestrained villification. In the process, Marshall, who had been Truman's surrogate in China in 1946, could not but be tarnished, and, once tarnished, he too would be "fair game."

America's "foremost expert on China" would know how to get at the great man and, in fact, had already taken an oblique swipe at him in his comment about those generals who had been "unsuccessful in dealing with Chinese leaders." For the

15. *China White Paper*, p. 582.

16. Interestingly enough, Wedemeyer had given the "unkindest cut" of all when he recommended in his report of September 19, 1947, that Manchuria be placed under a five-nation guardianship, which would have included the Soviet Union. It was this insulting suggestion that had led the Truman Administration to suppress the Wedemeyer Report. See pp. 25–27.

17. A perusal of the memoirs of Stuart and Wedemeyer reveals that, even after mature reflection, Chiang Kai-shek was enshrined in the hagiography of both of these men. See John Leighton Stuart, *Fifty Years in China* (New York: Random House, 1954) and Albert C. Wedemeyer, *Wedemeyer Reports!* (New York: Holt, Rinehart and Winston, 1958).

time being, however, it would be necessary to exempt th
World War II "architect of victory" from the worst charge
against the Truman Administration, and so Judd explaine
Marshall's mission to China in this fashion: "Never was
great soldier sent on a mission that was more hopeless. . .
The cards were all stacked against him before he left—in m
judgment, by people here at home." [18] But there was a flaw i
Judd's logic that would make it impossible to exclude Marshal
from the sweeping charge that "we have been assisting
Communist minority in China in its efforts to overthrow th
Chinese Government. . . ." If the China situation was as clea
and as simple as Judd said, and if General Marshall, who ha
spent a year in China, was not too stupid to see the obvious
then why had he accepted appointment as secretary of stat
to go on foisting allegedly ruinous policies upon the nation
Judd's argument could lead to only one end, and the time

18. Judd was hung up on the fact that President Truman's instructions
to Marshall in December 1945 had called for steps to secure the unity and
peace of China (presumably through coalition with the Communists) as the
prerequisite for American aid. Judd insisted that this made it possible for
the Communists to cut off American aid to China by simply refusing to
join Chiang's government, at the same time assuring themselves that they
could attack Chiang with impunity. But this assumes that the Communists,
whom Judd normally regarded as clever in super-human degree, were excessively simple. They probably were not at all impressed by American threats
to cut off aid to Chiang if he did not put his house in order and try to
bring peace to China. America had bluffed Chiang many times before, as
the Reds knew, and had never made good on its threats. It is more likely
that the Communists based their decision to fight on such solid considerations as these: (1) they had discovered that Chiang's armies could be
defeated when they met his ill-conceived attacks upon them in Manchuria,
(2) they perceived that their own popularity with the Chinese people was
rising as Chiang's declined, and (3) they were convinced that the United
States would not intervene on Chiang's behalf, not by what the United
States Government said, but by what the people's representatives in Congress
said, as they expressed their strong and unanimous opposition to American
intervention; Congressman Judd, for example, had said in 1948, "Not for
one moment has anyone contemplated sending a single combat soldier
in. . . ." *Congressional Record, op. cit.,* p. 3442. For Congressman Judd's
discussion of the Marshall mission, see *ibid.,* p. A4559.

would come when it would be spun out by others to that ultimate and ineluctable conclusion—treason.

Less tricky but hardly less important would be the task of discrediting the posthumous testimony of General Joseph Stilwell. And "laying that ghost" might not be a simple matter, for "Vinegar Joe" had recorded for the ages his pungent comments on Chiang Kai-shek. It was even possible that *The Stilwell Papers,* published in the early part of 1948, might deal the final blow to Chiang's dying cause. On the other hand, it might just serve as proof that the feud between the general and the Generalissimo had been so personal and so bitter as to invalidate everything the general had ever said about China. Walter Judd was quick to make the point: "The recent publication of some of his [Stilwell's] own papers reveals far more vividly than any other source could, how much earlier he should have been transferred to another type of command, for his sake as well as everybody else's." [19] The matter turned out as Judd doubtless expected and hoped; the Stilwell book was a six-month sensation, only to pass swiftly out of print and into limbo.

The job of dismantling Stilwell's reputation was undertaken by "Flying Tiger" Claire Lee Chennault in a series of articles published by the Scripps-Howard newspapers during March and April of 1948. Making certain that these articles were collected and bound as a single, comprehensive source, readily available to anyone with the price of a letter to his congressman or within reach of a moderate-sized library, Congressman Walter Judd read them into the *Congressional Record.*[20] This

19. *Ibid.,* p. A4490.

20. The dispute between Chiang and Stilwell grew out of the latter's efforts to build an efficient Chinese army for use against the Japanese during World War II, a project that Chiang steadfastly opposed because he feared that such an army would dispossess him of power. The latter attitude fell in perfectly with Chennault's plan for defeating the Japanese through the "magic" of air power, thus obviating the necessity for build-

was most astute of the congressman, for Chennault did a thorough job on Stilwell.

The "Flying Tiger" obscured the fact that Stilwell's feud with Chiang had been over the latter's refusal to fight the Japanese; he also failed to mention that his own difficulties with Stilwell had grown out of the fact that he (Chennault) had gone over Stilwell's head to secure permission from the White House to fight a dangerously unorthodox air war, which ended disastrously. With such matters neatly hidden away, it was possible to blame all of America's difficulties with Chiang, as well as Chiang's own endless derelictions, on Stilwell. It was even possible to reduce this able and colorful American general to the level of the "village idiot," which was very nearly done. Chennault stopped short of that, however, being content to damn with faint praise, as in this mean-spirited comment: "Joseph Stilwell was . . . one of the finest *divisional* commanders the United States ever produced" (italics supplied).[21]

General Stilwell's version of these events has never gotten a fair hearing. As previously mentioned, his diary was out of print within a year of publication; there were no additional printings, and it has never been reissued in any form. Moreover, no book on Stilwell was published from that time until

---

ing the efficient army that Chiang so feared. It naturally followed that Chennault and Chiang became allies in the scramble for the lion's share of the limited quantity of American supplies that could be flown over the "hump" into China.

Another matter that Chennault obscured—one that probably pained him a great deal and perhaps explains his fury against Stilwell—was the fact that Stilwell had predicted that stepped-up air attacks on the Japanese would force them to launch a campaign to capture the airfields from which the attacks came. This is exactly what happened, and when the Japanese came, the ground force that might have stopped them was not there, because Stilwell had not been permitted to create it. See Tuchman, *Stilwell in China,* particularly chapters 13 and 14, pp. 326–374.

21. *Congressional Record, op. cit.,* p. A4493.

1970, and, except for reviews of *The Stilwell Papers,* very few articles about him appeared in the popular press. The general did get one hearing that carried somewhat beyond the book-reading public when in April 1948 the *Ladies' Home Journal* published a selection from his diaries and letters edited and annotated by his admiring friend Theodore H. White.[22] This was the only brief on the general's behalf that was ever presented to a wide audience, and it came under immediate attack.[23]

Time magazine, as could have been predicted, had no intention of allowing it to go unchallenged and, in a lengthy article of April 5, 1948, set out to demolish both the general and Theodore White, saying of the latter that he "shares Stilwell's hatred of the Chinese government and his warm regard for the Chinese Communists." Having drawn the knife, *Time* made a few more deft thrusts, such as the following: "Like others, Stilwell fell for the 'liberal line' that the Chinese Communists were really agrarian reformers" (no instance was cited where the general ever used this expression); and again, "Much of the present U.S. governmental and popular attitude toward China [presumably, the declining affection for Chiang] has been distilled out of Stilwell's venom"; and finally, "Stilwell's colossal failure contributed to the war-born misunderstanding between the U.S. and China which has already brought a disaster to China and may have consequences for the U.S. as well." *Time* noted with approval General Chen-

22. "General Stilwell Reports," *Ladies' Home Journal,* April 1948.

23. Barbara Tuchman's excellent and wonderfully readable account of Stilwell's China mission, published in 1970, is easily the best account from the Stilwell point of view of America's problems in China during World War II. See her *Stilwell in China.* Certain other works, although generally fair, do less than justice to Stilwell in their very attempt at scholarly objectivity. See particularly Herbert Feis, *The China Tangle* (Princeton: University Press, 1953), and Tang Tsou, *America's Failure in China, 1941–1950* (Chicago: University of Chicago Press, 1963).

nault's series on Stilwell in the Scripps-Howard newspapers, without bothering to point out that the "Flying Tiger" was not entirely unbiased in this matter.[24]

As late as January 1950, in a three-part series in *The Saturday Evening Post,* Joseph Alsop was still pursuing the "ghost of Stilwell" with the sort of rancor that he claimed had animated Stilwell's dealings with Chiang Kai-shek. Far more venomous was this journalist's hatred for a man four years dead, concerning events seven years past. His series, published under the singular title "Why We Lost China," presented the thesis that Stilwell's feud with Chiang had created the misunderstanding between the United States and China that led to China's loss to the Reds, a thesis on a par with that which attributes the Russian Revolution to the evil machinations of Rasputin. And, while mercilessly flaying the dead bones of Joe Stilwell, the journalist did not reveal that, as General Chennault's wartime public-relations officer, he had been deeply and personally involved as a partisan of the Chiang-Chennault camp against Stilwell. He had not been simply a "witness on the scene," as the *Post* avers, but a very active participant.[25]

Besides the giants Stilwell and Marshall, it would also be necessary to get at the lesser actors in the China drama, such as John Paton Davies and John Stewart Service. These men were regarded by many as "America's foremost experts on China," and they held no exalted view of Chiang Kai-shek. But it would not be difficult to discredit men with no political following or other power base. It was likely that the "kiss of death" had already been put on them by Ambassador Hurley's charges that they had taken a pro-Communist position in

24. "Tragedy in Chungking." *Time,* April 5, 1948.

25. "Why We Lost China," *The Saturday Evening Post,* January 7, 14, 21, 1950.

China. In fact, they would serve as the living proof that America's China policy had been "sold-out" from within, as Walter Judd said, by "a handful of Communists, fellow travelers, and misguided liberals," who had thrown away the "victory over Japan which 4,000,000 brave Americans won at such a cost in blood and sacrifice." [26]

All this would now be grist for the mill of the "conspiracists" (China bloc, Asialationists, *et al.*), who could thank Congressman Judd for having provided them with such excellent source materials. He had worked hard to see to it that they had access to the "expert testimony" of "unimpeachable witnesses," carrying, wherever possible, the quasi-official sanction of the *Congressional Record*. Determined that they should have the very best of sources, Judd read into the *Record* on June 19 his own assessment of the China situation. This report of his junket to China of the previous fall was given to the world, said he, in response to wide popular demand.[27]

By an artful use of words, Judd reconstructed facts in such a way as to completely rehabilitate the Chiang regime, which he found to be no more corrupt or incompetent than other governments. In fact, he implied an efficiency performance of 70 percent, without any very clear indication of what that meant. Still, he confessed, this allegedly honest and able government, suffused with a democratic spirit, could not defeat the Communists without a great deal of outside help, another of Judd's contradictory propositions that was never cleared

26. *Congressional Record, op. cit.,* p. A45559. John Stewart Service had actually been arrested in June of 1945 when drafts of his reports from China, which he had foolishly loaned to the editor of the pro-Communist magazine *Amerasia,* were found during a raid on that magazine's offices. Service was cleared of any wrongdoing in the matter and reassigned to duty on General MacArthur's staff in Tokyo, but his troubles had just begun. See Charles Wertenbaker, "The China Lobby," *The Reporter,* April 15, 1952.

27. *Congressional Record, op. cit.,* pp. A4555–4562.

up. Finally, there were the usual charges that the Chinese
Communists were subservient to the Soviet Union and that
the China experts who advised the American government
were Communists or fellow travelers. Judd used the technique
of the generalized smear with consummate skill, as in the following: "It has been openly said that some of these experts,
both in and out of government, are members of the Communist Party, although I have no personal knowledge of that.
But certainly they have consistently followed the party line
with respect to the Chinese Communists." [28]

In September Ambassador Bullitt returned to his "save
China" crusade through the gaudy pages of *Life* magazine.
Taking a turn at "double-thinking" history, he transformed
the Yalta Agreement of 1945 into the Yalta sellout (although
he did not use that particular term).[29] While the Yalta Agreement was not one to cheer about, neither was it a sellout, but
rather a realistic, if unfortunate, bending to the exigencies of
power politics. The United States simply agreed that Russia
should be restored to substantially the same rights in Manchuria (regarding the South Manchurian and Chinese Eastern
Railways and the ports of Dairen and Port Arthur) that it had
enjoyed prior to the Russo-Japanese War of 1904–1905, provided the Chiang government agreed.[30]

Bullitt saw this as the price paid to Russia, unwisely in his
opinion, to get Russia into the war against Japan. But the
ambassador insisted on missing the main point, which was that
the Russians were conceded a little in order to forestall their
taking much, possibly all of Manchuria, and that this probably
had as much to do with the agreement as the question of

28. *Ibid.,* p. A4558.
29. *Life,* September 6, 1948.
30. *China White Paper,* pp. 113–126, 585–604.

Russia's participation in the war against Japan. Anyhow, Bullitt saw it as an act that sacrificed China's—and America's—vital interests and gave the Soviet Union a strategically advantageous position from which to press its campaign for "communizing China." [31]

Sinister possibilities were suggested in the loaded questions that, one way or another, were asked. Implicit in the article itself was the question, Why were America's vital interests in Manchuria given away? And quite explicitly put was the question, Who had the most to do with giving away these interests—George Marshall or Franklin Roosevelt? This sort of demagoguery transformed "Yalta" into a scare-word of such evil connotation that, in time, it would be capable of arousing the greatest emotion, even among people who had not the vaguest notion of what it was all about. The word would come to stand on its own, brooking little rebuttal, as the symbolic proof of treason in the American government.

Within four weeks of Bullitt's "spectacular revelations" about Yalta, a subcommittee of the House Committee on Foreign Affairs issued a remarkable document entitled "The Strategy and Tactics of World Communism," which seemed to confirm the worst fears about the world-conquering aims of "the Communists." The *Bolton Report,* as it was called after the subcommittee chairman Francis P. Bolton of Pennsylvania, was little more than a factual summary of the rise of Communism. Of course, the section on Chinese Communism emphasized that movement's relationship to world Communism through its membership in the Moscow-dominated

31. Apparently the Chiangs were satisfied with the Yalta Agreement; the Generalissimo thanked Ambassador Hurley for American assistance in helping China to achieve "rapprochement with the Soviets," and Madame Chiang, in Washington, thanked the President for helping China get a satisfactory agreement with Russia. *Ibid.,* pp. 120–121.

Comintern. As the subcommittee put it, "The Chinese Communist Party is as much a branch of world communism as any communist party in the world." [32]

There was nothing new or startling in all this. What was alarming was that the subcommittee did not even entertain the possibility that Communism, however hateful to Americans, might have been, for the wholly different people and circumstances of China, a quite legitimate expression of their revolutionary aspirations, or that the Russians, Communist or not, had no more chance than Americans of bending that revolution to their own purposes. The subcommittee, seeing a movement directed by and on behalf of international Communism and taking its orders from Moscow, actually entered into a serious discussion of the question, "Is it Communist or Chinese?" While granting that "the doctrines, the prophecies, and the commands [of the Comintern] have to be adapted to the conditions of the local scene," and while generously conceding that "Communists in China act like Communists in China and not like Communists in France," the subcommittee asserted that ". . . the diversity does not contradict the uniformity, however perplexing it may seem to some observers." The most sweeping, as it was the most incredible, assumption of the subcommittee was that China's mighty upheaval was but an experiment, "the pilot plant and proving ground for the development of Communist theory and strategy and tactics for all of the industrially backward areas of the world." [33]

While congressmen were thus claiming for themselves "gifts of prophecy" and while Walter Judd went on hailing Chiang

32. *The Strategy and Tactics of World Communism,* Report of the House Committee on Foreign Affairs (Subcommittee on National and International Movements), 81st. Cong., 1st Sess. (1949), House Document No. 154, Part I, Supplement III C, p. 2. Cited hereinafter as the *Bolton Report.*

33. *Ibid.,* pp. 2–3.

as the potential "savior of the world," the American people turned their attention to the more earthly concerns of a presidential election campaign, which would concern itself very little with foreign affairs and hardly at all with China. By now, both political parties were agreed that the main task of the nation's foreign policy was to "stop the commies." Toward this end, the Democratic Administration had discarded, without a qualm, the nation's traditional policy of avoiding foreign entanglements and, by an energetic application of the "commie-fear" stick, had bludgeoned a surly Republican majority into going along. To what degree this drastic departure had become the "new orthodoxy" was indicated when the Vandenberg Resolution, ostensibly designed to strengthen the United Nations but which called for "regional and other collective arrangements for individual and collective self-defense," passed the Senate in June with only four dissenting votes. Both political parties pledged themselves to this nebulous, adventurist policy, thus opening the way for endless "entangling alliances" and universal "containmentism."

This policy was conceived with reference to Europe, but the Vandenberg Resolution was too sweeping to be confined to half the globe. The Bolton subcommittee perceived this when it urged the nation to work with China "to seek the democratic and non-Communist way for the peoples of the earth" and noted that "assistance to China, military, economic, and political, and administrative assistance are unavoidable means to our ends." [34] The two political parties, however, were not all that sure what they should do about the "Communist conspiracy" in China. The Democrats, although insisting that Communism's main thrust was in Europe, had been willing to grant more than a half billion dollars to check its advance in China. And the Republicans, while arguing that its big

34. *Ibid.*, p. 61.

push was in Asia, were not willing to grant even so much as a half billion dollars to stop it.

With a determined consistency, the Republicans indicated in their 1948 party platform that this policy of "cheap" was precisely the view they took of the Vandenberg Resolution. Although they expressed a willingness to engage in programs of "self-help and mutual aid" to assist "peace-loving nations" to defend their "fundamental freedoms," they asserted that this should be done only "within the prudent limits of our own economic welfare." They were more worried about domestic Communism and expended more verbiage on it as they affirmed their desire "to expose the treasonable activities of Communists and defeat their objective of establishing here a Godless dictatorship controlled from abroad." If Republicans were truly more concerned about China than Democrats, they gave little indication of it in their 1948 platform, pledging themselves, in an inane generality, "to cherish our historic policy of friendship with China and assert our deep interest in the maintenance of its integrity and freedom." [35]

The Democratic Party, having everything to lose and nothing to gain by discussion of the China issue, left it strictly to the Republican candidate, Thomas E. Dewey, who talked very little on the subject but talked big when he did talk. Speaking at the Mormon Tabernacle in Salt Lake City on October 1, he waxed hot on the Communist menace, trotting out the "Munich shibboleth" as he warned against appeasing Russian aggression in China and other places.[36] On October 16 he expended an entire sentence on China with a promise to end "the tragic neglect of our friend and suffering ally China." [37] Two weeks later he was again pointing with alarm

35. *The New York Times,* June 23, 1948.

36. *Ibid.,* October 1, 1948.

37. *Ibid.,* October 16, 1948.

to the encroachments of Communism in Asia where Soviet power was being extended into "Manchuria, Northern and Central China, Outer Mongolia, Northern Korea, and to Port Arthur and Dairen." [38] What Mr. Dewey would do about all this had been spelled out at a press conference shortly after his nomination: he would provide "advisers, the kind of material the Chinese need and far greater financial assistance." [39] But he failed to explain how he proposed to get the money for this ambitious program from the Republican Congress he was asking the people to elect.

As the election campaign entered its final month, events in China were beginning to shape themselves toward the grand climax. Preparatory to his main thrust southward, Mao Tse-tung was consolidating his hold on the Northeast. The debacle began with the capture of Shantung's capital city of Tsinan on September 24, and proceeded at a rapid pace thereafter. Manchuria's capital city of Changchun fell on October 20 and its gateway city of Mukden on November 1. On the following day Harry Truman was elected to the American presidency over "sure winner" Thomas E. Dewey, and this was probably the most shattering blow of all to China's Nationalists, who had been counting on "a Republican election victory to boost the flagging spirits of field officers, troops and bureaucrats." [40] Actually, the election of Harry Truman had less significance for China than Kuomintang leaders supposed. At this point only massive, direct intervention by the United States would have saved the Chiang regime, and Mr. Dewey had no more stomach for that than did Mr. Truman. In fact, the election was no mandate to do anything about China, one way or the other, and certainly it was no mandate for intervention.

38. *Ibid.,* October 28, 1948.
39. *Ibid.,* June 26, 1948.
40. *Ibid.,* November 4, 1948.

Without waiting for election results, the administration had begun, during the previous summer, preparing for the worst eventuality in China. On August 12 and 13 policy statements had been dispatched to the embassy in China in an effort to prevent any possible misunderstanding about American policy. This was well enough, but one detects an alarming new note creeping into the policy pronouncements of Secretary of State Marshall. While holding steadfastly to non-intervention, he was beginning to employ the vague, emotional language of the "conspiracists" and to fret about "stopping the Communists." Laudable as this aim might have been in theory, it was not likely to be helpful in determining America's real national interests, placing uppermost, as it did, a moral-ideological concept so difficult of precise definition as to smack of abstraction.

The unrealistic hope was expressed that some kind of accommodation could be reached that would "leave as large an area of China as possible with a government or governments free of Communist participation." This chaotic regionalism was being wished upon China in the interest of American security and peace of mind; and the suggestion was actually made that the United States assist the process by providing economic aid for these projected regional governments so as "to permit basic anti-Communist Chinese characteristics to reassert themselves and correspondingly weaken sympathy for the Communists." [41] Such counterrevolutionary doctrine was being disseminated in policy papers at a time when there was the greatest need to take a calm and objective look at China and to see it as an independent entity whose real needs (in terms of its own national security and economic well-being), and not the mystical prognostications of Karl Marx or the jingoistic mouthings of Russian propagandists, would deter-

41. *China White Paper,* p. 279.

mine its future relationship to other Communist states as well as to the United States.

Happily, Marshall still had at least one foot planted firmly on solid ground. In the policy statement of August 12 he indicated that there would be no more meddling in China's affairs:

> 1. The United States Government must not directly or indirectly give any implication of support, encouragement or acceptability of coalition government in China with Communist participation.
>
> 2. The United States Government has no intention of again offering its good offices as mediator in China.[42]

What the United States would very properly do was consult its own national interests. It would keep its options open, said the policy paper of August 13, with regard to China, which was "entering into a period of extreme flux and confusion in which it will be impossible to perceive clearly far in advance the pattern of things to come and in which this Government plainly must preserve a maximum freedom of action." [43] In late October, after the China debacle had begun, the secretary was still holding firmly to the policy of non-intervention. "Present developments," said he, "make it unlikely that any amount of United States military or economic aid could make the present Chinese Government capable of reestablishing and then maintaining its control throughout all China." [44]

Desperately seeking to frustrate this non-interventionist policy by an appeal to the American people, Chiang Kai-shek, in an October 31 interview with A. T. Steele of the New York *Herald Tribune,* presented himself to the world as the great leader in the struggle for freedom and democracy. He trotted out all the scare-phrases, the hysterical slogans, and the nebu-

42. *Ibid.*
43. *Ibid.*
44. *Ibid.,* p. 281.

lous generalities of cold-war rhetoric. "It is the Communist principle," said he, "that in order to control the world, it is essential to control Asia, and in order to control Asia it is essential to control China." [45] If China were subjugated, Chiang continued, "I can decidedly affirm . . . the third world war would surely follow and mankind would once again be precipitated into a tragic disaster." [46] Finally, after a great deal of carping about receiving less American bounty than Europe, the Generalissimo asserted that saving China was "the great task unprecedented in human history. I hope that the American people and their statesmen will dedicate their lives to this task." [47] That this was indeed the Generalissimo's hope no one doubted.

The interview took place two days before the American presidential election; and while Chiang was not necessarily attempting to influence that event in Mr. Dewey's favor, he doubtless would not have been unhappy to have achieved that result. But, failing to move the American people either on his own or Mr. Dewey's behalf, Chiang had no alternative but to plead with the Truman Administration to come to his rescue. Thus it was that Mme. Chiang—against the Generalissimo's wishes, it was said—visited Washington in early December to make a last, desperate appeal for salvation. But neither the Madame nor her cause had the same power to captivate as during her triumphal wartime tour of America. The administration was totally immune to the lady's charms or, at least, did not wish to take any chances; neither the President nor the secretary of state was at the airport to hail her arrival. The latter duty devolved upon presidential aide Colonel Robert Landridge and Mrs. Marshall, who played hostess to the Gen-

45. *Ibid.*, p. 893.

46. *Ibid.*

47. *Ibid.*, p. 894.

eralissimo's lady.[48] Undismayed by this cold shoulder, Mme. Chiang took her forlorn cause to Walter Reed General Hospital to the very bedside of the ailing secretary of state. She came away empty-handed.

Meanwhile, the Chinese embassy in Washington was engaging in the most shameless rabble-rousing.[49] Ambassador Wellington Koo, with as much arrogance as his master, the Generalissimo, had the effrontery to place the Kuomintang in "the vanguard of the common cause of freedom and democracy" and to lecture Americans on their duty to world democracy. "China appeals," said he, "for your understanding of the great issues at stake for all the free peoples in her struggle against the Communist forces. . . . Above all, she appeals for your moral support and material aid." [50] Only in the last two words did he come to the point, and he spelled that out three days later in a comprehensive program of American assistance to China.

Ambassador Koo did not actually request that the United States intervene directly, only that its first step in that direction be a giant one. He asked for: (1) aid in the amount of $3 billion, (2) an outstanding American officer to take charge of supply services, training, and strategic planning, (3) accelerated delivery of equipment and supplies, and (4) an immediate declaration of American support for Generalissimo Chiang Kai-shek in his fight against the Communists.[51] Perhaps the wily ambassador thought the budget-balancing Asia-lationists would get hung up on the latter proposal—it did not

48. *The New York Times,* December 2, 1948.

49. Apparently Madame Chiang and the Chinese embassy were not working in concert, for as Secretary of Defense Forrestal noted at the time: "The President said that Wellington Koo and other Chinese in Washington were now busily undercutting Madame Chiang and the Generalissimo." *The Forrestal Diaries* (New York: Viking, 1951), p. 542.

50. *The New York Times, op. cit.*

51. *Ibid.,* December 5, 1948.

cost money—and force the government to give Chiang, at least, its moral endorsement. If such a forthright commitment had been made, however, it is likely that the pull of calamitous events in China would have dragged the United States the rest of the way to involvement. Fortunately, sanity still prevailed in the executive branch. Robert A. Lovett, acting secretary of state during Marshall's illness, stated very emphatically on December 16 that the United States would not intervene in China's civil war.[52]

Staying out of that war was a possible—even popular—policy in late 1948. No one was as yet so bold, or so stupid, as to suggest that American troops be sent to the continent of Asia to rescue Chiang Kai-shek, no matter how "Christian" or "democratic" he allegedly was. Not even *Life* and *Time* were prepared to cater to publisher Henry Luce's China fetish by such a suggestion. *Time* commented, gloomily but fatalistically, that the Communists would probably win, barring a miracle, and that this "would place forty percent of the world's population in Stalin's grasp." [53] *U.S. News & World Report*, as conservative as *Time* but far more rational, was actually so generous as to concede a degree of legitimacy to the Communist upsurge in China and to suggest that the movement might just possibly be more Chinese than Russian.[54]

This fatalistic acceptance of the inevitable was an attitude that could not last; there were evil portents in the wind. *Time* magazine desperately sought out grounds for intervention by the United States, as in its assertion of December 6: "Our objective in China is not that of aiding our friends. It is to roll back Communism in order to save our own—and Chinese —necks." [55] And as early as November 22 *Life* had thrown

52. *Ibid.*, December 17, 1948.
53. *Time*, December 27, 1948.
54. *U.S. News & World Report*, December 31, 1948.
55. *Time*, December 6, 1948.

down the gauntlet to the President, virtually daring him to recognize either a Red-dominated coalition government or an all-Red government in China. Before that government had yet come to power, and without even considering the possibility of dealing amicably with it, this respectable periodical was demanding that the United States, in effect, swear eternal hostility to it and resolve to retrieve China from its grasp.[56]

Worse yet, *The New York Times,* at the first news of Mukden's fall, rushed headlong into the camp of the "conspiracists," as it had long been tending to do. In what was surely one of the most absurd statements ever uttered by the *Times,* this great newspaper solemnly affirmed on November 1 that "Manchuria is being taken over by a Russian fifth column in a pattern of conquest which bears a startling resemblance to Japan's own pattern." Expressing the hope that "Chinese tenacity will again prove superior to all difficulties," the editorialist betrayed an apparent incapacity to understand, or to believe, that there were Chinese—even Chinese with tenacity— on the other side.[57]

This *Times* man then used "history in double-think" to demonstrate that the United States had contributed to the Kuomintang loss of Manchuria by "consenting to Soviet expansion into Manchuria." Having employed the "Yalta sell-out" gambit, it was inevitable that the next charge would be that the Truman Administration had "sought to bring Communists into the government, then canceled previous loan offers and imposed an embargo against China." Finally, it was noted by this presumably responsible—and certainly Republican—newspaper that "under Republican pressure the policy has been altered. . . ."[58]

---

56. *Life,* November 22, 1948.
57. *The New York Times,* November 1, 1948.
58. *Ibid.*

Such things were being said by reputable people before the worst had yet happened in China and before the Asialationists had even begun to mount their counterattack. The government's passive policy—while entirely correct—would not go well in a land of pragmatists to whom the words "do-nothing" were a reproach. A policy vacuum was created, and frenzied men rushed to fill it with their reckless charges and their angry recriminations, while government and press went on painting, in the most lurid colors, a "Communist conspiracy" of increasingly fearsome aspect. The people could not forever remain calm in the face of all this. Sooner or later they would demand the heads of traitors and, more tragically yet, require their sons to go out and do battle with Communists somewhere—almost anywhere.

CHAPTER FIVE

The Communists Win in China: "Hold 'Em! Harass 'Em! Hamstring 'Em!" (1949)

The theory of the "great commie-bogie" had been, in its beginnings, largely a creation of words, but two momentous events of 1949 seemed to give it terrifying life. The "loss of China" and the Russian acquisition of the atomic bomb apparently proved that "the Communists" were bent upon world conquest, that they were infinitely resourceful, and that their power was awesome—with the acquisition of "the bomb," very nearly unlimited.

Particularly unsettling to Americans was the swift disintegration of the Kuomintang before the Communist onslaught in China. Although another year would pass before the Chinese Communists would drive the last of Chiang's forces from the mainland, their decisive victories came in January, and well-informed persons knew that, for Chiang's government, it was all over but the shouting. So great a catastrophe required explanations, and, in a myth-making age, they were soon forthcoming. As the civil war rushed toward its climax during 1949, Americans increasingly accepted the view that the whole thing had been contrived by the Russians, against the will of the Chinese people, and that China was simply the puppet of Russia.

As the people watched their number one protégé, China, slip behind the "Red curtain," there burst upon them unexpectedly another of 1949's shattering news breaks: on September 23 President Truman announced that the Russians had "the bomb." Only four short years had the United States enjoyed its nuclear monopoly—now suddenly it was gone, along with China.

Americans were not willing to see these events as unconnected. How could the Russians have mastered so quickly the mysteries of "the bomb" or acquired so effortlessly dominion over the vast expanse of China? There were angry stirrings in the land, for surely something was amiss. "The shocks of 1949," said Eric Goldman, "loosed within American life a vast impatience, a turbulent bitterness, a rancor akin to revolt. It was a strange rebelliousness, quite without parallel in the history of the United States." This "strange rebelliousness" doubtless had explanations historically rooted in the American psyche, as Goldman suggests, but he was probably nearest the truth when he observed, "Most directly the restiveness resulted from the foreign policy of the Truman Administration." [1] Particularly, he might have added, from the Truman Administration's failure in China.

The people wanted to be shown that the cause of their country's failures lay neither in themselves nor in their stars but in calculated villainy. If they could find spys and traitors subverting the American government from within, they would have no difficulty in understanding the disturbing events of 1949. And it just so happened that Congressman Richard Nixon of California, having staked his political career on the rooting out of Communists from government, was using his

1. Eric F. Goldman, *The Crucial Decade and After: America, 1945–1960* (New York: Random House/Vintage Books, 1960), p. 113.

position on the House Un-American Activities Committee to track down just such a villain.

With the tenacity that was his outstanding characteristic, Nixon kept doggedly on the trail of Alger Hiss, a former high official of the State Department, through the summer and fall of 1948 and finally unearthed—or unpumpkined—the Whittaker Chambers microfilm, which proved, to the satisfaction of most people, that Alger Hiss was a traitor. The "pumpkin papers" (the State Department documents that Hiss had presumably turned over to Soviet agent Chambers, copies of which the latter had hidden away in pumpkins on his Maryland farm) would also provide for many the explanation as to how the Russians had gotten "the bomb" so soon and why America had failed in China. It seemed as though fate were conspiring to give credence to this dark suspicion when Hiss's trial in May 1949 (for the relatively minor offense of perjury) ended with a hung jury and the whole thing had to be gone through again in the last months of the year—after the Russians had exploded their first bomb and while the final chapters of the China drama were being written.

The grand denouement began in the second week of December 1948, *Time* magazine commenting at the time that "the howitzers could now be heard in Kansas City." During that week, while Congressman Nixon waited anxiously to see if a New York grand jury would crown the outstanding achievement of his career with success by indicting Alger Hiss, Mao Tse-tung was setting in motion a wholly different but truly earth-shaking chain of events in China. On December 11 he presented to his colleagues a paper entitled "Concept of Operations for the Peiping-Tientsin Campaign," a document that projected the doom of Chiang Kai-shek's government and, with it, American influence in China.[2] The stage was now set

2. *Selected Works of Mao*, Vol. I, pp. 289–293.

for the playing out of these two dramas, and, while there was
not the remotest connection between them, the fact that many
Americans saw them as two aspects of the same sinister plot
linked them strangely together.

Richard Nixon had the satisfaction of seeing Hiss indicted
on December 15, 1948, and the trial date set early the following year. Meanwhile, Mao Tse-tung had launched his
armies south of the Great Wall against the main force of the
Kuomintang. When this gigantic battle was over on January
31, 1949, Red armies held China's ancient capital of Peking,
while others swarmed into the rich and populous Yangtze Val-
ley. On April 20 these same armies crossed the Yangtze, and
ten days later Alger Hiss went to trial for the crime of perjury.

In January of that fateful year Dean Acheson took over the
onerous duties of secretary of state from the ailing George
Marshall. Chiang Kai-shek's government was entering the final
stages of collapse, and, as Acheson commented, "I arrived
just in time to have him collapse on me." [3] This was most unfortunate, for the extremely able Mr. Acheson would never
quite recover from having been "collapsed on." The little band
of congressional irresponsibles whom Acheson dubbed "the
primitives" would see to it that he did not recover. These
men, wielding excessive influence in a time of rising hysteria,
despised and distrusted the new secretary, holding against him
even the sophisticated intelligence that went far to qualify
him for his office. His moderation was a vice, and the fact
that he did not attack the Soviet Union in crude and violent
terms made him suspect.

Acheson would finally win confirmation from the Senate
but not before he had been thoroughly villified. Senator Kenneth Wherry of Nebraska noted that former Assistant Secretary of State Adolph Berle had said that "Mr. Acheson was

3. Dean Acheson, *Present at the Creation* (New York: Norton, 1969),
p. 257.

in the pro-Russia bloc of the State Department"; and Wherry was not impressed by the fact that Berle had later decided that "Acheson is now O.K., thoroughly solid, in his position that Russia's dictators are trying to rule the world and cannot be appeased." What mattered more to Senator Wherry, strongly seconded by Senator Jenner of Indiana, was that the American people simply did not trust this elegant fellow in striped pants: "As I have traveled around over the U.S. I have discovered a fact which cannot be denied . . . that somehow it is common knowledge that Mr. Acheson has been an appeaser of Russia." [4]

Even more incredible were the remarks of the moderate Senator Vandenberg, who came to Acheson's defense with the assertion that this man would not, in his opinion, "be a softy in dealing with Communism." By way of proof, the senator offered the fact that Acheson was not a good friend of Alger Hiss's (as was widely believed) but only of Alger's brother Donald (a member of the Acheson law firm). But the best thing in the secretary-designate's favor was the fact that the Kremlin had no use for him: "Upon at least one historic occasion it [the Kremlin] has officially and violently protested his statements about Russia and complained bitterly about his attitudes." [5]

Dean Acheson was irritated by this fantastic ritual of confirmation, but he clearly understood that it set the terms of his secretaryship—that he was being told that a mean-spirited rancor must inform all of his relations with Communist nations. It is to Mr. Acheson's credit that he accepted the terms with bad grace, but accept them he did. He affirmed that he would be tough on "commies," although he did it in a somewhat backhanded fashion: "The things I read about myself as an appeaser are so incredible that it is difficult to believe that

4. *Congressional Record,* XCV, 81st Cong., 1st Sess. (1949), p. 464.
5. *Ibid.,* p. 461.

even disinterested malevolence could think them up." [6] As Senator Vandenberg said, this man "would not be a softy in dealing with Communism."

Acheson got off easily this time, but he would soon become a favorite target in the vicious assault about to be unleashed against the makers of American foreign policy. The outlines of the sinister "conspiracy" with which they would be charged, as well as the leading heroes and villains and important places and events, had already been clearly delineated by Congressman Judd, ably assisted in the task by publisher Henry Luce, Ambassador Bullitt, and "Flying Tiger" Chennault. The important places were Yalta, Chungking, and Washington; the major events were the Stilwell-Chiang feud of 1942–1945, the Yalta Agreement of 1945, and the Marshall mission to China of 1946; the heroes were Generals Chennault, Hurley, Wedemeyer, and MacArthur, and the villains were Generals Stilwell and Marshall, along with their associates and advisers John Stewart Service, John Paton Davies, W. Walton Butterworth, and the wartime head of the State Department's Far Eastern desk, John Carter Vincent. Playing somewhat enigmatic roles as villains were Henry Wallace, a former Vice President turned radical, who had undertaken a special mission to China for President Roosevelt in 1944, and, of course, Alger Hiss, who was suspected of treason and, the ultimate damnation, had been at Yalta.

With Chiang's regime collapsing in China, with "commies" turning up in the most unexpected places in the United States, and with the American people growing daily more restive, it would now be possible to press the attack upon the government with unrestrained fury, the attackers knowing that, at last, they would be heard. There was no need to be very scrupulous about either facts or logic, which made possible

6. *Ibid.*

the emergence of a curious sort of circular argument. Those events that smacked of failure or of concessions to (appeasement of) Communists, such as the Marshall mission or the Yalta Agreement, were enough to taint any man who had been too closely associated with them. And once a man had been tainted, that very taint could then be turned around and used as evidence that the event that tainted him had been tainted. The circular argument also made it possible to deepen the guilt of one tainted man by the fact of his past association with another, and vice versa, *ad infinitum*. Marshall, for example, would be condemned by the fact that he had strongly upheld the suspect General Stilwell in China; and later, the case against Stilwell would be bolstered by the fact that he had been upheld by the suspect Marshall.

Senator Owen Brewster of Maine was a master at weaving names, places, and events into a pattern of treason.[7] It will be well to examine his technique at some length in an address he delivered to the Lincoln Club of Sacramento, California, on February 11:

> Stalin under the secret agreement at Yalta (of which not even General Marshall had been informed) was given control of Manchuria. The vast stores of Japanese war material and the even more important munition production of Manchuria were placed at the service of the Communists. Time was necessary to reorganize and mobilize this enormous military potential. Now note the coincidence.

> For 10 months all American military aid was cut off to Chiang while the State Department sought to force Chiang to take the Communists into his government. . . . Vast and insidious agencies of propaganda were operating full blast to discredit the Chiang regime with apparently the full sympathy of the responsible authorities in our State Department.[8]

---

7. The term "treason" was not yet being used; the operational terms were "softness on Communism," "fellow traveling," or "a fatuous liberal misunderstanding of the true nature of Communism."

8. *Congressional Record, op. cit.*, p. 1350.

Senator Brewster was not yet prepared to name the wrong-doers, but it would not be too difficult to guess who had imposed a ten-month embargo or who were the "responsible authorities in our State Department." And, of course, he delighted in calling the roll of the heroic nay-sayers: "Chennault, Wedemeyer, Hurley, and Bullitt might warn in vain," but apparently Chiang Kai-shek, "the only challenge to Communist domination," had been "doomed to destruction by the official voice of the State Department." [9]

Meanwhile, at the other end of the continent, John Fitzgerald Kennedy, a young Democratic politician who, like Republican Richard Nixon, had discovered that the Communists-in-government issue could provide a welcome assist to political ambition, actually outstripped Brewster in raising the "hue and cry." As a Democrat, he would eventually be forced to abandon the issue, but for now, Kennedy proved himself no mean myth-maker, as he recounted for a Salem, Massachusetts, audience "The Tragic Story of China." His sources were the fantastic Bolton Report, Ambassador Bullitt's doom-crying *Life* magazine article of September 6, 1948, and the paranoid rantings of General Hurley about those "senior foreign service officers in China" who had done him wrong.

Little wonder then that Congressman Kennedy was letter-perfect in the catechism of the China sellout: What did General Stilwell want to do in China? Arm one thousand Reds, in which he "was supported by the State Department." What happened at Yalta? "A sick Roosevelt, with the advice of General Marshall and other chiefs of staff, gave the Kurile Islands . . . Port Arthur and Dairen to the Soviet Union." What happened in Manchuria? "Russia left Chinese Reds in control of Manchuria and vast quantities of Japanese equipment. . . ." What did General Marshall do in China in 1946:

9. *Ibid.*

He embargoed shipments of war materials to China, so that "between the summer of 1946 and February 1948 not a single cartridge or shell was delivered to China." What was the purpose of all this? "To force Chiang Kai-shek to take Communists into the Chinese Government."

As a bonus, Kennedy dropped a couple of names not heard much previously when, in speaking of those who had lost sight of our "tremendous stake in a non-Communist China," he named "our diplomats and their advisers, the Lattimores and the Fairbanks." The congressman concluded on an emotional note that would drive home his message: "This is the tragic story of China whose freedom we once fought to preserve. What our young men had saved, our diplomats and our President have frittered away." [10]

"Old Asia hand" Douglas MacArthur thought this speech of "young veteran of the war in the Pacific, Congressman John Fitzgerald Kennedy," so excellent a piece of work that he quoted passages of it in his own speeches, and, taking little note of the "young veteran's" dubious sources, or perhaps approving them, he called it "one of the most accurate comments on this period. . . ." But it must be said for the general that, unlike the congressman, he was not a reckless name-dropper, and so these were deleted from passages he quoted. And while given to sweeping indictments of appeasement in American foreign policy, he charged it to ignorance rather than treason: "We have watched Communist imperialism spread throughout the world. We have seen thousands of our young men vainly sacrifice their lives in blind pursuit of sterile policies of appeasement based on ignorance of history and of this enemy." [11]

One who was not bashful about bandying names, or implying the worst, was the syndicated columnist George Sokol-

10. *Ibid.*, p. A993.

11. Douglas MacArthur, *Reminiscences* (New York: McGraw-Hill, 1964), pp. 320–321.

sky, who complained in the Washington *Times-Herald* of May 12 that President Truman had tried to convince Senators Wherry and Bridges that "it was Chiang Kai-shek, and not Generals Stilwell and Marshall, advised by John S. Service, Owen Lattimore, Lauchlin Currie, John Carter Vincent, W. Walton Butterworth, Jr., and several representatives of the Treasury Department suspected of Communist Party associations, who confused that situation." Striving desperately to fit "super-spy" Alger Hiss into the picture, Sokolsky let his imagination run free. He wondered if Hiss, being an underling, had not been acting under instructions from his superiors: "What were those instructions and who gave them and why did the Government suppress the Chambers-Hiss story, of which they had full knowledge for 10 years?" William Jenner thought this so rich that he quoted the entire article in a Senate speech.[12]

Those most devoted to conspiracy theories were usually quite as devoted to the idea that a "Communist take-over" equaled a "Russian take-over." The theory was already being given respectability as early as 1948, even by so reputable a newspaper as *The New York Times*. And before the "conspiracists" were finished, virtually everyone in America would believe it. Hard-liner William F. Knowland put it this way: "I will say . . . that I have no doubt that all the Communist forces throughout the world are tied together in a master plan. . . . I think they are all working toward the overthrow of what we like to think of as a free world of free men." [13] The more sophisticated Dean Acheson, not given to melodramatic references to "commie master plans" and "timetables of conquest," said the same thing somewhat differently in 1950: "We are interested in stopping the spread of communism because communism is a doctrine that we don't happen

12. *Congressional Record, op. cit.*, pp. 6391–6394.
13. *Ibid.*, p. 14340.

to like. Communism is the most subtle instrument of Soviet foreign policy that has ever been devised, and it is really the spearhead of Russian imperialism. . . ." [14]

These two—Knowland and Acheson—were very strange bedfellows indeed, and this Russia-in-China fantasy would bring together a whole assortment of poorly matched bedfellows. At one extreme, the very respectable C. L. Sulzberger of *The New York Times* expressed the view that Mao was the Kremlin's man, although he wondered if ideology alone would "serve to keep him the abject tool of Moscow." [15] At the other pole, *Collier's* magazine presented evidence from the inner circles of the "world conspiracy" itself, in an article by "old insider" and onetime *Daily Worker* editor Louis Budenz, that Moscow had been indoctrinating American Communists since 1927 with the line that "China is the master key to a Red White House." [16] An "authority" of yet another type was the Washington *Star*'s Constantine Brown, a favorite source of information for congressmen on matters of world intrigue and "commie" mischief. He was quoted by no less an "expert" than Walter Judd as having said that Russia had won an important "strategic victory" with the Reds' triumph in China. [17] Congressman John Sanborn of Idaho cited the same "global strategist" as authority for the unsupported claim that Russia gave the Chinese Reds much help and that they take orders from Moscow. [18]

Senator Knowland discovered a rich source of inside infor-

14. The Department of State *Bulletin*, XXII, January 23, 1950, p. 114; cited hereinafter as S.D. *Bulletin*. Dean Acheson was apparently of the same opinion when he wrote his memoirs in 1969: "Of course, we opposed the spread of Communism; it was the subtle, powerful instrument of Russian imperialism. . . ." Acheson, *op. cit.*, p. 356.

15. *The New York Times*, February 14, 1949.

16. *Collier's* March 19, 1949.

17. *Congressional Record, op. cit.*, p. A2526.

18. *Ibid.*, p. A4865.

mation about Soviet "master plans" and "timetables" in Russian defector Grigori A. Tokaev who, although only a lieutenant colonel, had carried out secret missions for Soviet leaders "and was privy to the innermost councils of the Kremlin. . . ." According to the colonel, Russia's plans for the conquest of Europe had been slowed because of fears about that eternal "vulnerable flank," but, with the Red conquest of China, the flank was now secure. The colonel could also explain, Knowland solemnly told the Senate, how the Red Chinese General Chu Teh had acquired his amazing aptitude for managing mass armies: "The higher staff posts [in the Chinese Red Army] are held by Soviet officers of Chinese, Korean and Mongolian nationalities. Many of these were recently serving in the Soviet Army, went through the Soviet military academies and colleges, or else commanded Soviet military formations in the East." [19]

Probably no myth-makers caused more trouble than the grimly serious commentators of the school of "hardheaded realism." Harold J. Noble wrote in this vein for *The Saturday Evening Post* and, while he did not claim that China was a puppet of Russia, he was impatient of those maudlin souls who supposed that China, having conquered all of Asia, would not, "in alliance with Russia," "bend every sinew to destroy us too." [20] Republican leader Thomas E. Dewey was another such "tough guy" who, in endless speeches on the subject of China, revealed the "true nature" of the "Russian conspiracy" in China. Professor John K. Fairbank took him to task in an open letter to *The New York Times* for stating as facts things that he could not possibly know to be facts and which probably were not facts.[21] But the governor was not to be diverted

19. *Ibid.,* p. 4601.
20. *The Saturday Evening Post,* July 9, 1949.
21. *The New York Times,* August 3, 1949.

from his patriotic mission by the likes of "the Lattimores and the Fairbanks."

No one, with the possible exception of *The New York Times,* could outstrip *Time* magazine in its devotion to "hard-headed realism." *Time* had no use for sentimentalists who would treat China as a real nation of flesh and blood creatures who worried more about where their next meal was coming from than about "timetables" of conquest. Rather, they must be seen in terms of their ideological orientation and of their presumed world view. Little hard evidence was required for *Time* realists to see that China was nothing more than a puppet of the Soviet Union.[22]

While myths were thus clothed with reality, congressional "realists" were crying for strong action on the part of the administration. Fifty-one members of Congress addressed a letter to the President on March 7, expressing their urgent demands:

> In view of the *grave threat to our national security* [italics added] presented by the crisis in China, it is our considered judgment that the public interest requires as a minimum the appointment of a commission of one or more eminent Americans, with top-level military, economic, and political advisers, to make an immediate reexamination of the situation and report its recommendations to you and to the Congress.[23]

But, however grave the crisis, these men were not willing to put aside partisan political rancor and scapegoat-chasing. They wanted to know to what degree American policy was based on the Wallace (villain) report of 1944 and to what degree on the Wedemeyer (hero) report of 1947.[24]

Four days later the Senate got into the act, calling for "an

---

22. *Time,* October 10, 1949.

23. *Congressional Record, op. cit.,* pp. 1950–1951.

24. *Ibid.*

affirmative policy for the United States with respect to Asia through providing effective assistance to the Government of China on a realistic basis." Fifty senators, including Arkansas Democrat J. William Fulbright and Wisconsin Republican Alexander Wiley, both members of the Senate Foreign Relations Committee, addressed a letter to the committee's chairman, Tom Connally, calling for swift action on the McCarran Resolution, which called for the swift spending of more money in China—$1.5 billion of it.[25] Secretary Acheson, in a letter to Senator Knowland, tried patiently to reason with the senators, explaining that Chiang's problem was not a lack of ammunition and equipment. Doubtless hoping to jolt them into a sense of reality, he pointed out that to provide "some prospect of successful military resistance would require the use of an unpredictably large American armed force in actual combat. . . ."[26] But the senators would not be panicked from their course by mere facts and common sense.

A frantic note began to be heard after the Chinese Reds crossed the Yangtze on April 20. *The New York Times,* in a tearful editorial of April 28, expressed regret that the United States had entered a "period of moral retreat. We have been obliged to compromise with our consciences in the name of expediency." What was moral, it turned out, was stopping the "Communists" and assisting "free peoples" (the very un-free people of China presumably) "to remain free."[27] Senator Knowland, another outstanding moralist, was pleased to have the moral support of the august *Times,* and he cited that newspaper's James Reston by way of proving that the United States had no China policy. All that Mr. Reston had said was that "Mr. Acheson, like Mr. Kipling, is following the policy of

25. *The New York Times,* March 11, 1949.
26. *Ibid.*
27. *Ibid.,* April 28, 1949.

'judicious leaving alone.' " Ah, ha! exulted Mr. Knowland, a "do-nothing" policy.[28]

But Knowland had "grounds more relevant than this"; he had "vulnerable flanks" and no less an authority than General Douglas MacArthur, who, said Knowland, had warned in 1948 that if the lower Yangtze fell to the Chinese Communists, "the American military bastion on Okinawa would be outflanked. . . ." [29] On May 3, that other great expert on "dominoes" and "vulnerable flanks" of the Far East, "Flying Tiger" Claire Lee Chennault, rushed to Congress with a plea for China's salvation (which, incidentally, would have meant the salvation of his own independent airline). If China falls, said he, the neighboring states (all dominoes presumably) of Indochina, Malaya, Siam, Burma, and Indonesia will fall and that will "bring grave pressure upon India and encourage the Soviets to resume their interrupted drive into the critical region of the Middle East." But the "Flying Tiger" had "a plan." It called for $700 million of military aid yearly to carry out a "holding operation" in South China, sustained by the "magic" of air power (the reactivated Flying Tigers or something of the sort), to "maintain a beachhead in the remaining free areas for the resurgence of Nationalist China." [30] While Chiang cowered in defeat in a rapidly shrinking corner of China, Chennault was already preparing to "unleash him."

Chiang was not too busy retreating to make his own pleas for help. This he did through an interview on July 5 with

28. *Congressional Record, op. cit.,* p. 5241.

29. *Ibid.,* p. 5240.

30. *The New York Times,* May 4, 1949. "The Chennault Plan" got very wide coverage, *Life* magazine running it in its issue of July 11, 1949, under the title "Last Call for China," and describing it in these terms: "A Fighting American Says that a Third of its Good Earth and 150,000,000 People Can Be Saved." An abridged version of it was printed under the extraordinary title "Hold 'Em! Harass 'Em! Hamstring 'Em!" in the *Reader's Digest,* October 1949.

Scripps-Howard writer Clyde Farnsworth; and Senator Knowland was happy to pass it on to the United States Senate. The Generalissimo warned the world against believing that China's Reds were independent of Russia or that they would, in the future, take "a Tito turn." Such talk was "just one more of their [the Communists'] propaganda tricks designed to mislead and confuse and will prove as false and unfounded as their previous efforts to confuse." Turning to the theme of Chiang-the-defender-of-peace-and-freedom, he asserted: "This fight against Communism in China isn't only a fight for Chinese freedom from the present Communist menace. It is a fight for the peace and security of the free world. . . ." Then, on the theme where his heart was, Chiang expressed the belief that the United States would not "exclude China from the scope of her aid." [31]

Not less terrified than Chiang was America's own doom-cryer William C. Bullitt. On April 23 the Texas legislature accorded him a standing ovation after he explained to them the mysteries of the chain reaction: "China is the key to all Asia. If China goes, Indo-China, Siam, Burma, the Malay States, and Indonesia will fall into the hands of the Communists. India will be at Stalin's mercy. . . ." The clincher was that America too was threatened: "Unless we oppose Communist conquest of China we assent to it. And our children will face assault by overwhelming masses of Communist driven slaves." [32]

Members of the United States Senate were also seeking out expertise on the phenomenon of the "chain reaction." Owen Brewster, at the suggestion of Robert A. Taft, read the Senate an entire article from the Washington *Post* of June 24 by columnist Joseph Alsop, the expert on Stilwell "villainy" and "vulnerable flanks" who, it seems, had also mastered the

31. Quoted in *Congressional Record, op. cit.*, p. 8821.
32. Quoted in *ibid.*, pp. 6307–6308.

Communist strategy of the chain reaction: "If the Soviet Union can extend its sphere beyond China, into Indochina, a chain reaction will become highly probable. All of Southeast Asia will be threatened. If Southeast Asia goes, Japan and India will be immediately menaced." But, Alsop, like Chennault, had a plan: He would begin to build a wall along the fringes of China; and, as farfetched as the scheme was, it would one day become American policy. He proposed that the line be held in Indochina by France's man, the Emperor Bao Dai, although admittedly this was not the columnist's first choice: "But the fact remains that although supporting Bao Dai is by no means an ideal solution to the Southeast Asia problem, it is the only solution available." [33]

But what was the import of all this doom-crying? If the menace to America was as grave as pictured, then surely it called for the most decisive American action. Tom Connally, chairman of the Senate Foreign Relations Committee, forced his colleagues to face the issue squarely when he put this question to Senator Brewster: "But let me ask the Senator from Maine if he would have wanted to send his son to China to take part in a fight between Chinese rival armies? The Senator from Texas does not have such a desire." Brewster attempted to avoid a direct answer, calling it a "red herring," but when finally pressed to the wall, said, "I had already made it very clear to the Senator from Texas that I had never proposed to send an American Army in China. . . ." Knowland, eager to get off the same hook, asked Connally this question, "Will not the Senator agree that there has never been a proposal on the part of those who are critical of the policy we have pursued in the Far East to send an Army to China . . . ?" [34]

33. Quoted in *ibid.*, p. 8294.
34. *Congressional Record, op. cit.*, pp. 8296–8297.

What then did these senators want? Miracles, apparently. But they would settle for a policy of "non-recognition" of Red China. Twenty-one of them addressed a letter to the President on June 27, asking for assurances that "no recognition of the Communist forces in China is presently contemplated and that we shall make it clear that a free, independent and non-Communist China will continue to have the friendship and assistance of the United States of America." This policy should be followed, they thought, because "Communist control of China means . . . a major victory for international communism with a corresponding threat to the national security of the United States. . . ." [35] A policy of non-recognition would neither prevent "a major victory for international communism" nor contribute to the security of the United States; but the State Department was not likely to reject a policy that had brought senators to so high a state of moral indignation.

Still, there was a remote possibility in the summer of 1949 that the United States might avoid this pitfall. Ambassador Stuart and other diplomatic officials had been left at their posts in China after the Reds took over; and while these officials studiedly avoided giving any formal signs of recognition to the Communist government, their continued presence amounted to *de facto* recognition. They were all withdrawn, either later that year or early the following year, as a result of abusive treatment by the Communists. But there was still a good chance that, once the Chinese Reds had vented their wrath over American support of the Chiang regime and once the latter had sunk into oblivion, normal relations could be established. It was not yet a pressing problem. This was one of those situations where "the best policy was to have no policy," or, as Mr. Acheson put it, to "wait until the dust settles."

35. *Ibid.*, pp. 8406–8407.

A number of America's most distinguished Far Eastern experts (scholars, businessmen, *et al.*), participating in a State Department "Round Table Discussion on China Policy" in early October, expressed a strong consensus in favor of early recognition of Communist China by the United States.[36] But this was not to be, for calamities were piling high in the fall of 1949. It was on September 23, during the very period when China's Red armies were rushing from one spectacular victory to another, that President Truman stunned the nation with the announcement that the Russians had "the bomb." And one week later, on October 1, Mao Tse-tung proclaimed the People's Republic of China in Peking. Americans, making little distinction as to the nationality of Communists and believing these events to be closely connected, envisaged armies of the Moscow-dominated "world Communist conspiracy," now nuclear-armed, sweeping across China. And in November the second perjury trial of Alger Hiss would begin, seeming to reaffirm the widely held view that these calamities had been caused by traitors within the American government. It was not a propitious time for granting recognition to China's Red government.

Certainly a State Department that was given to the most precipitate and disorderly retreats before its critics was not going to make a fight over the issue. In a formal statement of October 3 the State Department revealed that it was already preparing its lines of retreat. Department spokesman Michael McDermott set forth the standards that a new government must meet in order to be accorded recognition: It must be in control of the machinery of government; it must govern with the assent of its people and without resistance to its authority;

36. See "Round Table Discussion on American Policy Toward China Held in the Department of State, October 6, 7, and 8, 1949," *Hearings on the Institute of Pacific Relations*, 82nd Cong., 1st Sess. (1951). Cited hereinafter as *Institute of Pacific Relations*.

and it must be in a position to fulfill its "responsibilities and obligations" under international law. He emphasized, moreover, that Red China must not only be in a position to fulfill its international "responsibilities and obligations," it must also demonstrate a willingness to do so. Finally, as though to allay any doubts that the State Department could be bullied, McDermott gave the most solemn assurances that Congress would be consulted before any action at all was taken on the recognition question.[37]

Members of Congress kept strong pressure on the State Department to make sure it held steady on this issue, and no one worked harder at the task than the "senator from Formosa," William F. Knowland, who warned on October 11 that there was a great ground swell of popular opposition to recognition of Red China. He praised the A.F. of L. for adopting resolutions that indicated its awareness of "the betrayal that has taken place in the State Department of a wartime ally and traditional friend"; and he was delighted to report that the American Legion had adopted strong resolutions "condemning the policy of do-nothing or wait until the dust settles, which this country has followed in regard to the China policy." [38]

As exercised over this question as the "senator from Formosa," *The New York Times* observed in an October 4 editorial that if the Chinese Nationalist charge that the "Communist revolution is an instrument of the policy of the Soviet Union" were upheld by the U.N., it would impose upon the United States "the moral obligation to reaffirm the Stimson principle [of non-recognition] or satisfactorily to explain why we have departed from it." The *Times,* accepting the charges as already proven, insisted that Russia would have "to deny

37. *The New York Times,* October 4, 1949.
38. *Congressional Record, op. cit.,* p. 14182.

having given aid and support if its newest puppet state is to hope for even a tolerant reception in the family of nations." [39]

In an executive session with the Senate Foreign Relations Committee on October 12, Acheson was reported to have given no indication that the recognition of Red China was even being considered.[40] The secretary was still hoping that the "dust would settle" favorably for the United States, which would happen only if Mao's Communist armies quickly invaded the island of Formosa. Their failure to do so would give renewed life to the government of Chiang Kai-shek and impose an insuperable barrier to the normalization of relations between the United States and Communist China. Although Acheson did not know it, the dust had already settled—for at least twenty years—on a policy of non-recognition of the *de facto* government of China. And within little more than a year, Secretary Acheson would be stoutly defending this policy and just as stoutly denying that he had ever considered any other.[41]

Thus did the United States assume the right to determine the legitimacy of every government on the globe, employing, in the process, its own self-determined standards and values. Anti-Communist governments, no matter how corrupt, reactionary, and unpopular, could count on receiving the American stamp of approval. Since they were on "our side," they were, by definition, "defenders of the free world" and of the "people's freedom." On the other hand, radical leftist movements, even if indigenous and no matter how popular, were certain to be branded as illegitimate usurpations of power. This made it possible to condemn even internecine revolutionary movements as aggression, if they were Communist-led, the

39. *The New York Times, op. cit.*
40. *Ibid.,* October 13, 1949.
41. *Military Situation in the Far East,* p. 1778.

proof being that they got some of their arms (one single rifle would be proof enough) from independent Communist states. American arms were, of course, supplied to established governments, already stamped as "legitimate authority."

The American people developed a genuine fondness for this policy; it appeared to be the very embodiment of high principle and, what was more important, there seemed little possibility that it would ever cost them very much. For similar reasons, many American politicians conceived an intense devotion to the policy, some actually growing quite passionate about it. After all, it provided them endless opportunities for doing the things they loved so well to do: delivering grand moralizing orations, mouthing inane patriotic slogans, and denouncing foreigners—particularly Europeans who did not go along with American policy and Asians who did not adopt the "American way." And these same politicians—men whose reactions to foreign affairs were almost entirely emotional— would set the terms of America's Far Eastern policy. They would demand a policy of vigorous and apparently endless support for the discredited government of Chiang Kai-shek and one of calculated and relentless hostility toward the government of Red China. Any departure from such policies would be regarded as immoral and unpatriotic and, in time, as downright treasonable.

CHAPTER SIX

The State Department's *White Paper* Defense: Disengagement Proclaimed (1949–1950)

While "waiting for the dust to settle" during the summer of 1949, the secretary of state decided that it would be a very good thing for the American people to have all the facts about China. Believing that the "human mind could be moved by facts and reason," Mr. Acheson had the State Department prepare a thorough factual study of recent Sino-American relations, which, he hoped, would dispel some of the misrepresentations and general nonsense that were being uttered on the subject.[1] Even that hardheaded realist Harry Truman thought it might do some good, saying when he released the study that its object was to "insure that our policy toward China, and the Far East as a whole, shall be based on informed and intelligent public opinion." [2] Thus it was that one of the most controversial government documents ever issued was presented to the public, carrying the imposing title *United States Relations*

1. Dean Acheson, *Present at the Creation* (New York: Norton, 1969), p. 302.

2. *Presidential Papers: Truman* (1940), p. 408.

with China with Special Reference to the Period 1944–1949,
commonly known as the *China White Paper.*

The *White Paper* was both a complete success and a total
failure. It proved conclusively what it set out to prove, but
in the end, served only to strengthen the case of those who
damned the administration for its alleged failure in China.
Any fair and intelligent person who read all 1,054 pages of the
document would have had to conclude, with Mr. Acheson, that
"The unfortunate but inescapable fact is that the ominous
result of the civil war in China was beyond the control of the
United States." [3] But who was going to read 1,054 pages of a
dull, tedious government document? Hardly anyone, as a matter of fact—not even the "fair and intelligent." The *Paper* was
not capsulized (an impossible task) in a form that would
grab, let alone hold, the mind of the average person. Thus it
became the happy hunting ground for scavengers. Anyone
could make what he would of the *White Paper,* and, needless
to say, they did.

The main trouble with the *White Paper,* as some astute
observers noted, was that it had not asked, let alone answered,
the right question. But the right question was one that no
government was going to ask of itself, let alone attempt to
answer, namely, why was an obviously hopeless policy ever
attempted in the first place? Actually, there was no indication
that the State Department believed this to be the case. The
White Paper was itself an implicit reaffirmation of the basic
premises of that policy: (1) that a friendly—that is, non-Communist—government in China was important to the security
and well-being of the United States and (2) that, by an astute
manipulation of the political forces in China, this result could
be brought about. The first premise was not necessarily true,
and even if it were, the second was presumptuous foolishness.

3. *China White Paper,* p. xvi.

But the belief that the American government could manipulate foreign governments into paths of America's choosing would continue to be a tragic presupposition of the nation's policy-making in the Far East.

The *White Paper* challenged only the chosen instrument of that manipulation, not the principle of manipulation. It demonstrated that the Kuomintang had been a woefully inadequate instrument to the task assigned it and, what was worse, that the State Department had been keenly aware of that fact from the beginning. It was not at all inappropriate then for critics to ask the very disturbing question, as did the distinguished China scholar John K. Fairbank, "Were we well advised to try [to save Chiang's government] in the first place?" [4] But the Truman Administration, as noted, dared not ask the question and was probably relieved to see that very few people asked it or were even aware that John Fairbank had asked it. After all, the State Department had requested renewed aid for the Chiang government in April 1948 and as recently as April 1949 had accepted, without visible protest, a congressional authorization for the President to go on providing Chiang with China aid money to the bitter end.[5]

Still so committed to the Chiang government, the State Department could not afford to be forceful and explicit in its indictment of that regime. If the case were too strongly put, the department would convict itself of the most reckless and irresponsible behavior. Consequently, only a very few who, like Professor Fairbank, were equipped to read the *White Paper* with understanding would ever be aware of how damning had been its indictment of the Chiang regime. The negative side of the argument (America's innocence rather than China's guilt) was emphasized, as in this key statement of

4. *New Republic*, August 22, 1949.

5. *China White Paper*, pp. 408–409.

Secretary Acheson in the *White Paper*'s "Letter of Transmittal": "Nothing that this country did or could have done within the reasonable limits of its capabilities could have changed that result; nothing that was left undone by this country has contributed to it." [6] The worst that was said of the Kuomintang was that decay had sapped its powers of resistance and that its leaders had "proven incapable of meeting the crisis confronting them." [7]

Congressman Walter Judd was quick to see the administration's dilemma over the *White Paper* and to notice that it had not dared to condemn the Chiang regime out of hand but had buried its indictment in the tedious detail of a thousand pages. Being free then to make his own judgment of the generally un-read *White Paper,* Judd simply stood the document on its head and drew the opposite conclusion from that which was meticulously documented on virtually every page. "My first impression. . . ," said he, "is that on balance China's record is not as bad as expected, while that of the American government is worse." [8] Judd perceived how innocuous the *White Paper* would prove to be, and he had ready answers for what little substance he was willing to concede it: "The weaknesses of the Chinese Government at the end of an 8-year war and occupation were well known. They were and still are the problem to be solved—not our alibi for not solving it." [9]

The Judd view would prevail in the end, and, ironically, his position was that which the administration had originally held, namely, that a non-Communist China was important to the United States and that this could be achieved by giving

6. *Ibid.,* p. xvi.

7. *Ibid.,* p. xiv.

8. *The New York Times,* August 6, 1949.

9. *Congressional Record,* XCV, 81st Cong., 1st Sess. (1949), p. 10875.

adequate aid and support to the government of Chiang Kai-shek. The State Department had abandoned the latter part of this position, while Judd and the China bloc had clung ever more tenaciously to Chiang as his fortunes declined. They were not willing to concede that Chiang was a "loser," and they insisted that he had failed to become a "winner" only because American aid had been inadequate. This was a devilishly shrewd argument, which could not be disproved by any number of *White Papers*. The very fact of Chiang's failure seemed to prove it. The Kuomintang's weaknesses were beside the point, thought Judd: "It is our problem, not our alibi. The greater the difficulties in helping China keep free of Communist control, the greater the problem it is our job to solve." Just in case anyone might try to battle his way out of this semantic trap, Judd had provided a catch: "Those who are resisting Communist forces in China are on our side, and to the extent that we refuse to help effectively those who are on our side, we are intervening in favor of those who are mortally opposed to us." [10]

The State Department had badly miscalculated if it thought the *White Paper* would persuade the American people to unburden themselves of the deadweight of Chiang Kai-shek. The China bloc and Asialationists were able to convince the people that the Kuomintang's continued dominance in China was important, if not absolutely vital, to American security. So long then as Chiang occupied one square foot of Chinese ground, his American friends would carry on their impassioned struggle for his—and, as they saw it, America's—salvation. Only by effecting that salvation could the administration redeem itself for its sins against China (Chiang).

Judd and Senator Knowland believed that the Kuomintang

10. *Ibid.*, p. 11677.

leaders were great, good, and wise. How completely Judd deferred to them, in matters of fate and history (and how certain he was that no one would read the *White Paper*), is revealed in this incredible statement:

> The one fact that overshadows every other is that on the most important issue of this century—the one on which our very survival depends—the Chinese Government was right and our own Government was tragically wrong. Chinese leaders understood the nature, the objectives, the methods, and the insidious threat of the worldwide Communist conspiracy. Our leaders did not.[11]

Close behind Judd in admiration of Oriental wisdom (or inscrutability) was Knowland, who was lavish in his praise of Chiang for resisting the wicked efforts of the American government to force him to consort with Communists: "It is to the everlasting credit of Generalissimo Chiang Kai-shek that he stood then as he stands today uncompromisingly against this tie up with international communism." [12]

Not surprisingly, strong support for the general theme of the Judd-Knowland group came from *The New York Times* on the day after the *White Paper* was issued. With the smug assurance of one who had spent an evening mastering the thousand pages of that document and preparing an editorial on it for the morning edition, the editorialist assured the world that "This White Paper, an attempt at vindication, is actually a sorry record of well-meaning mistakes." This superficial remark suggests a real ignorance of the *White Paper*, and the remainder of the editorial bears out that suspicion. It is no more than a rehash of preconceptions that the *Times* man had derived, not from reading the *White Paper*, but from double-thinking history, as in the remark about "the long-continued efforts of our government to force the Communists into the Government of China," and in the assumption that

11. *Ibid.,* p. 10875.
12. *Ibid.,* p. 10813.

the Wedemeyer report, made public for the first time in the *White Paper,* had provided a solution to the China problem.[13]

The *Times* had stated what was to become a common theme: The *White Paper* was an alibi for a sellout. Generally, commentators derived nothing new from this sensational document; they went on parroting their old charges, adding the *White Paper* as yet another act of perfidy. Senators Bridges, McCarran, Wherry, and Knowland issued a "Memorandum on the White Paper," in which they reviewed the story they loved so well, the "Yalta sellout" and the attempt of General Marshall "to force Chiang into coalition with the Communists." Then they concluded that the *White Paper* was a "1,054-page whitewash of a wishful, do-nothing policy which has succeeded only in placing Asia in danger of Soviet conquest with its ultimate threat to the peace of the world and of our own national security." [14]

The fury over the *White Paper* emboldened Senator Homer Ferguson of Michigan to make one of the strongest attacks yet made on General Marshall, although he did it in the words of one Ray Richards, a reporter for the Hearst newspapers:

> Whether he [Marshall] played his role willingly, unwillingly, or unwittingly, the symbol of mediation was George C. Marshall, Army Chief of Staff, Ambassador to China, Secretary of State. It was General Marshall who sent General Stilwell to China, where he engaged in bitter personal bickering with Chiang and took advice in support of the Communist cause from John Carter Vincent and John Stewart's service [sic, surely he said John Stewart Service] in the American embassy.[15]

This is an excellent example of the insidious techniques that would be increasingly employed against the makers of America's China policy. It should be noticed that no one is

13. *The New York Times, op. cit.*
14. *Congressional Record, op. cit.,* p. A5450.
15. *Ibid.*

accused of anything in particular; Marshall's only sin was that
he had sent Stilwell to China, and Stilwell's only sin was that he
had bickered with Chiang. Even the underlings, Vincent and
Service, are not charged with being Communists or traitors,
but only with having given advice "in support of the Communist cause," for whatever reasons they may have had (possibly
ignorance).

Having learned to play this fascinating game (weaving
names, places, and events together, with innuendo and leading
questions, into sinister patterns), Senator Ferguson, with the
help of Senator George Malone of Nevada, played it out in
minstrel-show fashion for the edification of the Senate. Interlocutor Malone began the act by asking if General Marshall
was not the same man who had gone out to China in 1946.
Assured by end-man Ferguson that they were indeed one and
the same, the innocent Malone then inquired if this was not
the same general who had been an adviser to Franklin Roosevelt at Yalta when Russia was given a foothold in Asia.
Reassured on this point, the astonished interlocutor then
wondered if it could have been that same general, advising
that same President, "when Berlin was given to the Russians
without any means of access to the city." Sadly, Ferguson
confessed that this was the case.[16]

Kenneth Wherry used the "name game" to get at W. Walton
Butterworth when the latter was nominated to be an assistant
secretary of state. As Wherry played the game, the secretary
of state himself, not surprisingly, was "it." Acheson had been
an under secretary at the time when "pro-Communistic policies," as Wherry called them, were adopted for China. But
what did this have to do with Walton Butterworth? Simple,
crowed Wherry, he had been Acheson's assistant at the time.[17]

Going after the scalp of the same Mr. Butterworth, Senator

16. *Ibid.,* p. 10961.
17. *Ibid.,* p. 11900.

Knowland demonstrated that he was no slouch at "name games." Serious doubts were raised in his mind about this man Butterworth by the mere fact that he had once been in China and had been sent there by none other than John Carter Vincent. Moreover, Butterworth had held "a responsible position in China during part of the time General Marshall was there . . . urging the Nationalist Government to take the Communists into the government on a coalition basis." And lurking in the background had been "super-spy" Alger Hiss, although Knowland did not quite know how to work him into the plot: "How much part Alger Hiss played in the shaping of our conduct in China, I do not know. He was present at Yalta, he was associated with the Far Eastern division for a part of the time he served in our State Department. . . ." [18]

To serious "gamesmen," nothing was more infuriating than the case of former Vice President Henry Wallace. The man had proved himself a dangerous radical in his bid for the presidency on the Communist-backed Progressive ticket in 1948. Surely he had perpetrated some villainy or other during his famous mission to China in 1944. But the *White Paper* had left him "clean as a hound's tooth," and there seemed even a possibility that he had been on the Chiang-Chennault side against Stilwell at that time. Judd and Knowland were irritated by this fact and insisted that something was being held back. Judd contended that the original report on the Wallace mission had been written by John Carter Vincent and Owen Lattimore (whom Asialationists regarded as a very suspicious character). The State Department replied that Vincent alone had written the report and that it had been printed in its entirety in the *White Paper*. Judd went on insisting, however, that the alleged *original* report "must be produced from wherever it is and published." [19] Determined to squeeze something

18. *Ibid.*, p. 13264.
19. S.D. *Bulletin*, XXI, September 5, 1949, p. 352.

out of the issue, Knowland pointed out, for whatever sinister implication it might have, that "Wallace was accompanied [to China] by John Carter Vincent, at that time the Chief of the Division of Chinese Affairs of the State Department." [20]

In October a senatorial nonentity from Wisconsin, Joseph Raymond McCarthy, quietly entered the game when he read into the *Congressional Record* an article by one Richard L. Stokes. This slanderous piece of hack journalism had no value except as an indication of the trend of thought of the senator who, a few months hence, would begin a "reign of terror" against the makers of American foreign policy. As an augury of the coming "McCarthy storm," the Stokes article centered its fire on General George C. Marshall who, it was said, had gone to China in 1945 not as one simply carrying out instructions but as one "in personal sympathy with the instructions that had been drafted by the left-wing cell which then controlled, and still controls, the State Department's Far Eastern Division." [21]

Stokes insisted that Marshall had saved "the doomed Communist armies" by forcing Chiang into a truce with them at the moment when the Generalissimo had "victory in his grasp." He had then "coerced Chiang Kai-shek into opening the Kalgan pass" so that the Reds could move into Manchuria, where they equipped themselves with surrendered Japanese equipment. To accomplish all this, said Stokes, "Marshall had applied pressure after the Stilwell manner by shutting off American aid, including war supplies already paid for by the Chinese." [22]

The stirring up of this hornet's nest was about all the *White Paper* accomplished. What it had proven about the Chiang

20. *Congressional Record, op. cit.,* p. 13264.

21. *Ibid.,* p. 13264.

22. *Ibid.*

regime went unnoticed, and the State Department was damned for having compounded its sins by attempting to lay them upon the "innocent" head of Chiang. The critics had their way, as they branded the *White Paper* a "cover-up," a "white-wash," an "alibi." Even those who were charitably disposed toward the *Paper* could not deny that it amounted to an apologia. Under the circumstances, it could hardly have been anything else.

Having brought down upon its head charges of covering up wrongdoing, the State Department proceeded to further complicate its problems by adopting the position of those critics who insisted that China's civil war was a Russian "take-over." In his "Letter of Transmittal" accompanying the *White Paper,* Secretary Acheson seems to have already made that assumption: "We continue to believe that . . . however ruthlessly a major portion of this great people may be exploited by a party in the interest of a foreign imperialism, ultimately the profound civilization and the democratic individualism of China will reassert themselves and she will *throw off the foreign yoke* [italics added]." He then went on to warn the Chinese Communist regime that it should not "lend itself to the aims of Soviet Russian imperialism and attempt to engage in aggression against China's neighbors. . . ." [23]

Again, on August 22, the secretary asserted gratuitously that "there is in China a Communist regime which, while in fact serving the imperialist interests of a foreign power, has for the present been able to persuade large numbers of Chinese that it is serving their interests. . . ." He further spoke of the Chinese Communists' attempts "to establish a totalitarian domination over the Chinese people in the interests of a foreign power," and affirmed it to be a basic American policy to oppose "the subjection of China to any foreign power, to any

23. *China White Paper,* p. xvi.

regime acting in the interest of a foreign power, and to the dismemberment of China by any foreign power, whether by open or clandestine means." [24] Containmentism's very own prophet, State Department Counselor George F. Kennan argued, in a CBS radio broadcast of August 22, that the Chinese Communists were "being utilized as a means of deceiving the Chinese people and of inducing them to accept a disguised form of foreign rule." [25]

The Chinese Nationalists, not likely to miss an opportunity to encourage the State Department in this line of thought, appeared before the United Nations on September 30 to press these formal charges against the Soviet Union: "Threats to the political independence and territorial integrity of China and to the peace of the Far East resulting from Soviet violations of the Sino-Soviet treaty of friendship and alliance of 14 August 1945." [26] Supporting the action, American Ambassador Philip C. Jessup told the Political and Security Committee of the U.N. General Assembly that "some of the evidence and of the reports create grave cause for concern that groundwork is in fact once again being laid for a further Russian attempt to dismember China. . . . The United Nations must be alert," he continued, "to see that the domination of China by one totalitarian power has not been displaced only to make way for the subjugation of that country to any other

24. S.D. *Bulletin,* XXI, August 15, 1949, pp. 236–237.

25. S.D. *Bulletin,* XXI, September 5, 1949, p. 324.

26. *The New York Times,* October 1, 1949. During the previous summer Chiang Kai-shek had been engaged in other activities calculated to bring the United States to his assistance. Following the rule that what was good for Europe was good for Asia, and noting the negotiation of the North Atlantic Pact for Europe (ratified by the Senate in July 1949), Chiang tried to put together a Pacific defense pact. Seeking allies, he visited Syngman Rhee of Korea on August 6, the only other interested party being Elpidio Quirino of the Philippines (said to be the prime mover of the scheme); but they were not able to arouse any enthusiasm for their project in the United States. See *The New York Times,* August 7, 1949.

imperialism." [27] Explaining his support of this cause to the press, Jessup insisted that China's position "is sound." [28]

One is not prepared to accept it as fact that Acheson, Kennan, and Jessup actually believed that China was the puppet of Russia. They had too much information available to them from the most accurate and perceptive reporters. Kennan, at least, betrayed a degree of skepticism on the matter in sessions of the State Department's "Round Table Discussion on China Policy," October 6, 7, 8, 1949. As to Russia's primacy in matters ideological, Kennan had this to say: "How that will work out in terms of relationship between them [the Russians] and the Chinese Communist regime I don't know." He offered the observation, however, that where one people cannot overshadow another militarily, "ideology is in itself an untrustworthy means with which to hold them." [29] As Kennan said, he just did not know.

George C. Marshall, participating in the same Round Table Discussion and speaking out of his experience as Army chief of staff and secretary of state, was able to provide some hard information as to Russia's role in China's civil war:

> They [the Chinese Communists] did not make any pretense of their association with the Communists of Russia; that was natural. They were Communists; they were Marxists, and that [Russia] was the seat of that development. When it came to Soviet assistance at all, I never could get my hands on it. I was given all kinds of schedules, but, in the opinion of all my advisers and Intelligence, they [the Russians] were not supporting them [the Chinese Communists]." [30]

This was borne out by a Colonel McCann of the Central Intelligence Agency who briefed the Round Table on the

27. S.D. *Bulletin,* XXI, December 12, 1949, pp. 900–901.
28. *The New York Times,* October 1, 1949.
29. *Institute of Pacific Relations,* p. 1563.
30. *Ibid.,* p. 1654.

military situation in China. He reported that when American representatives in China asked the Nationalist government for evidence that the Russians were aiding the Chinese Reds "They were not given proof of the allegations." [31]

The most competent journalists and scholars in the field of Chinese affairs did not for an instant believe that China was, or was likely to become, a puppet of Russia. Edgar Snow, the journalist who had introduced Mao Tse-tung to the world, was contemptuous of this view and was at pains to refute it in popular magazines.[32] Theodore White, another astute journalist with a vast firsthand knowledge of China, gave no indication in his book on wartime China that the Communists of that country were under the domination of anyone.[33] China scholar John K. Fairbank observed, in a letter to *The New York Times,* that "the Chinese Communists, although certainly genuine Communists, are not foreign invaders like the Japanese and are not generally regarded in China as the agents of a foreign power." [34]

It is of further significance that the nation's popular newsmagazines, with the exception of *Time,* had not yet accepted the idea that China's civil war was a Russian affair. The *U.S. News & World Report,* as already shown, regarded China's Communist movement as an indigenous one.[35] *Newsweek* was even more emphatic, as in its assertion that Russia would be in for serious trouble if it attempted "to impose the same kind of totally docile submission on China that it does on its

31. *Ibid.,* p. 1581.

32. See Edgar Snow, *Red Star Over China* (New York: Random House, 1938); see also his closely reasoned argument in "Will China Become a Russian Satellite," *The Saturday Evening Post,* April 9, 1949.

33. White and Annalee Jacoby, *Thunder Out of China* (New York: William Sloane, 1946).

34. *The New York Times,* August 3, 1949.

35. See p. 67.

Eastern European satellites. . . ," and in its suggestion that the United States encourage the nationalistic tendencies that were bound to develop among China's Communists.[36] The liberal periodicals, *The Nation* and the *New Republic*, were somewhat more cautious. Walter L. Briggs, writing in the latter in February, noted that China's leaders, despite their pro-Russian talk, did not really trust the Russians and that their Communism was "conspicuously Chinese"; however, by December, the editor was worried about the domino tendencies that would develop if China should "pass within the Soviet world." [37] Maxwell Stewart warned in *The Nation* that the United States must not take action that would drive China into Russia's arms.[38]

One wonders then why Secretary Acheson had embraced so precipitately the theory that China was the puppet of Russia. It is true that Acheson was worried that an older Russian imperialism, having nothing to do with the so-called "Communist conspiracy," was at work in China, detaching the inner provinces of Manchuria, Inner and Outer Mongolia, and Sinkiang.[39] But many of his statements on the Russia-in-China theme were more general than that. Perhaps this was simply a "manner of speaking," calculated to prove that he was no "softy on Communism." But it is also possible that Mr. Acheson was coming to believe somewhat in the "commie-bogie" theory or, at least, to accept it operationally as a useful —even necessary—concomitant of the policy of "containment." It might prove as useful in Asia as it had in Europe as the justification for strong action on behalf of American interests. The great danger, however, was that it might build up unbear-

---

36. *Newsweek,* January 3 and 31, 1950.

37. *New Republic,* February 21 and December 12, 1949.

38. *The Nation,* February 12, 1949.

39. S.D. *Bulletin,* XXII, January 23, 1950, p. 115.

able pressure for action that was not at all in the national interest, as it had already forced adoption of the mischievous "non-recognition policy." [40]

Still, there was good reason to believe, in the fall of 1949, that once Chiang Kai-shek had been swept into "the dustbin of history" the pressure would abate, for surely then Chiang's champions in America would lose interest in harassing China's Communist government. Acheson had no way of knowing, of course, that the Communists were not going to invade Formosa and settle the "two Chinas" dilemma for him. Until they did, the secretary would confront, in even more dangerous form, the same problem that had plagued the nation for three years: How to prevent America's Chiang-infatuated politicians from forcing the United States to intervene, in some manner, in China's civil war; and, above all, how to keep the United States from becoming involved in a land war in Asia. And it was almost certain that involvement with Chiang on Formosa would lead the United States straight back to the continent, a calamity that Acheson was as determined to prevent as General Marshall had been.

On December 8 Chiang absconded to the island of Formosa with the last remnants of his beaten army. Once ensconced on that island fortress, his air and naval superiority over the Communists gave him a new lease on life, and it was this consideration, most likely, that delayed the Communist attack on the island. It was also probable that Mao's generals were given pause by the fact that the new situation opened up anew the possibility of American intervention. Certainly it opened up interesting new possibilities for America's "China specialists." *First,* so long as Chiang's government was still in business, he would need American assistance of every kind, and his American friends would renew their efforts to get it for him. *Second,* the very fact that Chiang's position was now

40. See pp. 120–124.

more defensible would create greater pressures on the American government to help him defend it. His island fortress made possible the "clean" sort of intervention that Americans would come to love. One could shoot at the enemy from the relative safety of planes and ships without the messy business of occupying his soil. *Third,* and most important of all, was the fact that the argument could be advanced that Formosa had *strategic value* for the United States. And who could say for sure that this was not true?

The storm over Formosa broke on the first day of the new year (1950) when James Reston of *The New York Times* divulged the government's Formosa policy as summarized for him by a "responsible official." An accurate report, it asserted that there would be no military action by the United States in defense of Formosa or Hainan. While the "responsible official" conceded that Formosa was strategically important, it was not important enough to create "another 'Spanish situation' in which the Soviet Union might back the Communists in an assault on Formosa and the United States might mastermind the defense." Both the State and Defense departments agreed that occupation of the island was not justified.[41]

Adding a note of gravity, and no little partisan heat, to this evolving controversy was the sudden appearance in the midst of it of two of the most influential and highly respected Republican leaders, former President Herbert Hoover and Senator Robert A. Taft. It is of some interest that neither of them, in statements issued on January 2, appeared as champions of Chiang Kai-shek. Rather, they were concerned with stopping the spread of Communism, and both thought that Formosa would have value for the United States in the building of a military wall in Asia. Hoover actually accepted the necessity of recognizing Red China, although he wanted re-

41. *The New York Times,* January 1, 1950.

strictions imposed, such as denying that government a seat in the U.N. Security Council and preventing its legations and consulates from becoming "nests of Communist conspiracies." Taft, characteristically, stuck closer to the issue at hand. He would use the Navy to keep Communists out of Formosa, for purely military reasons, but he was not prepared to support the Nationalists or any other Chinese government.[42]

The following day something of a sensation was created over the leaking to the press of a State Department advisory memorandum on Formosa. The memorandum instructed American officials in the Far East to expect the fall of Formosa at any time and to put up the best possible front when that unfortunate event occurred. This was a routine sort of thing to do, since no government wants its officials crying in public. But Senator Knowland, as might have been expected, was outraged that these officials should have been instructed to take the position that "Formosa has no military significance."[43]

Some Republican leaders were sobered by this event. Perhaps the fact that the memorandum was leaked from General MacArthur's headquarters in Tokyo (still something of a mystery) and that it assumed an imminent attack on Formosa warned them that the time had come to "put up or shut up." Henry Cabot Lodge, Jr., expressed "grave doubts that we should undertake military action in Formosa. I think we have got to stop the military aspect of communism somewhere, but I don't think that's the place." Even Walter Judd, while still tirelessly demanding more aid for Chiang and a noncombatant military mission such as that sent to Greece, said he would not be willing to "go to the extent of seeing the country send any military or naval force."[44]

42. *Ibid.,* January 3, 1950.
43. *Ibid.,* January 4, 1950.
44. *Ibid.*

This seeming "moment of truth" made it possible to see what meaning, if any, there had been in all the verbal pyrotechnics of the previous months. It must be said for Taft and Hoover that while they had been among those who talked least, at the time of decision they had been prepared to recommend a specific line of action. Judd and Lodge, on the other hand, backed away completely from the hard decision, leading one to doubt that they had ever believed that Chiang's cause was as vital to America as they had claimed.

Then there was the interesting position of Senator H. Alexander Smith of New Jersey who insisted that Formosa should be occupied. Such a bold, fighting stance attracted considerable attention, but when pressed for specifics, Smith would only express the vague hope that "we will find a formula for occupying Formosa."[45] Senator Connally, irritated at not being able to get Smith to designate the "occupying force," asked if he perhaps planned to occupy the island with tourists or with two or three senators.[46] But the most abstruse position of all was that of Senator William F. Knowland, who would not recommend definite military action but insisted, like the most tiresome of hair-splitting theologians, that the United States government make public obeisance to the theory that Formosa was of strategic importance to the United States.

Knowland's position was not very different from that of the Joint Chiefs-of-Staff, who were not willing to say that the island had no strategic value but were not willing to fight for it either. In the MacArthur hearings of 1951, General Omar Bradley, chairman of the Joint Chiefs, would summarize their position this way: "We have always had the view that Formosa had considerable strategic value, if held by the enemy. We

45. *Ibid.*
46. *Congressional Record*, XCV, 81st Cong., 2nd Sess. (1950), p. 170.

have always said it did not have sufficient value to justify occupying it by our own troops." [47] Secretary Acheson, at the same hearings, found himself in a similarly equivocal position when he undertook to convince Senator Knowland that the State Department's controversial "advisory memorandum" of January 3, 1950, had not been serious when it said that "Formosa has no military significance." This was simply the "cover story" that was to be used to put a presentable face on an unavoidable misfortune. [48] Having implied, in his exchange with Senator Knowland, that he thought Formosa did have strategic value, the secretary then stated emphatically: "It was the clear unequivocal recommendations of the military services [from October 1948 to June 1950] that we could not deploy any of our forces for the defense of Formosa." [49]

Those who were determined to prove the strategic value of Formosa always cited their hero, General Douglas MacArthur, believing that here was an authority on Far Eastern matters against whom no one could stand. It was reported in the press on January 6 that the general would urge the United States "to draw a definite line in the Far East [including Formosa] beyond which Communism will not be permitted to spread. . . ." This was the word he was expected to give to Ambassador-at-Large Philip Jessup, already enroute to Tokyo as the first in a long line of emissaries who would make that journey in an effort to set the general straight on America's Far Eastern policy. Meanwhile, the MacArthur headquarters went on making its own policy. High staff officers, presumably expressing MacArthur's views, were reported as saying that "the State Department is wrong in trying to

47. *Military Situation in the Far East*, p. 930.
48. *Ibid.*, pp. 1675–1682.
49. *Ibid.*, p. 1681.

write off that island as virtually lost already and as of insignificant strategic value." [50]

On this subject MacArthur was not on solid ground, as was
demonstrated in an exchange between the general and Senator
Richard Russell of Georgia at the MacArthur hearings of
1951. Russell could not see why an enemy possessing Formosa would be in an appreciably better position to menace
the American defense line (running from the Philippines
north through Okinawa to Japan) than one operating from
the Chinese mainland. This would put them perhaps a few
hundred miles (Russell said 90; MacArthur said 165) nearer
to the line, which would make no substantial difference to
fast-moving aircraft. MacArthur's first attempt to explain it
went like this: "Because it gives them another bastion, Senator. The continental line there [pointing to a map] has a
certain capacity, but when you take it out and put it here
[presumably pointing to Formosa on the map] where it is
immediately north of the Philippines, immediately south of
Japan, you give them the additional capacity that goes with
that." [51]

This did not even touch Russell's question, which was concerned with minor differences in air mileages (that is, min-
utes), and so he pressed the point again. The general's second
attempt to explain was a ridiculous and irrelevant lecture on
the Formosan economy. He spoke of "a great nation of
8,000,000 people," "an enormously wealthy potential country
agriculturally," troops there could "live off Formosa," and "a
great population . . . stronger than both Australia and the
Netherlands put together." [52] Perhaps sensing the weakness of
his explanations, General MacArthur resorted to rabble-

50. *The New York Times,* January 6, 1950.
51. *Military Situation in the Far East,* p. 184.
52. *Ibid.,* p. 185.

rousing to scare off opposition to his point of view: "I have seen a number of statements in current literature about the weakness of Formosa. . . . All were made by men whose ideals were closely linked with the Communist cause. There had been an enormous propaganda put out about it which is false." [53]

There can be little question that MacArthur's statements at that time were politically motivated. They were intended to savage the President who had just fired him and to win favor with the Asialationists who might conceivably be able to get him the Republican presidential nomination in 1952. Earlier statements of the general, however, had already cut the ground from under his newly discovered strategic concept. On January 2, 1949, when speaking in strict military terms and without political malice, he had outlined a grand strategy for the United States in the Pacific area that ignored Formosa. America's defense perimeter, he said, "starts from the Philippines and continues through the Ryukyu Archipelago, which includes its main bastion Okinawa. Then it bends back through Japan and the Aleutian Island Chain to Alaska.

And General MacArthur could not argue that he had changed his position because of the establishment of Red power in China; he had taken that factor into account from the beginning. Noting that the advance of Red armies in China would put them on the flank of his defense perimeter, he had argued that this "did not alter the fact that the only possible adversary on the Asiatic continent does not possess an industrial base near enough to supply an amphibious attacking force." The secure bastion of Okinawa could then launch 3,500 heavy bomber missions per day, bringing the whole of East Asia from Singapore to Vladivostok within range.[54]

53. *Ibid.*, p. 186.

54. *The New York Times*, January 2, 1949. General MacArthur was never called to account for his contradictory views other than in the

The time had come for the administration to make a definitive statement on Formosa. "For the past week or 10 days," Secretary Acheson observed on January 5, "this subject of Formosa has become one of the foremost subjects of discussion throughout the country. . . . There has been a great deal of amateur military strategy indulged in in regard to this matter." [55] That same day the President delivered this ringing statement on Formosa:

> The United States has no predatory designs on Formosa, or on any other Chinese territory. The United States has no desire to obtain special rights or privileges, or to establish military bases on Formosa at this time. Nor does it have any intention of utilizing its Armed Forces to interfere in the present situation. The United States Government will not pursue a course which will lead to involvement in the civil conflict in China.[56]

In extemporaneous remarks on the President's statement, Mr. Acheson pointed out that this was not a new policy and that it was not a temporary one, but one that had to do "with the fundamental integrity of the United States and with maintaining in the world the belief that when the United States takes a position it sticks to that position and does not change it by reason of transitory expediency or advantage on its part." [57]

One week later Secretary Acheson delivered a major foreign policy address in which he expanded the Formosa statement into a general principle of America's Far Eastern policy. Speaking to the National Press Club in Washington, he outlined an American "defensive perimeter" in the Far East that

---

grousing of a few liberal commentators, nor did he bother to make explanations. Writing in 1964, he had the gall to criticize Acheson for having left Formosa and Korea outside the American defense perimeter: "I felt that the Secretary of State was badly advised about the Far East. . . ." *Reminiscences* (New York: McGraw-Hill, 1964), pp. 321–322.

55. S.D. *Bulletin*, XXII, January 16, 1950, pp. 79–80.

56. *Presidential Papers: Truman* (1950), p. 11.

57. S.D. *Bulletin, op. cit.,* p. 80.

"runs along the Aleutians to Japan and then goes to the Ryukyus. . . . [then] runs from the Ryukyus to the Philippine Islands." [58] This was precisely General MacArthur's defense perimeter, and it meant that the American military presence in Asia would be maintained offshore; only at this easily defensible line (one that was not even likely to need defending) would there be a commitment of American military power. And so, despite all his past concessions to critics, Mr. Acheson remained firm and resolute on this essential point. There would be no squandering of America's substance (particularly its young men) in the endless quagmire that was the Asian continent.

In terms of America's vital interests, this was the best of all possible policies, negative though it was. But the policy was not likely to prove durable, for it was not accepted in all its ramifications. This would have required the acceptance of the fact that a policy designed to avoid any possibility of a military confrontation with China on the Asian continent must also accept the fact that the small states around the fringes of China (Korea, Formosa, Indochina, Burma, and Thailand) are merely extensions of the Asian land mass and that their societies are, in large measure, racial and cultural extensions of China. Since this is China's natural "sphere of influence," it follows that any strong and independent government established in China will never rest until it has reestablished the same sort of dominance in the area that was once enjoyed by the Chinese Empire. This means that a policy of avoiding military confrontation with China requires non-involvement anywhere on the East Asian continent, including the island of Formosa.

Unfortunately, these facts were not accepted by the United States, and so its offshore policy was an extremely tenuous

58. *Ibid.*, January 23, 1950, p. 116.

thing from the beginning. Even before the Reds had won their final victory in China, the "domino theorists" were wringing their hands over the probable fate of Southeast Asia, and, of course, they were right. China, if permitted, would certainly have dominoed its way right around its own borders. But this was not the sort of thing that would have been done immediately (China had other problems), or by outright conquest (other forms of dominance serve just as well and are cheaper), or to carry out somebody else's "timetable of conquest" (even if it had possessed the power). China would have imposed some form of hegemony over its small neighbors exactly as the great powers of the earth, including Russia and the United States, have always done; and almost any relationship established was likely to have been a more natural and harmonious one than any relationship that might have been established between these nations and Western powers, the latter never having been carried on in any other manner than "under the gun."

The United States was not yet prepared in January 1950 to build a defensive wall along the fringes of the Asian continent, but tentative steps toward some kind of involvement in the area were already being considered. The State Department's Round Table Discussion of October 1949 had been told by a departmental Southeast Asia expert that there must be "long-range encouragement, reassurances, and planning with and for the South Asians if we are to counteract Communist intrusions." [59] And, on January 6, 1950, it was announced that the State Department was making plans to provide various forms of assistance to the small states on China's

---

59. *Institute of Pacific Relations,* p. 1606. Nathaniel Peffer was the only participant in the "Round Table Discussion" whose voice was raised against interfering with revolutionary movements, even those conducted by Communists: "I don't think I would go looking for Ho Chi Minhs where they don't exist . . . but I would not obstruct." *Ibid.,* p. 1614.

periphery, particularly Korea and Vietnam, by way of demonstrating to critics that the department was as determined to "stop the expansion of Communism" in Asia as in Europe.[60]

Here was "manipulation" in its economic and political planning stages, "containment" at its inception. There was a bare possibility that the level-headed Secretary Acheson might be able to curb this dangerous propensity to "fix things." He told the Senate Foreign Relations Committee on January 10 that while the problems of Southeast Asia—Burma, India, Thailand, Indochina, and Indonesia—were being considered, "the most we can do is to encourage them and give them some aid under Point Four." [61] But, as already seen, Acheson had begun to waver badly on the China question. Besides, he probably did not have as great a popular following in America as Chiang Kai-shek; and, as long as the Generalissimo was alive and well, somewhere on Chinese soil, there would be increasing pressure on the secretary to adopt a strong Asian policy. This meant that Chiang Kai-shek must be saved, at all costs, but that the United States must not intervene directly, at any cost. This was not logical, but then logic was never a strong point with Asialationists. All they knew was that they wanted a strong policy, and the fury of their attack increased the possibility that they would get it. America had yet to learn that staying out meant *staying out*.

60. *The New York Times,* January 6, 1950.
61. *Ibid.,* January 11, 1950.

CHAPTER SEVEN

The McCarthy Attack on the State Department: Disengagement Postponed, Harassment of China Begins (1950)

There probably never had been a time in the nation's history when the State Department was forced to submit its policy-making process to so much raucous public debate or to attempt to carry out policy in an atmosphere so rife with fear and suspicion as during the 1950s. Needing public support for its policies, like all government agencies, the department could not escape the debilitating effects of attempting to accommodate its views to those of its critics, to whom it conceded a great deal more than was probably necessary. It had yielded to them when it asked for a renewal of China aid in 1948 and when it agreed to a continuation of that aid in April 1949. And, by issuing the *White Paper,* it had condescended to debate the China question with them, thus legitimizing their lunatic attacks by raising them to the level of serious discussion. Finally, it had tacitly agreed with the "China haters" in their irrelevant moral assault upon China when it backed away from recognition of that country's Red government.

The critics of America's Far Eastern policy would expect a great deal more of the State Department, however, than a temporary withholding of recognition from China's Communist government. They wanted the secretary of state to make it absolutely clear that at no time in the foreseeable future could that government expect either recognition by the United States or membership in the United Nations. And they were determined that Mr. Acheson should prove that he was "no softy in dealing with Communism" by joining enthusiastically in the chorus of moral outrage against the "Red bandits" who had dared unseat a pro-American government in China. Meanwhile, as hysteria grew in the nation, it was becoming increasingly difficult to determine, from one day to the next, what new level of moral outrage was considered appropriate. In the end, nothing less than pure hatred and unceasing villification of Red China would be demanded.

The secretary was a fast learner. Since August he had been speaking glibly of Russian imperialism in China. But his greatest fear was that Russia, not as the leader of a "world conspiracy" but in pursuit of its traditional policy of eastward expansion, would detach China's four interior provinces—Manchuria, Inner and Outer Mongolia, and Sinkiang. Even in this more substantial concern, Acheson was moved by the "hate China" (or the hate-Russia-through-China) spirit into violating his own rule against dogmatism, as he told the National Press Club on January 12. Going out on a very shaky limb, he confided to the assembled newsmen that "the fact that Russia is taking the four northern provinces of China is the single most significant, most important fact in the relations of any foreign power with Asia." [1]

Russia's sins were many, but this was not among them. While it supported Outer Mongolia in its determination to escape Chinese domination, there was no indication that Russia was making a determined effort to detach the other prov-

1. S.D. *Bulletin*, XXII, January 23, 1950, p. 115.

nces. When Soviet Foreign Minister Andrei Vishinsky denounced the charge as "false and crudely slanderous," the State Department petulantly repeated the foolish charge. In doing so, it drew upon the conspiracists' beloved myth of the "timetable of conquest." "How long this process of penetration and detachment will take will depend on the Soviet timetable—and of course on any resistance that may arise in China." [2] This acrimonious, public brawl with the Russians over serious but unsubstantiated charges of aggression is an indication of how far the moderate, sensible men of the State Department were willing to go in suiting the nuances of their speech and opinion to the tastes of their detractors.

There were very few Americans who were not susceptible to the "commie-bogie" madness. Scholars, newsmen, statesmen, were swept along, helping to make "fear of Communism" a great national cause. Although it was these notables who had created the monster, it must be said on their behalf that they had tried to keep the thing within reasonable bounds. Indeed, they drew back in horror when they saw it personified in the frightening image of one Senator Joseph Raymond McCarthy. But it was too late to draw back; in the end, they would learn to ape the senator's ways and to conduct foreign policy as he would have it.

Not many people had ever heard of Senator Joseph McCarthy when, on the evening of February 9, 1950, he addressed the Republican ladies of Wheeling, West Virginia, and casually told them that there were 205, or 57, or 81 (afterward, no one could remember the number) known Communists working in the State Department. Within a matter of months McCarthy would become the most feared man in America, and still most Americans knew virtually nothing about him and never would learn very much. There was very little to

2. *Ibid.,* February 6, 1950, p. 219.

know, and that little was not good. Morally and physically un attractive, the senator's career had been undistinguished, a best, frequently skirting the unethical, if not the downrigh criminal. His small claim to fame—or notoriety—rested upo: his championship of two extremely shabby causes: one, o: behalf of the Nazis charged with the massacre of unarme Americans at Malmédy, Belgium, during World War II, an the other, on behalf of the Pepsi-Cola Company's grab fo: more than its share of war-rationed sugar, for which he earne the proud title "the Pepsi-Cola Kid." [3]

This was the disreputable nonentity who, for four years stalked unimpeded through the legislative and executive branches of the American government, literally setting the terms under which they could operate. The unbelievable reach of his destructive power has been assessed by Richard Rovere as follows:

> He held two Presidents captive—or as nearly captive as any Presi- dents of the United States have ever been held; in their conduct o: the nation's affairs, Harry S. Truman and Dwight D. Eisenhower from early 1950 through late 1954, could never act without weigh- ing the effect of their plans upon McCarthy and the forces he led, and in consequence there were times when, because of this man, they could not act at all. [4]

The nature of the terror that made possible this irregular ex ercise of power was well described in a Washington *Post* edi- torial of May 22, 1950: "For weeks the capital has been seized and convulsed by a terror . . . a roaring bitterness, the ranging of Americans against Americans, the assault on free- dom of inquiry, the intolerance of opposition." [5]

3. Jack Anderson and Ronald W. May, *McCarthy, the Man, the Senator, the "Ism,"* (Boston: Beacon Press, 1952), pp. 128–165.

4. Richard H. Rovere, *Senator Joe McCarthy* (New York: Meridian Books, 1960), p. 5.

5. Quoted in James Aronson, *The Press and the Cold War* (New York: Bobbs-Merrill, 1970), p. 66.

Strangely enough, McCarthy came late to the "Communists
n government" issue. A number of politicians had, for some
ime, been harranguing the people on the dangers of sub-
ersives in government, particularly in the State Department,
ut McCarthy topped them all by supplying what they omitted
—names and numbers. Little matter that he kept changing the
numbers and that he had no proof against the persons named.
Since he was not hauling anyone into a court of law, he
needed no proof. And so long as he kept naming names, the
people listened and were impressed. Besides, as many good
citizens said, the brutal tactics of this man were necessary to
flush the "commie-coddlers" out of government.

There seemed to be an element of truth in this latter observation. If half the things being said about the "Communist
conspiracy" were true, then McCarthy was justified in what he
did. Surely desperate expedients were required to combat the
grave peril that threatened the nation. The President himself
apparently believed this; for three years, he had been deeply
preoccupied with the building of walls against Communism's
external threat—an economic wall in the Marshall Plan and a
military wall in the North Atlantic Alliance.

When not building walls, the President was summoning the
people to a holy crusade against that epitome of modern evil—
Communism. He alerted the people to the defense of everything they held dear, for, as he said, "Communism denies the
very existence of God. Religion is persecuted because it stands
for freedom under God. This threat to our liberty and to our
faith must be faced by each one of us. . . ." [6] Senator McCarthy
did not, therefore, have to prove that Communists were bur-
rowing from within as well as attacking from without; he had
the President's word for it. And events such as the Hiss case
seemed to bear out McCarthy's contention that the Truman

6. Quoted in Athan Theoharis, *Seeds of Repression: Harry S. Truman
and the Origins of McCarthyism* (Chicago: Quadrangle Books, 1971), p. 56.

Administration was not purging itself of Communists and fellow travelers.

The President had further prepared the ground for McCarthyism when he established the Federal Employee Loyalty Program in 1947. By that act he revealed his own fears about internal subversion and, in the vast, arbitrary powers given the Loyalty Review Board, even betrayed a degree of alarm. Under the President's program, derogatory information against any federal employee could bring a full field investigation by the FBI, in which the accused was not permitted to confront his accusers (or even to know who they were) or to demand substantive proof of the allegations against him. If an accused person were not sustained by the Loyalty Board of the agency that employed him—an unlikely event in a time of rising suspicion—his only recourse was appeal to the President's Loyalty Review Board, which could bring about his dismissal on the vague and self-determined basis of "reasonable grounds for belief" in his disloyalty.[7] This was precisely the "McCarthy method"—the sweeping charges, the anonymous witnesses, and the unsubstantiated evidence accepted as proof of disloyalty. The difference between the two methods was that the government sandbagged people in the dark, while McCarthy did his work in the glare of a publicity spotlight.

There was sensation aplenty to feed his cause in late 1949 and early 1950 when it seemed that there were nearly always spies and subversives, of one sort or another, on trial. The sensational, brawling trial of the eleven top Communist leaders in October 1949 was followed by the second perjury trial (and conviction) of Alger Hiss in November. Far more disturbing was the trial in February 1950 of Klaus Fuchs, the German-born British physicist, who was convicted in London of turn-

7. Cabell Phillips, *The Truman Presidency: The History of a Triumphant Succession* (New York: Macmillan, 1966), pp. 360–364.

ng over atomic secrets to the Soviet Union. Fuchs' betrayal
had been carried out while he was working at the top level
of the American atomic bomb project, and the trail of his
crime led to two American accomplices, Harry Gold and
David Greenglass. In March Justice Department employee
Judith Coplon was tried and convicted of conspiracy and attempted espionage, along with her accomplice, Valentin Gu-
bitchev, a Soviet consulate official. The Truman Administration's vigorous prosecutions of Communists and their agents
did not, however, redound to its credit. Rather, they tended to
bear out Senator McCarthy's charges and helped prepare the
people's minds for acceptance of the senator's wildest claims,
whether he said the number of Communists in the State Department was 205, 57, or 81.

How thoroughly the administration had prepared the ground
for its own undoing has been noted by Athan Theoharis:
"Through its own rhetoric, the Truman Administration had
closed the vicious circle on itself. All the McCarthyites had
to do was chase around it." [8] And the only thing left for the
administration to do was to try to "chase around" the circle
faster than the McCarthyites; that is, it must make every
effort to distract attention from the McCarthy crusade against
the internal threat of Communism by stepping up its own
crusade against the external threat. There was no other possible course for an administration that, on the very weekend
that McCarthy made his first sensational charges, was busy
heating up the rhetoric of the cold war and doing all it could
to enhance the fearful image of the "commie-bogie."

Only two days after the senator's famous Wheeling speech,
and before its impact had been felt, the secretary of state was
gratuitously disseminating such vague generalities as this:
"The United States cannot do business with Russia (just as it

8. Theoharis, *op. cit.,* p. 67.

could not do business with Hitler) except where a set of facts creates entrenched realities that force the Kremlin to adjust its aggressive policies downward." As grim as though full-scale war had broken out, Acheson went on to say that the making of foreign policy will "take purpose, continuity of purpose, perseverance, sacrifice, and . . . more than anything else, steady nerves." [9]

The strain of building a global "containing wall" against the Soviet Union and of alerting the people to the insidious threat of domestic Communism was taking its toll of bureaucratic nerves. Arthur Krock of *The New York Times* observed that Acheson, in particular, was showing the wearying effects of his heavy burden and that in other executive departments and at the Capitol "nerves show signs of high tension." Krock did not "attribute that to panic in any degree [one wonders why he used the term] or to lack of any of the items in Mr. Acheson's formula," but he found that a number of the President's sub-executives were worried about "fifth-column activities in the Government itself":

> One such official told this correspondent he felt certain there was such a column at work in the department where his jurisdiction is just short of the top, but that he was still unable to bring persuasion for forceful purging. Another said he would be uneasy over the successful execution of any foreign policy, however sound and strong, until "five or six individuals" are removed from a very important government office indeed.[10]

It was a "vicious circle," as Theoharis said, and administration officials were already chasing each other around it.

"Crusader" Joe McCarthy must have been amused and delighted at *The New York Times'* unexpected support for his cause. Although doubtless unintended, Arthur Krock's column

9. *The New York Times,* February 12, 1950.
10. *Ibid.*

of February 12 provided sufficient confirmation, if any were needed, that the State Department, which the senator had attacked on the previous Thursday evening, was torn by fear and suspicion and that the secretary, who would bear the brunt of the attack, was already reeling under his burden. In the beginning McCarthy smeared Secretary Acheson only by implication, as in his letter to President Truman in which he asserted that Dean Acheson could supply—the implication being that he would not supply—the full list of "those whom your board listed as being disloyal and who are still working in the State Department." [11] This oblique attack opened the way for those who were already spoiling for a knockdown brawl with the secretary over his statement of January 25 that he "would not turn his back on Alger Hiss."

On March 1, in an "extraordinary scene of ill-repressed bitterness before his Republican antagonists in a Senate Appropriations Subcommittee," Mr. Acheson publicly abased himself and turned his back, at least somewhat, on Alger Hiss:

> So far as public avowals of loyalty are concerned, I have on numerous occasions taken the most solemn oath of allegiance and loyalty to my country and to its Constitution.
>
> But for the benefit of those who would create doubt where none existed, I will accept the humiliation of stating what should be obvious, that I did not and do not condone in any way the offenses charged, whether committed by a friend or by a total stranger, and that I would never knowingly tolerate any disloyal person in the Department of State.[12]

Mr. Acheson had begun his ordeal by slander, and it would never abate during his term of office.

Not even Acheson was attacked so brutally, however, as Ambassador-at-Large Philip C. Jessup. Having been charged

---

11. *Ibid.*
12. *Ibid.*, March 1, 1950.

by McCarthy with an "unusual affinity for Communist causes,"
he, like the secretary, thought it necessary to humble himsel
before the Senate Investigating Committee: [13] "Although I believe I have made it clear from what I have already said, I
wish to repeat categorically and without qualification that I
am not a Communist and never have been a Communist. I am
not and never have been a Communist sympathizer." He then
gave a blanket endorsement to the President's Loyalty Review
program. Although admitting that he did not have "any detailed knowledge of the process," he had high praise for its
efficacy in seeing to it that "Communists or Communist sym-
pathizers are kept out of our government." Pleading his orthodoxy as a "commie-fighter," the ambassador ended with
this patriotic flourish: "You know that the stakes are high.
. . . We are opposed by the efforts of a well-organized Communist organization which is seeking to destroy our democracy." [14]

But Jessup had committed the unforgivable sin: He had
participated in "formulating topflight policy in the Far East."
And McCarthy had shrewdly centered his attack on America's
Far Eastern policy, where there had never been any bipartisanship and where the administration's failure had been monumental. Not only was the administration vulnerable here, but
it was an area in which the senator could find ready and willing allies. Men of the Asialationist group and the China bloc
would give strong support; and even such upright men as Senators Knowland and Taft would be lured into supporting the
cause, the latter actually being quoted by reporters as saying
that McCarthy should "keep talking and if one case doesn't

13. This was a subcommittee of the Senate Foreign Relations Committee,
set up under the chairmanship of Democrat Millard Tydings of Maryland
to investigate the McCarthy charges.
14. *The New York Times,* March 21, 1950.

work out he should proceed with another." [15] Particularly tenacious in its support of the senator would be the China lobby, "a hard core of hired lobbyists, influential friends, and outspoken advocates of Chiang Kai-shek," of whom Jack Anderson and Ronald May have written, "few other lobbies ever exerted such relentless pressure on American foreign and domestic policy." [16]

One would not suggest that McCarthy was the tool of the China lobby, but he did make repeated use of old, discredited charges of that group's chief lobbyist, Alfred Kohlberg, particularly in his attack upon Ambassador-at-Large Philip Jessup. As early as 1944 Kohlberg had attempted to discredit the *Far Eastern Survey,* the publication of the very respectable Institute of Pacific Relations, by charging it with following the Communist Party line. McCarthy simply revived the old charge of fellow traveling against the magazine, made Jessup its guiding light, by virtue of a year's service on the Institute's Research Advisory Committee, and thus created within the councils of government a purveyor of the Communist Party line on China. As McCarthy saw it, however, Jessup had been manipulated in his China views by Professor Owen Lattimore of Johns Hopkins University. This evil genius, McCarthy asserted in a letter of March 20 to Senator Tydings of the Senate Investigating Committee, had been the "architect of our Far Eastern Policy," and so Jessup's continued employment by the State Department should depend upon whether he "continues running with the same pack that has to date done everything in the Far East that Russia wants" and whether he "continues to be the voice of Lattimore." [17]

15. William S. White, *The Taft Story* (New York: Harper and Brothers, 1954), p. 85.

16. Anderson and May, *op. cit.,* p. 192.

17. *The New York Times, op. cit.*

Ten days later McCarthy told the Senate that Jessup "was such a dupe that he did not know that he was being used by Owen Lattimore." Parroting the "Kohlberg line," McCarthy insisted that *Far Eastern Survey* was "Jessup's magazine" and that it parroted the "Communist Party line":

> Professor Jessup must, therefore, be credited by the American people with having pioneered the smear campaign against Nationalist China and Chiang Kai-shek, and with being the originator of the myth of the "democratic" Chinese Communists.
>
> From that time onward we witnessed the spectacle of this three-horse team of smears and untruths thundering down the stretch—Jessup's *Far Eastern Survey,* the *Daily Worker,* and *Izvestia.* What an effective job they did can best be demonstrated by the fact that this was the line which the State Department followed in formulating its Far Eastern policy, right down to the last comma.[18]

Everything was falling neatly into place: Acheson and Jessup were the Kremlin's men in the State Department, and the "tie-up" (a favorite expression of the "conspiracists") between them and the Kremlin was Professor Owen Lattimore.

This Johns Hopkins professor was ideally suited to McCarthy's purpose, which was to completely discredit Secretary Acheson, who refused to "turn his back on Alger Hiss," and Ambassador Jessup, who was "formulating topflight policy in the Far East." Since Lattimore had never been employed by the State Department, it would be difficult to prove anything against him, but, at the same time, it would be virtually impossible to clear him of anything. He had been an occasional consultant of the State Department on Far Eastern affairs, so who could say how much influence he had had on China policy? The vagueness of the case was all to the good. McCarthy knew what could be done with conjecture and innuendo, and so he knew that he was taking no serious risk when he offered to stake his whole case on proving that the professor was the "top Soviet agent in America."

18. *Congressional Record,* XCV, 81st Cong., 2nd Sess. (1950), p. 4402.

It seemed that he might actually win his gamble when ex-Communist Louis Budenz testified before Senator Tydings' committee on April 20 that, while Lattimore was not "the top Soviet agent," he was a Communist and had "helped bring down the China nationalists . . ." [19] *The New York Times'* distinguished columnist Arthur Krock was impressed by this witness and observed, for what it was worth, that the "progressive and fair" Senator Ralph Flanders of Vermont found the testimony "disturbing." Further to establish the credibility of Budenz, Krock observed that the man had returned to his Catholic faith after he left the Communist Party, that he was a professor in good standing at Fordham University, and that he had been a frequent witness against Communists.

What Mr. Krock did not reveal was that Budenz had already acquired an unsavory reputation as one given to "sudden recall" and an eagerness to testify about past Communist activities of persons already thoroughly damned by repeated accusations of such activities. And buried deep in the Krock article was the information that ex-Communist Bella Dodd testified that she had never heard of Lattimore, that Budenz himself confessed that he had never before seen the man, and that Budenz was not able to satisfactorily explain why his newfound patriotic fervor had not prompted him to come forward earlier with his information against Lattimore.[20]

Whatever the credibility of the witness, it was not likely that McCarthy would ever admit that he had failed to make his case against Lattimore or that the guilt of Lattimore did not implicate Acheson and Jessup. On May 15, in a famous speech to the Sons of the American Revolution at Atlantic City, he dubbed the latter two gentlemen "pied pipers of the Politburo" and further confided to his congenial audience of "professional patriots" the breathtaking news that Secretary

19. *The New York Times,* April 2, 1950.
20. *Ibid.,* April 23, 1950.

Acheson had bought a plan for the Far East "masterminded by Professor Owen Lattimore" that was "gigantic in its fraud and complete in its deceit." This plan "conceived by Mr. Acheson's architect is to deliver vast areas and millions of people into Communist slavery. . . ." [21] There were no limits to which this man McCarthy would not go, and, unhappily, none had been set by the Truman Administration.

Secretary Acheson apparently thought the outer limits had been reached when, in April, he told newsmen that the State Department had taken the offensive against the "mad McCarthy charges." Having taken the offensive, he then spoke defensively, and at some length, about the high caliber of State Department personnel, calling particular attention to John Peurifoy of South Carolina, Jack Hickerson and George McGhee of Texas, Ed Barrett of Alabama, Dean Rusk of Georgia, and Walton Butterworth of Louisiana. Since these men were from a region known for its rock-ribbed conservatism, Mr. Acheson could not resist the ironic comment that they were all "old-fashioned Southern Communists like former Secretary of State Cordell Hull and Senator Tom Connally of Texas." [22]

But the secretary was whistling in the dark; there was no very good reason for his jauntiness. Deputy Under Secretary John Peurifoy was kept busy defending the State Department's people, and, by April, analysis and refutation of McCarthy's charges had become almost a regular feature of the department's weekly *Bulletin*. Even the President had been badly stung, as was demonstrated at a press conference on March 30 when he permitted himself to be baited into saying "I think the greatest asset the Kremlin has is Senator McCarthy."

21. *Ibid.*, May 16, 1950.
22. *Ibid.*, April 23, 1950.

He broadened this into a charge that certain Republicans are "trying to dig up that old malodorous dead horse called isolationism. And to do that, they are perfectly willing to sabotage the bipartisan foreign policy of the United States." [23] Whatever they were willing to do to "bipartisan foreign policy," the McCarthyites were quite prepared to destroy careers and reputations.

A Marshall or an Acheson, although terribly battered, could withstand the McCarthy attack, but lesser figures could not. As Foster Rhea Dulles has observed, while McCarthyism "significantly served to paralyze any further moves toward disengagement from the Chinese civil war, it also led to the dispersal of many veteran China experts in the State Department at a time when their first-hand experience could hardly have been more needed." [24] Among those so dispersed and ultimately driven from the State Department, their careers hopelessly blighted, were such knowledgeable China experts as John Carter Vincent, John Paton Davies, and John Stewart Service. When they came under attack, the State Department did not take up their cause but left them to fend for themselves as best they could, and, according to State Department Counselor George F. Kennan, "The same was done in other cases— why? I never knew. I would have suspected pusilanimity except that this was the last thing one would suspect in Dean Acheson." [25]

The damage done to a few individuals was, of course, a relatively small matter compared to the devastating and long-lasting effects such attacks clearly had on the nation's foreign

23. *Presidential Papers: Truman* (1950), pp. 234–235.

24. Foster Rhea Dulles, *American Foreign Policy Toward Communist China, 1949–1969* (New York: Thomas Y. Crowell, 1972), p. 80.

25. George F. Kennan, *Memoirs, 1925–1950*, II, (Boston: Little, Brown, 1967), p. 208.

policy. How great the effect cannot be determined with precision, and it is doubtful that the policy-makers concerned
will ever confess that they had any at all. These men are not
likely to confess it even to themselves, if indeed they are aware
of it, which is unlikely, given the infinite capacity of the
human mind to rationalize away the intolerable. In his memoirs, not surprisingly, Acheson took pains to deny it in emphatic terms: "A great deal of nonsense has been written
about the effect of the attack of the primitives, both before
and during McCarthy's reign, on the China policy of the
Truman Administration. Whatever effect it had on our successors, it had little on us." [26]

At the risk of speaking more nonsense, one is bound to ask
why, if the attack of the "primitives" had so little effect, Mr.
Acheson bothered to raise the question when writing his
memoirs twenty years later? And one might also ask why an
unruffled secretary and his ambassador-at-large should have
subjected themselves to the humiliating ritual of publicly
denying that they were traitors or that they condoned treason?
And why should Deputy Under Secretary Peurifoy have spent
so much time analyzing and refuting the McCarthy charges?
Above all, one would question why the State Department
moved so swiftly from a stoic acceptance of the new government of China to a policy of relentless hostility and harassment of that regime?

But were there not better reasons than the "McCarthyite
terror" to explain why the United States abandoned its sensible policy of disengagement from the continent of Asia in
favor of the very foolish opposite course? Neat and plausible
explanations for such behavior are always to be found in
"economic interest," as, for example, in William Appleman
Williams' assertion that there was, among America's postwar

26. Dean Acheson, *Present at the Creation* (New York: Norton, 1969),
p. 369.

leaders, a "firm conviction, even dogmatic belief, that America's well-being depends upon . . . sustained, ever-increasing overseas economic expansion." [27] Certainly no one was ever more firmly committed to this belief than President Truman and his two postwar secretaries of state, Marshall and Acheson.

But economic interests, potent as they were, do not adequately explain America's rising passion for adventures on the Asian continent. Mr. Truman, as he said in his Marshall Plan address, was primarily concerned with integrating Latin America and Western Europe into his "vast trading system." The Far East continued to be of secondary importance economically, as it had been in the heyday of the Open Door, and militarily, as it had been during World War II. That this was the case is clearly demonstrated by the fact that the men who had shown the greatest sensitivity to America's economic needs—Truman, Marshall, and Acheson—were the very men most determined that the United States should take no dangerous risks to keep China, with its half-billion potential customers, out of Communist hands.[28] And yet these same men would later carry out a large-scale military intervention in Korea, which had not the slightest economic value for the West. Clearly something other than economic interest was eating on them.

Only "McCarthyism" had the demonic power to force the administration to reverse policies that, for four years, it had vigorously defended as wise and good, and only "McCarthyites" were battering down the doors of the State Department during the period when the policy reversal occurred. As

27. William Appleman Williams, *The Tragedy of American Diplomacy* (New York: Dell, 1962), p. 11.

28. Acheson was at pains to point out that, during the period of 1946–1948 when the United States was the largest China trader, exports to China were less than 5 percent and imports from China less than 2 percent of America's total foreign trade. S.D. *Bulletin*, XXII, March 27, 1950, p. 470.

Richard Rovere has said, "He [McCarthy] had enormous impact on American foreign policy at a time when the policy bore heavily on the course of world history, and American diplomacy might bear a different aspect today if McCarthy had never lived." [29] Under the McCarthy lash, both the American people and the State Department abandoned, as they had long been tending to do, their commonsense view that Communist nations were discrete power entities who played power politics very much as other nations did. They fastened their terrified gaze upon that vague, menacing collectivity known as "the Communists," whom they learned to regard only as fanatical ideologues bent upon world conquest.

How completely this intellectual confusion had become the accepted norm is well illustrated in an article of February 12 by *The New York Times'* Southeast Asia expert Foster Hailey. Mr. Hailey began with this astonishing proposition: "Until the Chinese Communists, and then Moscow, recognized Ho Chi Minh . . . there had been some question in the minds of the Western countries just where Indo-China was on the Communist timetable for the conquest of Southeast Asia and the world." [30] Tiny Vietnam is thus seen as an important step in the "Communist timetable for the conquest of . . . the world," on the strength of Russian and Red Chinese recognition of Ho Chi Minh's government. And yet Mr. Hailey knew that this government had been promised independence by the French (the only foreign aggressors in the country) who, upon regaining some of their power, had promptly repudiated the promise. Mr. Hailey also knew that the Vietnamese struggle, Communist-led or not, was an indigenous one, for, as he pointed out in a later article, "Ho Chi Minh's strength never has been military alone. His forces have always been outnumbered and outgunned. . . . The great strength of his movement has been in the strong nationalism of the Indo-Chinese people." [31]

Nonetheless, having fixed Vietnam in the Communist scheme of "world conquest," Hailey then considered the question of what the Chinese would do next: "It had been thought that the Chinese would be so busy consolidating their control over the 450,000,000 Chinese that they would have little spare energy to keep on moving south." Indeed, this is exactly what one would have thought and, being sensible, would go on thinking. But not hardheaded American journalists of the 1950s who were far too shrewd and worldly-wise for that. And so, Hailey continues, "The acts of recognition of Ho Chi Minh [by Russia and China] were a clear signal that there is to be no lull in the 'hot war' in the Far East, that the Communists intend to try to push on South and swallow up that rich area of the world as they already have populous China and northern Korea." [32]

Hailey, it will be noticed, had raised the question as to whether the *Chinese* would have the energy to "keep on pushing South," but when he answers, the Chinese have completely disappeared, only to reappear as Ho Chi Minh and the Vietnamese. Apparently the latter, being Communists, were interchangeable with Chinese; thus, Ho and his Vietnamese followers, who were fighting for their country's independence from France, were denationalized. As though outsiders, they were lumped into that vague collectivity known as "the Communists," or "the Chinese" as Hailey would have it, who had decided to "push on South and swallow up that rich area of the world as they already have populous China and northern Korea."

This was "McCarthyism" in international affairs, seen here

31. *Ibid.*, May 14, 1950.
32. *Ibid.*, February 12, 1950.

working its mind-boggling mischief in the columns of *The New York Times,* which was not only America's greatest and most influential newspaper but one which, in the past, had not been unmindful of the requirements of hard fact, sound logic, and respectable semantics. In this article are to be seen all the worst elements of "McCarthyism," applied to external affairs—the same fevered imagination (the wild statements about the Communist timetable of world conquest); the same "guilt by association" (among nations, in this case); the same cavalier treatment of logic (transforming a Vietnamese independence movement into "Chinese pushing South"); and the same emotionalism.

This was before the name "McCarthy" had yet impinged upon the American consciousness, all of which is to say that Senator McCarthy did not invent "anti-Communism" and, in fact, did not even invent muddleheaded "anti-Communism." Moreover, it should be carefully noted that the term "McCarthyism" would become a term of opprobrium only in domestic "commie-hunting," whereas the McCarthyite rhetoric of fear and hate, only slightly modified, would soon attain full respectability in the realm of foreign affairs ("external McCarthyism").

The administration's defenders, both within and without the State Department, were not long in discovering that this "external McCarthyism" would be indispensable in defending themselves against "internal McCarthyism." James Reston of *The New York Times* had noticed the emergence of the strategy even before the appearance of McCarthy when he commented in early January that the State Department was busy devising assistance programs for China's continental neighbors as a way of demonstrating to its critics that it was as determined to stop Communism in Asia as in Europe.[33] When McCarthy transformed criticism into a vendetta, the

33. *Ibid.,* January 6, 1950.

State Department perceived that it would have to escalate its Asian assistance programs, again, not so much in defense of Asia as of itself. And liberal opinion-makers, in a similar plight, discovered that they would have to heat up their rhetoric against Communism abroad in order to validate their anti-Communist credentials at home.

Although anti-Communism was already well established as the moving force in American foreign policy, there is little doubt that McCarthyism gave it renewed impetus and encouraged many normally mild-mannered persons to raise their voices to a strident pitch. This was the other side of the coin, which Lord Bertrand Russell failed to notice when he so astutely observed that McCarthy had shown Americans of isolationist and budget-balancing proclivities how they could attack, at the same time, their two obsessive fears, Communism and the income tax: They could cut expenses and balance the budget if they restricted their anti-Communist crusade to the relatively cheap business of fighting it at home.[34] Russell failed to show that liberals and moderates had just as great a need for a Communist threat—an external one—which they could furiously attack by way of proving that they were not "commies" or "fellow travelers" when they fought for liberal reforms or when they defended civil liberties against the McCarthy assault.

This emerging controversy over priorities in the anti-Communist struggle could only be debated obliquely. Stated simply and directly, it would have come out in this not altogether rational form: Should Communists be fought mainly at home, because that would be cheaper; or should they be fought abroad, because that would make it possible to preserve liberalism at home? The President called attention to this strange dichotomy and gave his view as to how it should be handled when he

34. "Looking Backward—to the 1950's," *The New York Times Magazine,* April 26, 1953, p. 12.

defended his loyalty program before the American Bar Association on April 23, 1950:

> We know that the greatest threat to us does not come from the Communists in this country, where they are a noisy but small and universally despised group. The greatest threat comes from Communist imperialism abroad, where the center of its military and economic strength lies. The real danger is that communism might overrun other free nations and thus strengthen itself for an ultimate attack against us.[35]

Here was an invitation to all good citizens to prove their "Americanism" by strong support of the Truman Administration's anti-Communist foreign policy.

The invitation was eagerly taken up by those whose domestic political position was made precarious by the implications of McCarthyism. The liberal writer Richard Rovere noted with approval the observation of fellow liberal Philip Rahv that the great danger of McCarthyism was its insistence "that Communism was a danger, not *to* the United States, but *in* the United States, when in truth it was the other way about." Rovere then added his own comment: "It [McCarthyism] was focusing attention on the spy rather than on the power for whom the spy spies, on the Communist or ex-Communist . . . rather than on the Red Army, combat ready and nuclear-armed. Indeed, most of its votaries opposed all reasonable efforts to deal with these matters." [36]

Probably no one stated the "either or" position on battling Communism better than the liberal Professor Arthur Schlesinger, Jr.:

> How are the New Isolationists to get around the fact that their proposals are greeted with loud cheers in the Kremlin? Somehow they must cover their retreat; and what better way to do so than by

35. *Presidential Papers: Truman* (1950), p. 268.
36. Rovere, *op. cit.*, p. 43.

raising a great outcry about the supposed danger of Communism within our own country? Such a sham battle at home might well distract attention from the stealthy desertion of our allies abroad.[37]

Not only did Schlesinger make use of the McCarthyite technique of branding his political foes tools of the Kremlin, he made use of their "crack-of-doom" rhetoric when he warned that policies of the "New Isolationists" would amount to a steady retreat, in the face of Soviet power, "until we are forced back into the Western Hemisphere, or, what is more likely, until we perceive what we are doing and then, having invited Soviet expansion, strike back in the panic of total War." "Without McCarthyism," he continued, "the New Isolationism would be almost indistinguishable from a policy of appeasement." [38] And so, while McCarthy branded as "fellow travelers" those who did not run furiously in pursuit of domestic "commies," Professor Schlesinger labeled as "appeasers" those who did not run furiously in pursuit of overseas "commies."

It is possible that Schlesinger took his cue from the President who, in the March 30 press conference previously mentioned, had accused Senator McCarthy and his Republican supporters of "trying to dig up that old malodorous dead horse called isolationism" and of trying to "sabotage the bipartisan foreign policy of the United States." Since the President insisted that his foreign policy was designed for no other purpose than to defend the nation (and the free world) against Communist aggression, he tended to regard any vigorous, sustained criticism of the policy as unpatriotic. Those who engaged in such activity, beyond quibbling over minor details, were attempting to return the nation to "isolationism" for their own partisan reasons (such as chasing alleged "commies" at home), and this would be suicidal, the President

37. "The New Isolationism," *Atlantic Monthly,* May 1952, p. 38.
38. *Ibid.*

believed, for "isolationism" would weaken the nation's defenses in the face of an aggressive enemy.

During a speech-making trip across the country in early May, the President repeatedly warned against the McCarthyite sins of "isolationism" and "partisanship" and defended the expansionism of his administration's foreign policy as a plan for securing the peace and freedom of the world's peoples. On May 9, at Laramie, Wyoming, he said: "All our international policies taken together form a program designed to strengthen the free world in its resistance to the spread of Communism"; and then in Butte, Montana, on May 12: "We are engaged in a great worldwide struggle to demonstrate that the free way of life is the way to the highest level of well-being for all the people of the world"; and in Fargo, North Dakota, on May 13: "There is no room for economic isolationism in a world torn between freedom and the Communist tyranny." Finally, at a Democratic Party conclave in Chicago on May 15, Mr. Truman blasted the Republican wreckers of bipartisan foreign policy and defended his own party's bipartisanship in seeking world peace (against external Communists).[39]

If there was any doubt as to the President's purpose in his speech-making trip that May, his daughter, Margaret, has set it to rest: He would "turn the tables on the Communist witch-hunters in Congress," saying to them that if they wanted to fight Communism, "Then join me in making America and its allies so strong, we can frustrate Communism's dream of world conquest—and guarantee a century of world peace in the bargain." [40] The conclusion: Overseas commie-hunting ("external McCarthyism") was true Americanism; domestic commie-hunting ("internal McCarthyism") was not.

39. *Presidential Papers: Truman* (1950), pp. 337, 391, 403, 444.

40. Margaret Truman, *Harry S. Truman* (New York: William Morrow, 1973), p. 434.

Meanwhile, the State Department was attempting to refute the charges of Senator McCarthy against leading officials of the State Department by demonstrating that they were faithful "external McCarthyites." In a letter of May 12, sent out to the five hundred members of the American Society of Newspaper Editors, Assistant Secretary of State for Public Affairs Edward Barrett undertook to disprove McCarthy's contention that there are "those in the State Department who say that Soviet Russia's aims have changed in the last few years and that she no longer wants to enslave America. . . ." [41] Barrett answered this "have-you-stopped-beating-your-wife" question by quoting from speeches of Secretary Acheson, Ambassador Jessup, and State Department Counselor Kennan, proving that these men had not stopped beating their wives and had no intention of stopping, which is to say that they all had impeccable credentials as anti-Communist rabble-rousers.

Ambassador Jessup was shown warning the press of India on February 23, 1950, that "where Communism gains control, it becomes immediately apparent that the peoples are not allowed to determine their own future, but must conform to a single policy laid down in Moscow." State Department Counselor Kennan was proudly presented as the author of an article in the *Reader's Digest,* no less, telling the readers of its March issue that "The Russian leaders believe our downfall is inevitable. They would do anything they can to hasten it. . . ." And Secretary Acheson was triumphantly revealed as the "granddaddy of them all," in a speech on March 16 at Berkeley, California: "We can see no moral compromise with the . . . theses of international communism: that the end justifies the means, and that any and all methods are therefore permissible, and that the dignity of the individual is of no importance as against the interests of the state." The secretary

41. S.D. *Bulletin,* XXII, June 12, 1950, p. 969.

then went on to speak of Communism in terms of "regimentation," "the police state," and "slave labor," and finally, not to neglect the Almighty, as a "denial of the fundamental truths embodied in all the great religions of the world." [42]

Truly, as Assistant Secretary Barrett demonstrated, the men of the State Department needed no lessons from Senator Joseph McCarthy in rabble-rousing. Of course, it was entirely proper that they should have defended themselves against the charges of irresponsible politicians. But it was a very sad thing that, in their desperation, these very able and dedicated public servants should have aped the ways of their tormentors. It was particularly distressing to see the sophisticated Dean Acheson taking up the emotional, demoralizing language of the rabble-rousers. His August 1949 warnings against Russian attempts to dominate China had by February 16, 1950, within a week of McCarthy's first blast, been developed into this absurdly simplistic doctrine:

> What they [the Russians] did was to invite some Chinese leaders who were dissatisfied with the way things were going in their country to come to Moscow. There, they thoroughly indoctrinated them so that they returned to China prepared to resort to any means whatsoever to establish Communist control. They were completely subservient to the Moscow regime. These agents then mingled among the people and sold them on the personal material advantages of communism. They talked to the people in their own language. They promised to turn over the land to them.[43]

Not only was this oversimplified view of China's civil war unworthy of Mr. Acheson, it was entirely at variance with earlier views of the State Department, as expressed by Marshall and Kennan.

The rhetoric of the secretary of state and the President

42. *Ibid.*
43. *Ibid.,* March 20, 1950, p. 428.

heated up so remarkably during the spring of 1950, not because of new threatening actions by the Soviet Union, for there were none, but because of threatening attacks upon the Administration by Senator Joseph McCarthy. Acheson had given himself up wholly to the theory that the Soviet Union was determined to bring about the swift and total destruction of the United States. And on April 22 he explained to the American Society of Newspaper Editors what was meant by this sweeping assumption of American foreign policy: "We mean that the Soviet authorities would use, and gladly use, any means at their command to harm us." He then told of Soviet schemes to confuse and divide America and make it "doubt the desirability of helping other free nations," because, he continued, the Kremlin had another objective, "which is to pick off members of the free community of nations one by one." [44]

The secretary knew that it would not be wise to excite American newspaper editors about a threat to the nation's very existence without, at the same time, convincing them that effective measures were being taken to frustrate that dark scheme. And so he assured them that America had the capacity to defend itself militarily and that this was being attended to by the competent men of the Defense Department. More than that, however, there was a need to guide people into a pro-American path: "Beyond faith and preachment and defense there lies the necessity of translating all of this into terms of the daily lives of hundreds of millions of people in this free world of ours." Lifting people out of poverty would give them hope and an alternative to Communism, but, Acheson continued, "the question is whether these people will choose a way out that leads to freedom. The question is

44. *Ibid.,* May 1, 1950, p. 674.

whether these people will move ahead in the free world with us." [45]

The most alarming thing about all this was that the secretary was beginning to discuss American security within the context of a vague idealism, as when he spoke of leading the "hundreds of millions of people" into choosing "a way out that leads to freedom," and then went on to assert that this was "tremendously important to the United States, to our security and well-being." [46] American policy was being "ideologized," which would prove to be the irretrievable calamity of "McCarthyism." It probably explains why Mr. Acheson felt it necessary to keep shifting his ground between "hard-headed realism" and "fuzzy-headed idealism" and why he seemed to find it increasingly difficult to tell the difference between the two. It also explains why the United States abandoned its policy of disengagement from the Asian continent and embraced instead a policy of calculated hostility and persistent harassment of China's Communist regime.

It was during the early stages of the McCarthy onslaught that all discussion of the recognition of Red China abruptly ceased, never again to be considered as a viable possibility or even raised as a subject for serious discussion during the ensuing twenty years. A decision on that question had been postponed in October 1949, in the face of congressional opposition, but as late as January 1950 it was still being said that the State Department favored an early normalization of relations with Red China. Here is Mr. Acheson's explanation for the change in policy: "The Chinese clearly found the United States more useful as an enemy than in any other relationship, and went out of their way to insure that an enemy we remained." [47]

45. *Ibid.*, p. 675.
46. *Ibid.*, pp. 675–676.
47. Acheson, *op. cit.*, p. 369.

But the Chinese Reds were inflicting a great deal less injury on Americans during this period than the Chinese Nationalists, who were actually attacking American ships that attempted to run their blockade of the China mainland. The Reds were indeed harassing American diplomats, but this was to be expected, seeing that the latter had no official standing whatsoever in Red China. Legally speaking, they were private citizens, residing in a country that was being attacked by Nationalist China with arms supplied by the United States. And their accreditation was to the latter government, which the United States went on insisting was the only legitimate government of China. In view of all this, and of the unceasing vilification of Red China by the press and politicians of America, one cannot imagine what measure of "Christian" forbearance the secretary expected from Communists.

In fact, Mr. Acheson knew exactly what the United States would have had to do to normalize relations with Red China. It would have had to live up to its own solemnly given pledge *not to intervene* in China's civil war—that is, it would have had to *cease intervening* in the war, which, in violation of its own policy, it had been doing almost continuously for three years. And this meant that the United States would have had to withdraw recognition from the defeated and discredited regime of Chiang Kai-shek and stop supplying it with the means to impose its unwanted dominion over the people of Formosa. It would have meant fulfillment, at last, of the policy of disengagement from the continent of Asia, which the Administration had been trying so hard to effect since the beginning of Marshall's secretaryship in 1947 and which had been announced as official policy by Dean Acheson on January 12, 1950.

It is said that congressional opposition prevented recognition of Red China, and certainly that was a major stumbling block. But Mr. Acheson had made it virtually impossible for

Congress to alter its position when he decided to interpret China's revolution as an act of Russian imperialism. And after the McCarthy attacks forced the secretary to regularly demonstrate his anti-Communism by frequent moral diatribes against China, one would doubt that he ever again approached Congress on the subject. In any case, Mr. Acheson, who was not averse to pointing an accusing finger where appropriate, did not blame Congress for the policy of non-recognition of Red China. He used the lame excuse of the latter's misbehavior.

Herbert Feis, in a recent study of the cold war, accepts the "smoldering opposition in Congress," in conjunction with the Chinese Communists' "insult and hostility" toward the West, as the explanation for America's non-recognition policy.[48] But it is probable that, had the secretary of state continued to press strongly for recognition, both obstacles could have been surmounted. If Red China had been accepted as a "great power" and treated as what it was, in fact, the one and only government of China, doubtless its behavior would have improved. And continued pressure on the Congress might have secured at least grudging acceptance by the Senate of a policy of "recognition." That is, these things might have happened except for the unleashing of the "McCarthyite terror." It was the latter fact that made all the difference; Mr. Acheson had stopped trying.

Another striking change in America's China policy, although little noticed at the time, came on the question of China's representation in the United Nations. As late as March 1950, the secretary of state had said that the United States, while it would not vote for the seating of Red China in the U.N., would not oppose that action. But when later that spring the Secretary-General of the United Nations again

48. Herbert Feis, *From Trust to Terror: the Onset of the Cold War, 1945–1950* (New York: Norton, 1970), p. 406.

pressed for a settlement of the question, Secretary Acheson said, "Our position of supporting the National Government and opposing the seating of the Chinese Communists remains unchanged." [49] This seemingly routine statement that "our position . . . remains unchanged" was neither routine nor true. It obscured the fact that the United States had reversed itself on the "China representation" question—from a policy of tacit acceptance of Red China in the United Nations to one of outright opposition.

The secretary's further statement that the United States would abide by the majority view of the U.N. membership was misleading. Since a majority of the U.N. members were under the military and/or economic domination of the United States, they were not likely to support what their "patron" opposed. It was the United States then that denied representation in the world's only peace-keeping body to the world's largest nation. The consequences of this action could not conceivably be anything but bad, and it was done in a vain effort to placate the McCarthyites.

The most drastic—as it would prove the most far-reaching and tragic—policy change to occur during the period of the "McCarthy storm" was in the area of America's relations with China's tiny continental neighbors. Although Secretary Acheson had told the Senate Foreign Relations Committee on January 10 that "the most we can do is encourage them and give them some aid under Point Four," the following months would bring a rapid escalation of American meddling in their affairs.

On March 7 Mr. Acheson pleaded with the Senate Foreign Relations Committee to supply economic assistance to South Korea. He quoted the President's statement of the year before

49. S.D. *Bulletin*, XXII, June 26, 1950, p. 105.

that "the Korean Republic, by demonstrating the success and tenacity of democracy in resisting communism, will stand as a beacon to the people of Northern Asia in resisting the control of the Communist forces which have overrun them." [50] In actuality, Korea was not democratic, it had no value for the United States, and it was outside the perimeter of genuine American interest laid down by the secretary on January 12. Any responsibility for that country that the United States had assumed, by virtue of having accidentally liberated it from the Japanese, had been fulfilled, and as for continuing to support it, the secretary noted that some members of Congress have indicated that they "doubt the wisdom of the United States' giving a helping hand in this effort." [51] But Acheson, like the President, wanted to make Korea into a beacon light of democracy.

Plans were also in the making for bolstering governments on China's southern flank. And these, being mostly reactionary, militarist cliques, were likely to be dependable enemies of China and eager recepients of American military and economic aid, referred to euphemistically by the State Department as "friendly support to the states in Asia which may desire such aid." When American envoys in the area of Southeast Asia met in Bangkok on February 15 to discuss ways and means of expediting such "friendly support," high on the list of those said to be threatened with subordination to the "control of the international Communist movement" were the so-called "independent governments of Viet Nam, Cambodia, and Laos." [52]

More would be needed than economic aid, however, and on

50. *Ibid.*, March 20, 1950, p. 455.

51. *Ibid.*

52. *Ibid.*, March 27, 1950, p. 502.

June 1 the President asked Congress to provide it. "Recent events make it evident," he said, "that the forces of international communism do not want these countries to grow in freedom—instead the Communists seek to dominate them." Despite the $75 million provided during the previous year "for assistance to countries in the general area of China," the general area of China remained unsettled. Therefore, because of America's "readiness to act in the interests of peace," the President continued, ". . . I recommend the authorization of an additional 75 million dollars for military assistance to countries in the general area of China during the next fiscal year." Indochina was singled out as a country (or countries) "in the general area of China" where guns were particularly needed to further the cause of peace.[53]

On the following day Secretary Acheson told the Senate Foreign Relations Committee that "the menace of Communist China threatens the people of Indochina, Burma, Thailand, Malaya, and the newly created United States of Indonesia." Speedy action, he thought, was required in Indochina: "Thus, we have been able to announce our determination to support France and the States of the French Union in Indochina—Vietnam, Laos, and Cambodia—in their struggle to preserve the freedom and integrity of Indochina from the Communist forces of Ho Chi Minh."[54] The senators were apparently unastonished by the astonishing news that the United States was going to help imperial France "preserve the freedom and integrity of Indochina," which was very much like helping the fox guard the hen house.

This emerging Asian policy, which actually constituted a fundamental and dangerous shift in American policy, occa-

---

53. *Presidential Papers: Truman* (1950), p. 448.
54. S.D. *Bulletin,* XXII, June 12, 1950, p. 944.

sioned no great public clamor in America. There was relatively little discussion of it and no strong or sustained opposition in the national press. Among the few news weeklies to demur was *U.S. News & World Report,* which grumbled that "the United States and Britain are being drawn into Indo-China." [55] Liberal journals such as *The Nation* and the *New Republic* were not so much concerned about American meddling as about the reactionary cliques through whom the meddling was done. *The Nation,* noting Russia's recognition of the Ho Chi Minh regime and America's counter-support of the French in Indochina, offered this petulant remark: "Once again she [Russia] maneuvered us into giving support to a regime which only offers anti-communism." [56] Apparently it was thought that manipulation through "liberal reformers" would have turned the trick in Indochina.

On the other hand, there was much support for casual adventures "in the general area of China." *Life* and *Time,* bellicose as usual, were avid for any kind of policy that called for hitting Reds, little caring how tenuous the ground on which the hitting was done. And Joseph Alsop, it will be remembered, had been pleading the Indochina interests of France and the Emperor Bao Dai in his nationally syndicated column since June 1949. In March 1950 his brother, Stewart, returned from a journey through the Far East to report in *The Saturday Evening Post* that "We Are Losing Asia Fast." Stewart, like brother Joe, feared that the nations of Southeast Asia would fall like a row of dominoes, and he came close to winning the small immortality that would have gone with inventing the term "domino theory" to describe that hypothetical phenomenon. But the pithy and extremely mischievous

55. *U.S. News & World Report,* February 24, 1950.

56. *The Nation,* March 4, 1950.

ttle phrase would have to await the coming of phrase-maker Dwight Eisenhower. The best Alsop could do was a bowling analogy, in which he perceived that a strong bowler had already hit the head pin. "The head pin was China. It is already down. The two pins in the second row are Burma and Indo-China." [57]

Foster Hailey of *The New York Times* asked the only important question about America's increasing involvement in Indochina: "What are the probabilities that aggressive intervention there might lead to war?" Finding no reason for caution, and concluding that Indochina was a prize worth a considerable risk, Hailey gave this extremely interesting assessment of the Indochina situation:

> The French are convinced, and apparently they were able to convince Mr. Acheson and his advisers, that, before Indo-Chinese Nationalism can express itself, a real military victory must be won over Ho Chi Minh's regular army and the hard core of his movement either destroyed or driven out of the country.
>
> For better or worse the United States now seems committed to that belief and policy. Since it is, time would seem to be an important factor: the need to get all necessary military equipment there as fast as possible before the Chinese Communists can lend any material support to Ho Chi Minh's movement.[58]

Hailey was somewhat dubious about the political situation in Indochina, but he had no doubts at all that the military situation was "one capable of solution; even a quick solution, as surplus American war material, not necessarily the latest weapons, should suffice." [59]

The secretary of state apparently hoped to give this interventionist policy a rational purpose when he explained to the

57. *The Saturday Evening Post,* March 11, 1950.

58. *The New York Times,* May 14, 1950.

59. *Ibid.*

Senate Foreign Relations Committee that developments i
"the general area of China" were "of great importance to th
security of the United States." If the secretary believed this
he had become convinced of it since his announcement of th
offshore policy on January 12 when he had avowed that h
would never "put the cart before the horse"—that is, place a
ideological struggle above national interest in foreign policy
Apparently he had changed his mind: "Our policy is an
must be devoted to doing everything within our power t
prevent the further spread of Communism." [60] Acheson wa
equating American security with an ideological struggl
against Communism, thus submerging the nation's security i
an ideological haze. But the solid fact remained that the littl
states on China's border could not provide a bulwark agains
an expansive China, no matter how much material aid the
were given. And the President's previously quoted statemen
about helping these nations "ward off the threat to thei
security from subversive Communist forces within their coun
tries" did not make a great deal more sense. Unpopular
reactionary governments would be no better able to put dow
viable insurgencies within their borders than to ward off
Chinese attack.

Nonetheless, they were now being aligned with the Unite
States and placed in a stance of armed defiance of thei
powerful neighbor. The arms provided them were utterl
useless to effect either of the purposes for which they wer
intended and, in fact, were more likely to invite attack tha
to deter or repel it. Having placed them in this vulnerable
position, the United States would be obliged to go to thei
defense if they were threatened by either external attack o
domestic insurgency; the moral obligation, so casually assumed, would be too strong to ignore. Asia's militarists under-

60. S.D. *Bulletin, op. cit.*

tood, if the State Department did not, that the only conceivable value of American military and economic assistance for them was that it *virtually guaranteed American intervention on their behalf.*

A frightening thing was happening to the men who made America's foreign policy. They were no longer being guided by a hard, objective analysis of the nation's real interests, although this method had served them well enough in the past. It had taught them during the difficult years of dealing with the Chiang regime, for example, that the United States must never, under any circumstances, get itself involved in a land war in Asia and that, to avoid all possibility of that calamity, its power must be kept well back from the Asian continent, not even pressing so close as the island of Formosa. This hardheaded realism had also informed them that the little states along China's periphery, being geographical and cultural extensions of China, would almost certainly fall under the domination of their powerful neighbor but that this mattered not at all to the United States, since they served no vital American interest. But the policy-makers were now being forced to think in moral-ideological terms, and so they must abandon their hard-won knowledge. In a time of rising hysteria, their emotions—particularly those of fear and hate —would serve better.

This was, in fact, demanded by the McCarthyite dispensation, and the McCarthyites were moving into possession of America's Far Eastern policy. They had already forced the nation into a "hate China" policy, which was being carried forward by a ceaseless stream of invective, the withholding or recognition from the *de facto* government of China, the denial of that government's rightful seat in the United Nations, and, most dangerous of all, the harassment of China by arming its small neighbors and encouraging them to believe that they were safe in assuming a bellicose attitude toward China. Since all of this happened before North Korea's attack upon South Korea, it cannot be argued, as it often has been, that the Korean War was a major cause of McCarthyism. What can be legitimately argued, as it is herein, is that McCarthyism exerted a very powerful—possibly decisive—influence on America's Far Eastern policy.

CHAPTER EIGHT

"McCarthyism" and the Korean Intervention: Harassment of China Becomes Military Encirclement (1950)

It was on Sunday, June 25, 1950, around noon, that President Harry Truman got word that the North Korean attack upon South Korea, which he had first learned of the evening before, was a general offensive, apparently aimed at the complete conquest of the South; and it was only a little more than twenty-four hours later that American military forces were actually fighting in defense of South Korea. The strong, swift response of the United States to this new cold war crisis had all the appearance of a reflex action, as though the precise nature and scope of the reaction had been carefully planned in advance. Nothing could have been further from the truth, for the fact was that all prior consideration given to the problem of South Korea had led to only one conclusion: That its value to the United States was absolutely nil—that it was not worth fighting for. Korea was a remote land that provided neither strategic nor economic advantage for the United States; it was outside the perimeter of America's vital interest as defined by the secretary of state on January 12; and it was a land about which Americans knew nothing and cared less. Surely then President Truman's decision to intervene there was one of the most astonishing—and, in the end, tragic—ever made by a President of the United States.

The action was taken under the authority of a United Nations resolution, and this provided a great deal of moral comfort for many people. But the administration knew perfectly well that Americans, although as given to moralizing their violent acts as others, are not fond of spilling their blood in idealistic causes that are unrelated to real national interests. Thus, President Truman was careful to make it appear that his action was a continuation of the cold war by other means and that his main purpose was to defend America by thwarting Russian "aggression." This is how he explained it to the nation on June 27: "The attack upon Korea makes it plain beyond all doubt that Communism [that is, Russia] has passed beyond the use of subversion to conquer independent nations and will now use armed invasion and war." [1] This explanation was generally accepted at the time, and it continues to be a widely held view.

But, even if all of this were true, or assumed to be, the only important question for the United States was whether or not Korea was a good place to make a stand. The answer to this was an obvious and emphatic *no,* for, as *The New York Times'* military analyst Hanson W. Baldwin said ". . . militarily and strategically Korea was perhaps the least advantageous place in the world for American forces to make a stand." [2] And the Joint Chiefs of Staff, according to Secretary Acheson, had never been enthusiastic about the strategic value of Korea: "I do not think that the Joint Chiefs of Staff have ever determined, or rather I think they have not determined that Korea is of strategic importance to the United

1. *Presidential Papers: Truman* (1950), p. 492.
2. *The New York Times,* July 2, 1950.

tates." [3] The Joint Chiefs' own chairman, General Omar Bradley, confirmed this view: "Korea is a poor place to fight war, and a lot of military implications are involved in exending the war." [4]

As early as September 25, 1947, the Joint Chiefs of Staff —one of the most distinguished ever, with Admiral William D. Leahy as chairman, General Dwight Eisenhower for the Army, Admiral Chester Nimitz for the Navy, and General Carl Spaatz for the Air Force—advised the President to abandon the nation's military commitment to Korea. Their reasons for making this recommendation are of more than passing interest and deserve quoting at some length:

> The Joint Chiefs of Staff consider that, from the standpoint of military security, the United States has little strategic interest in maintaining the present troops and bases in Korea for the reasons hereafter stated.

> In the event of hostilities in the Far East, our present forces in Korea would be a military liability and could not be maintained there without substantial reinforcement prior to the initiation of hostilities. Moreover, any offensive operation the United States might wish to conduct on the Asiatic continent most probably would bypass the Korean peninsula. [5]

Clearly the Joint Chiefs of Staff did not think Korea was worth fighting for.

Politically and ideologically, Korea had even less to recommend it as an American protégé. The Joint Chiefs had as low an opinion of the country's political possibilities as of its strategic advantages and cited the former as among the reasons for departing the country: "Authoritative reports from Korea indicate that continued lack of progress toward a free and independent Korea, unless accompanied by an elaborate

3. *Military Situation in the Far East*, p. 1818.

4. *Ibid.*, p. 891.

5. Truman, *Years of Trial and Hope*, p. 325.

program of economic, political and cultural rehabilitation, i
all probability will result in such conditions, including violen
disorder, as to make the position of United States occupatio
forces untenable." [6]

President Truman, for all his own propaganda abou
Korea's budding democracy, was not taken in by the reaction
ary bunglers of Syngman Rhee's governing clique: "I did no
care for the methods used by Rhee's police to break u
political meetings and control political enemies, and I wa
deeply concerned over the Rhee government's lack of concern
about the serious inflation that swept the country." [7] Fo
such very good reasons as these, President Truman withdrev
all but 500 of the 45,000-man garrison from Korea durin
the next two years.

The man whose opinion on this subject probably mattered
most, General Douglas MacArthur, was also strongly opposed
to military adventures on the Asian continent. His actual view
were obscured by his close association with those favoring a
stronger policy in Asia, but the fact is that, even when giving
testimony on behalf of a strengthened Asian policy in 1948
MacArthur had warned against an excessive commitment of
American resources to Chiang Kai-shek. And the defensive
perimeter that he outlined for the United States in January
1949 was the line that Dean Acheson followed when he defined the limits of the American military commitment on January 12, 1950. MacArthur later moved his defense perimeter
up to include Formosa, but he clung to his offshore views
right through his experience of the Korean War. When, during
the hearings concerning his dismissal from the Far Eastern
command in 1951, he was asked if he had ever said that any-

6. *Ibid.*, pp. 325–326.
7. *Ibid.*, p. 329.

one who "commits the land power of the United States on the continent of Asia ought to have his head examined," he replied, "I don't know whether I made the statement, but I confirm absolutely the sentiments involved." [8]

The President and the secretary of state were sufficiently impressed by these views of the nation's senior military officers that, on January 12, 1950, they formally declared the principle of non-involvement on the Asian continent to be the official policy of the United States. And it is abundantly clear that the secretary of state regarded this as a permanent policy which, like the policy of non-involvement in Formosa (far more defensible than Korea), had to do "with the fundamental integrity of the United States and with maintaining in the world the belief that when the United States takes a position it sticks to that position and does not change it by reason of transitory expediency or advantage on its part." [9] The secretary's later efforts to prove that this policy had not been reversed by the Korean intervention were lame indeed, as lame as if he had attempted to prove that black is white.

One man who believed that the policy of non-involvement on the Asian continent meant what it said was Tom Connally, chairman of the Senate Foreign Relations Committee and chief spokesman for administration policy in the Senate, and he was quite certain that it precluded all possibility of intervention in Korea. When asked by a reporter in early May if the suggestion that South Korea be abandoned would be seriously considered, he answered, "I am afraid it's going to be seriously considered because I'm afraid its going to happen whether we want it or not." On the question of whether Korea had strategic importance for the United States, Connally's

8. *Military Situation in the Far East,* p. 156.
9. See p. 147.

answer was an emphatic "no." "Of course," he continued, "any position like that is of some strategic value. But I don't think it is very greatly important." [10]

Republican critics of administration policy had no more doubts than Connally as to the full implications of the Truman policy, and they insisted that it be made consistent by cutting loose from the small but dangerous commitment to Korea. Supported by dissident Democrats, they had defeated the administration's request in January for supplemental aid to Korea in the amount of $60 million. Although the funds were later restored, this action was an indication of congressional displeasure with a policy of casual meddling that had no clear purpose in view. It was thus possible that simple logic and good sense, rather than resentment over the abandonment of Chiang Kai-shek (Acheson's explanation), had prompted Republican Congressman Donald L. Jackson of California to ask: "What kind of policy for the Far East would put economic aid into Korea, which bears no relationship to our national defense, and at the same time refuse a request to put aid into Formosa?" [11]

From the foregoing it should be clear, beyond any possibility of doubt, that, when President Truman ordered American troops into Korea, he was acting against the best judgment of the Joint Chiefs of Staff, the State Department, and Congress. After the decision was made, his advisers, the Congress, and the entire nation rushed to pledge him their vigorous support. But there is no evidence that, at the moment of crisis, before the President's decision was known, a single person urged him to go to Korea. What is known for certain is that, in the months and years preceding the crisis, the President's

10. *U.S. News & World Report,* May 5, 1950.

11. *Congressional Record,* XCVI, 81st Cong., 2nd Sess. (1950), p. 649.

advisers, almost unanimously and in the strongest terms possible, had advised against such action.[12]

However that may be, once the decision was made, it had to be justified. The administration could not claim that its Korean intervention had been primarily for the purpose of improving the nation's defensive posture. This would have been to boast of substituting an extremely hazardous policy (a bloodily held beachhead line) for a very sound one (an easily held offshore line). On the other hand, an admission that American lives were being expended in the service of a vague United Nations-based ideal would not have gone well with the American people. But, since neither the idealistic argument nor the security argument had much substance, the one being no more rooted in true idealism than the other in genuine realism, an explanation was needed in which each argument propped up the other. And so the explanations usually began with the United Nations ideal that, by a circuitous logic, was brought into the service of American security.

This is how Secretary Acheson performed that delicate balancing act during the MacArthur hearings of 1951: "Their [the American people's] conviction grew that the best way to protect the security of our nation and other people was to prevent war and that the way to go about it was through an international system of collective security." Such things as the Four Freedoms, the Atlantic Charter, the United Nations

12. In 1974 the Senate Foreign Relations Committee released the reports of its hearings conducted in executive session during 1950, and there one finds the final confirmation that the Truman Administration had never had any intention of fighting in Korea. When asked by Senator Tom Connally if the United States would go to the defense of South Korea in the event of an attack upon it by North Korea, Mr. Acheson answered: "I do not believe that we would undertake to resist it by military force." *Reviews of the World Situation: 1949–1950,* Hearings Held in Executive Session Before the Committee on Foreign Relations, United States Senate, 81st Cong., 1st and 2nd Sessions (1950), p. 191.

were not cynical slogans, he thought, "They represented the ideas which our people felt in their hearts were worth fighting for." Korea was a test of this idealism: "If we stood with our arms folded while Korea was swallowed up, it would have meant abandoning our principles, and it would have meant the defeat of the collective security system on which our own safety ultimately depends." [13] Actually, Acheson would have been one of the last people to place America's security in the bumbling hands of the United Nations.

Senator Owen Brewster of Maine, noticing the tenacity with which Acheson clung to the two mutually supporting pegs of his argument, tried to get him to throw away one peg or the other. By close questioning, he attempted to force the secretary to admit that the administration had reversed its offshore policy—which it had but did not admit—or else that the United States had intervened in Korea for no other purpose than to support a U.N.-centered idealism—which it had not, but which it claimed to have done in the interest of national security. But Acheson had no intention of giving up either half of his argument, as he indicated in this answer to one of Brewster's questions, taking care to put the American security interest first:

> It [American action in Korea] is motivated by the security of the United States, because this whole question of collective security is one of the bases of our own security; and, therefore, when this attack occurred in Korea and Korea appealed to the United Nations for assistance against an unprovoked armed attack, it was of the greatest importance that the collective-security system should work, the United Nations should come to the assistance of Korea, and that this attack should be repelled, because, if that is not done, then I think the whole system of collective security will begin to disintegrate.[14]

13. *Military Situation in the Far East,* pp. 1714–1715.
14. *Ibid.,* pp. 1818–1819.

Brewster thought the answer evasive and gave his own version of what the secretary had said: "Our action in Korea was not because Korea was a part of our defense perimeter or vital to our security, but because of our interest in collective security along with the United Nations. That was my question, and I gather that your answer to that is 'Yes.' " [15] But Acheson would not accept the one peg without the other.

Actually, collective security, if it meant anything more idealistic than an old-fashioned military alliance, had nothing at all to do with America's reasons for intervening in Korea. The United Nations was used as the instrument of that intervention and provided a convenient moral cover for it, but the United Nations was not a truly universal peace-keeping body at the time of the Korean action. China, the world's largest nation and the great power most vitally concerned by what happened in Korea, was not even a member, and Russia was boycotting it at the time. It was thus possible for the United States and its allies and dependents to use this "rump" United Nations for their own purpose and that purpose was to make war on Communism, which was not a legitimate U.N. objective, assuming it was not spread by force.

That the United States was determined to intervene, with or without U.N. authorization, is demonstrated by the fact that sea, air, and logistical support for South Korea was ordered by President Truman on June 26 and not called for by Security Council resolution until the afternoon of June 27. "Thus," Acheson confessed in his memoirs, "some American action, said to be in support of the resolution of June 27, was in fact ordered, and possibly taken, prior to the resolution." [16] The President confirmed the essentially unilateral American character of the intervention when he sent a note

15. *Ibid.*, p. 1819.

16. Dean Acheson, *Present at the Creation* (New York: Norton, 1969), p. 408.

to his secretary of state on July 19 thanking him for his swift action in calling the Security Council into session: "Had you not acted promptly in that direction we would have had to go into Korea alone." [17]

The plain fact is that, despite the smoke screen of moral idealism, the United States had reversed its offshore policy and had done it in the most sweeping fashion. All hope that the Korean affair might prove to be a temporary, localized aberration was dashed when President Truman dispatched an American fleet to guard the island of Formosa and, at the same time, enlarged the nation's commitment to the French in Indochina. All of this meant that the American defense perimeter had been moved forward to positions on or near the Asian continent. The Philippines-Ryukyus-Japan defense perimeter, so nearly impregnable that it was not likely to be attacked by the most reckless of aggressors, had been abandoned in favor of the Korea-Formosa-Indochina perimeter, anchored on precariously held beachheads that were certain to be under constant threat from a China steadily growing in power and in its resentment of the menacing beachheads.

Knowing full well how dangerous this policy reversal was and hoping that, having abandoned its own best judgment, it might be saved by good luck, the Truman Administration attempted to edge its way onto the Asian continent surreptitiously, doubtless hoping that, in time, it could edge its way back off again. The actions taken would have to be camouflaged. Just as the true nature of the Korean intervention had been obscured by a U.N. sanction, the Formosa intervention was covered by the theory that it was a neutral act (preventing military action both to and from the island) and that its main object was to provide for the security of American troops fighting in Korea. The deepening Indochina involvement had

17. *Ibid.*, p. 415.

its own ready-made cover, being carried on through the favored device of a proxy—in this case, the French, who would gobble up $4 billion of American money before abandoning their hopeless task to American soldiers.

Senator Robert A. Taft was not flummoxed by the administration's sleight of hand. He saw very clearly that its Far Eastern policy had been reversed on a broad front, while its spokesmen persisted in denying the fact. In a Senate speech of June 28 he cited the three main instances in which the reversal had occurred. First, "The use of United States air and sea forces in Korea overrules the policy of American withdrawal [from the continent] and the defense of the Okinawa-Japanese line." Second, "The statement that 'the occupation of Formosa by Communist forces would be a direct threat to the security of the United States forces performing their lawful and necessary functions in that area' is directly contrary to the statement of Secretary Acheson that Formosa has no military value and that 'we are not going to get involved militarily in any way on the Island of Formosa.' " And finally, "The furnishing of military assistance to Indochina contradicts Secretary Acheson's statement that all the United States could do in Southeast Asia was to provide advice and assistance when asked, and that the responsibility was not ours." [18]

If, Taft argued, the administration had now decided that it was entirely proper for the United States to involve itself directly on the Asian continent, then the Marshall-Acheson policy of leaving the continent strictly alone, which had been doggedly pursued for three years, had been tragically wrong. Taft's logic was flawless, for the North Korean attack was the sort of contingency that the administration must surely have taken into account when it pledged itself to the sound principle—one to which even General MacArthur subscribed—that

18. *Congressional Record, op. cit.,* p. 9322.

anyone who committed American forces to a land war in Asia "should have his head examined." One can scarcely believe that the administration had committed itself to non-involvement on the continent of Asia with the understanding that the policy was to be abandoned the moment an incident occurred that made it applicable. It was not, therefore, either illogical or improper, as was charged, for Taft to demand the resignation of Secretary Acheson whose policy had been reversed.[19]

Recalling how his earlier demand for the naval defense of Formosa had been called foolish, Taft suggested that "intervention in Korea from a military standpoint is a good deal more foolish an adventure than intervention in Formosa." It was over this Formosa question that Taft (and General MacArthur, for that matter) had disagreed with Acheson's offshore defense perimeter; and it seems obvious, from his speech, that he still preferred the offshore line, provided it included Formosa. And he just as clearly had no enthusiasm for the Korean adventure: "It seems to me that the new policy is adopted at an unfortunate time, and involves the attempt to defend Korea, which is a very difficult military operation indeed." Having brought his sharp knife to the very jugular vein of the Truman Administration foreign policy, Taft then drew back, pledging his support to the new adventure, "I see no choice except to back up wholeheartedly and with every available resource the men in our Armed Forces who have been moved into Korea." [20]

One wonders why Senator Taft did not press the administration hard on the point where it was vulnerable, not on questions of where or how it would fight its Asian wars, but of *why* it should fight them at all. And why had Senator Brewster failed to drive Acheson to the wall over his mixing of vague

19. *Ibid.*
20. *Ibid.*, p. 9320.

ideals with security interests? Why, indeed, if the nation's security was the "central and dominant objective of American foreign policy," as Acheson claimed, did someone not force the Administration to explain why it had moved the nation's defense perimeter from an impregnable and easily defensible line to one that could be held only with great difficulty and at the sacrifice of many lives?

The fact is that the Korean intervention, in all its ramifications, did not readily lend itself to rational analysis. Why had it suddenly become important for Americans to die in large numbers to save the insignificant (to America) little state of South Korea from "the Communists" when saving the infinitely more important Nationalist China from "the Communists" had not been thought worth the life of a single American soldier? The crucial difference was that, between the time of Chiang's collapse and the outbreak of the Korean War, a radical transformation had occurred in American thinking. *It had been completely ideologized by the McCarthyites.*

The nation had become obsessed with making war on Communism, everywhere and with every resource. This was the new "orthodoxy," which it had become exceedingly dangerous to oppose, and it explains why no loud and influential voices were raised against the Korean War, but, rather, were all raised stridently in support of it. It also explains why Secretary Acheson could get away with his mixing of moral and military objectives in explaining the war, and why he could have the temerity to claim that America would be most secure if it depended for its defense upon the "collective might" of the United Nations, when, in actual fact, the administration had placed the nation's defense upon unilaterally held beachheads perched precariously around the fringes of a vast, remote, and hostile China. Under the McCarthyite dispensation, all of this mattered very little; what mattered was that Americans were fighting Communists.

The pernicious effects of McCarthyism upon the State Department have been noted: the abasement of the secretary of state and other high department officials before their congressional critics; the constant explanations—even apologies—in reply to the McCarthy charges; and the tragicomic efforts to present the State Department's top men as anti-Communist rabble-rousers. It has also been shown how all of this had culminated in a policy of "hate and harassment" of China, which was being carried forward most recklessly in the State Department's policy of placing the small nations of the Asian continent in a position of armed defiance of Red China. Finally, and possibly most mischievous of all, had been the application to foreign policy of the McCarthyite rhetoric of fear and hate.

The President himself has been observed in his ever more strident demands for all-out support of his increasingly tough anti-Communist foreign policy and in his tendency to lump all his critics with the McCarthyites as irresponsible "partisans," "isolationists," and "friends of the Kremlin." The highly emotional and excessively moralistic state of the President's mind during this period is revealed in virtually everything he said on the subjects of Russia and Communism. On June 27 he explained the Korean situation in this sweeping statement: "The attack upon Korea makes it plain beyond all doubt that communism has passed beyond the use of subversion to conquer independent nations and will now use armed invasion and war." [21] Thus, an attack by half of one country upon the other half had been transformed into the conquest of "nations"; and "communism" (Russia) had been adjudged guilty of aggression, without any substantiating evidence whatsoever. On the same day, when speaking at the cornerstone-laying for a federal court building, Mr. Truman went out of his way to describe Soviet governing techniques in terms of "kidnapping,

21. *Presidential Papers: Truman* (1950), p. 492.

torture, slavery, murder." [22] And at a press conference two days later, he called the North Koreans a "bunch of bandits," happily assuring newsmen that they could quote him.[23] The President's simplistic moral view of the cold war was no more than this: The American "good guys" were standing up firmly against the Communist (Russian) "bad guys."

Only against this background of violently inflamed moral-ideological attitudes can one readily understand how the President could have moved so quickly and decisively along his new, bloody course in Asia, apparently without a single regret or so much as a backward glance. His own account of how he reached that fateful decision deserves repeating:

> It was about ten-thirty on a Saturday night, and I was sitting reading right here in our house in Independence. The phone rang, and it was Dean Acheson calling from his home in Maryland. He said, "Mr. President, I have serious news. The North Koreans are attacking across the 38th Parallel." Instead of going right back to Washington I waited for further developments, and the next day we were at my mother's for an early Sunday dinner. About eleven-thirty the phone rang, and Margaret went to answer it. She came back and said, "Daddy, it's Dean Acheson, and he says it's important." I went to the phone and said, "What is it, Dean?", and he said, "Mr. President, the news is bad. The attack is in force all along the parallel," and I said, "Dean, we've got to stop the sons-of-bitches, no matter what."

This version of the decision to intervene was recounted to Robert Allan Aurthur during the filming of a television special on Korea. When Aurthur asked to hear more of the details of the decision-making process, what he got was the same story, twice repeated. There was no more to tell, insisted Mr. Truman, "And that's all there is to it." [24]

22. *Ibid.*, p. 494.
23. *Ibid.*, p. 504.
24. Robert Allan Aurthur, "The Wit and Sass of Harry S. Truman," *Esquire* (August 1971), pp. 66–67.

The matter was probably not all that simple for Secretary Acheson, for his own "offshore policy" (no military intervention on the continent of Asia) had been reversed. Having completed his telephone conversation with the President, Acheson undoubtedly knew that he was confronting one of those "awful moments of history" when unhappily "the Gods are silent." He set in motion the engines of intervention and then gave himself up to contemplation:

> During the afternoon I had everyone and all messages kept out of my room for an hour or two while I ruminated about the situation. "Thought" would suggest too orderly and purposeful a process. It was rather to let various possibilities, like glass fragments in a kaleidoscope, form a series of patterns of action and then draw conclusions from them.[25]

One would have liked to get a closer look at those "glass fragments" forming on the "kaleidoscope" of Acheson's mind, for this was surely his *moment of truth*. But he gives us very little.

Whatever Hamlet-like doubt disturbed that Sunday afternoon's reverie, Acheson gives no hint that he was even aware that his offshore policy had been reversed. The close collaboration between him and the President continued as before, neither of them being prepared to admit that a sweeping reversal of policy had taken place. And certainly neither the President nor the secretary was ever going to admit to anyone—not even to themselves—that, under the goad of McCarthyism, they had been marching steadily along the route of increased continental involvement since February.

The transformation of Secretary Acheson's thinking about the Far East is clearly marked. In January he had made strong, clear statements indicating that the United States had no intention of becoming directly involved on the Asian main-

25. Acheson, *op. cit.,* p. 405.

land or on the island of Formosa. And, in his National Press
Club speech of January 12, Mr. Acheson had emphasized the
dangers of assuming that America's principal overseas interest was to stop the spread of Communism. This, he thought,
was "to get the cart completely before the horse"; the United
States was concerned to "stop Communism" primarily where
it was the "subtle, powerful instrument of Russian imperialism."[26] But within six weeks' time, such views had been
branded as heresy by the McCarthyites, and by June the secretary had concluded that it was entirely proper to "put the
cart before the horse": "Our policy is and must be devoted to
doing everything within our power to prevent the further
spread of Communism."[27] The administration's surrender was
complete with its three-pronged lunge at the Asian continent.

It was to be hoped that so great a capitulation would, at the
least, bring domestic peace, and so it did. The respite proved
short-lived, but for a time Washington was pervaded by an
unaccustomed spirit of peace and harmony. David Lawrence
commented on June 28 that there was "such a sigh of relief
throughout Washington today that it's like a breath of fresh
air in a stuffy room. The Republicans and the Democrats are
again united on an unpartisan foreign policy."[28] This was a
macabre thought—that the Korean bloodletting could bring a
happy euphoria to Washington—but it was a fact, and David
Lawrence was not the only one who noticed it. James Reston
of *The New York Times* observed that "there is in Washington
tonight [June 27] a spirit of far greater cooperation than at
any time in the last few years."[29]

Reston was favorably impressed by this upsurge of national

26. *Ibid.*, p. 356.

27. S.D. *Bulletin*, XXII, June 12, 1950, p. 944.

28. Quoted in Denna Frank Fleming, *The Cold War and its Origins,
1917–1960*, Vol. II (Garden City, N.Y.: Doubleday, 1961), p. 601.

29. *The New York Times*, June 28, 1950.

unity and by the alleged moral purpose of the Korean intervention. But he was too perceptive a journalist not to have at least glimpsed the sinister aspect of that action: "Moreover, the somber spectacle of American planes engaged against a Communist aggressor 7,000 miles away from home . . . has finally overwhelmed the atmosphere of McCarthyism that has pervaded this city for months." [30] Reston did not suggest (and probably did not think) that the Korean action might have been taken for the very purpose of "overwhelming the atmosphere of McCarthyism," or, what is more likely, that the administration itself had been so "overwhelmed [by] the atmosphere of McCarthyism" that it could no longer summon up the courage to avoid violent action in the Far East. It was *U.S. News & World Report* that perhaps came nearest to stating the harsh truth about the connection between McCarthyism and the Korean intervention in its offhanded remark that the latter action "lets Secretary Acheson off the hook on the Communist issue." [31]

Many people at the time were trying to get off the hook or to stay off it. On the day before the Korean crisis broke (June 24), John Stewart Service had spent seven hours before a Senate Foreign Relations subcommittee writhing on that terrible hook. Although he had cleared himself several times already, including unanimous acquittal by a New York grand jury in 1945, the State Department had ordered him home from his overseas post to clear himself once again of the McCarthy charges that he had tried to "scuttle Chiang Kaishek" and to "sabotage American policy in order to aid the Communists." Subjected to the same humiliating ordeal as his superiors Acheson and Jessup, Service desperately pled his innocence, "Never have I been a Communist. . . . As my re-

30. *Ibid.*

31. *U.S. News & World Report,* July 7, 1950.

ports written from China clearly indicate, I had full appreciation of the dangers of Russian domination and sought means
of preventing such domination." [32]

Another McCarthy "favorite," Owen Lattimore, hurried to
get himself on record as endorsing the Korean intervention.
Scarcely a year earlier he had been urging the United States
to relinquish its Korean commitment, but he had changed his
mind by June 26, 1950: "Under the present conditions, voluntary withdrawal is, of course, unthinkable." [33] Another who
rushed to join the Korean crusade was Henry Wallace, the
eager, if naïve, "fellow traveler" of 1948. Branding Russia the
guilty party in the North Korean attack, he went on to say
that "when my country is at war and the United Nations sanc-
tions that war, I am on the side of my country and the United
Nations." [34] Even the most independent of China scholars
noticed the emergence of an orthodox line that must not be
trespassed. Harvard's John K. Fairbank, writing in the *Atlantic*
in November, continued to talk good sense about China,
urging the administration to normalize its relations with Red
China and, above all things, not to renew its involvement with
Chiang Kai-shek. But Professor Fairbank dared not embrace
this heresy without making his obeisance to right thinking with
a stern warning against "appeasement of Mao." [35]

No prominent citizen in the land dared oppose the Korean
intervention. After all, it involved the shedding of American
blood in the killing of Communists; to have opposed it would

32. *The New York Times,* June 25, 1950.

33. *Ibid.,* June 27, 1950.

34. *Ibid.,* July 16, 1950.

35. John K. Fairbank, "China," *Atlantic Monthly* (November 1950).
Apparently, Professor Fairbank would have regarded it as appeasement of
Mao to refrain from intervening in Korea, which action he supported, or
to refrain from meddling in the nations of Southeast Asia, which he had
urged since the "Round Table Conference" of October 1949. *Institute of
Pacific Relations,* p. 1588.

have been to spit on the flag. It was very likely this consideration that caused such Truman-hating Asialationists as Taft
and Brewster to modify their attacks upon the Truman interventionism, which they clearly suspected to be a very grave
error. And it is probable that a terrible dread of the wildly
swinging axe of Senator McCarthy at least partially accounts
for the eager queuing up of liberal senators to pledge themselves to the Korean cause. They had never previously favored
a bellicose policy in Asia; rather, they had adamantly opposed
such a course. But it was certain that they could not go on
fighting McCarthy's "domestic anti-Communism" and, at the
same time, oppose Mr. Truman's "overseas anti-Communism."
Besides, they were already strongly committed to the President's globe-girdling foreign policy, which had now been sanc-
tified by the shedding of American blood.

Thus it was that America's liberal senators, like those of
other political hues, dutifully took turns at "waving the flag."
The liberal Democrat Herbert Lehman of New York was one
of the first to grab up Old Glory and try to wrap it around all
of mankind (at least, non-Communist mankind): "Anxious
millions, hundreds of millions, are watching what we do or
say in these historic hours." [36] The liberal, maverick Republican Wayne Morse of Oregon growled out his pleasure that
the United States had, at last, "made it clear to the freedom-
loving peoples of the world that the false, lying, vicious Communist propaganda which would make it appear that they
cannot count on the United States to defend freedom in the
world is really false and lying and vicious." [37] And so it went,
as, one after the other, they came forward to "troop the
colors," the liberal Estes Kefauver of Tennessee, the moderate
Henry Cabot Lodge of Massachusetts, and the "China special-

36. *Congressional Record, op. cit.,* p. 9155.
37. *Ibid.,* p. 9231.

ists" Alexander Smith of New Jersey and Styles Bridges of
New Hampshire. Meanwhile, Tom Connally of Texas labored
mightily to unsay all the strong things he had said against the
very sort of action (commitment of American troops to the
Asian continent) that was now being hailed as the ultimate
in liberty-loving Americanism.[38]

Not intending to be outdone by anyone in patriotic sloganeering and all-round "commie-hating," the liberals' liberal
Hubert Humphrey of Minnesota declared himself proud to
be associated with such men as Smith of New Jersey and
William Knowland of California, the "save Formosa" fanatics,
who had expressed their support of Korean intervention "so
courageously and in such statesmanlike words. . . ." Humphrey, a man given to saying more than was necessary, went
on to praise all aspects of the President's sweeping intervention
in Asia. The Korean action was justified as a "selfless act taken
under the charter of the United Nations," while the Formosan
involvement was hailed as a nonpartisan act "to preserve a
condition of peace" in the area. Having run out of fine phrases,
or grown weary of them, the senator characterized the President's action in Southeast Asia in orthodox "containment"
terms: "The fact that he [the President] has acknowledged the
request of the French Government and the request of the
Government of Bao Dai in Indochina to bolster the defenses
in that area, where Communism has moved into southeast
Asia, is most encouraging." [39]

No one watched these strange developments with more interest, or with a greater sense of outrage, than Senator Joseph
Raymond McCarthy. He perceived that the very men he had
been attacking for their "softness on Communism" were now
about to take the "anti-Communist" issue away from him by

38. *Ibid.*, pp. 9154–9188, 9227–9234, 9319–9340.
39. *Ibid.*, p. 9233.

focusing on the fight against external Communists. Irritated that others should treat logic as cavalierly as himself, he pounced upon the contradictions involved in the administration's dramatic reversal: "Either Acheson was wrong when he referred to the suggestion of the Senator from Ohio [Mr. Taft] that we aid the anti-Communist forces on Formosa as a 'silly venture,' or, if Acheson was then right, the President is now engaged in a 'silly venture'!" [40]

McCarthy was right: If it had been foolish to aid the "incompetent bunglers" of the Kuomintang, as Acheson called them, then it was even more foolish to assist Syngman Rhee's reactionary bunglers in the inconsequential little state of South Korea; and if it had been a "silly venture" to defend Formosa in January 1950, it was just as silly a venture in June 1950. Shrewd demagogue that he was, McCarthy was quick to notice that there was a great deal of hypocrisy in the liberals' strong support of the Truman-Acheson interventionist policies which, so short a time before, they had joined the President and secretary of state in denouncing as foolish. Of course, liberals would never have dreamed of urging military intervention as a means of getting themselves "off the hook on the Communist issue," but, once the war was begun, they were not averse to using it for just that purpose.

McCarthy was determined that they should not get away with it. He denounced them as "political war profiteers" who used the word "unity" as a "mere catchphrase to center the attention of the American people solely on the fighting front. They argue that if we expose Communists, fellow travelers, and traitors in our Government, that somehow this will injure our war effort." [41] Communists "within our borders" had been more responsible for the success of Communism abroad than

40. *Ibid.*, p. 9716.
41. *Ibid.*, p. 9715.

Russia, McCarthy asserted, and "the blood that is being shed in Korea is upon the hands of the men who now shout that we must leave them alone or we shall not have unity in the war effort." [42] He served notice on "Communists, fellow travelers, and dupes that they are not going to be able to hide and protect themselves behind a war which would not have been necessary except for their acts." [43]

Particularly exciting the senator's ire were the liberal columnists who had "headed the smear brigade against those who would expose Communists and traitors at home" but who had now "wrapped themselves in the American flag." [44] Joining in the attack upon the Johnny-come-lately flag-wavers of the press, Senator Hugh Butler of Nebraska (in the words of James Daniel of the Washington *News*) castigated those liberal columnists who had scoffed, as recently as January, when Taft demanded that Formosa be defended but who were now just as loudly praising such action. Among those berated for having learned so tardily the joys of waving the flag and denouncing Communism were Tom Stokes, Doris Fleeson, Marquis Childs, and Mrs. Eleanor Roosevelt.[45] McCarthy could scarcely believe that these people would attempt to wrestle the flag away from him. With a fine sense of irony, or perhaps on the theory that "it takes one to know one," he applied to these latter-day flag-wavers the dictum of Dr. Samuel Johnson, "Patriotism is the last refuge of a scoundrel." [46] But, scoundrels or not, just about everybody was scurrying for that "last refuge" and learning to wave some kind of anti-Communist flag.

Waving this flag required one to "view with alarm" and "point with horror" at those alleged facts which proved that

42. *Ibid.*, p. 9716.
43. *Ibid.*
44. *Ibid.*
45. *Ibid.*, pp. 9719–9920.
46. *Ibid.*, p. 9716.

"the Soviets are out to do us in." On July 17, for example, *Time* magazine came up with this frightening information: "On many evenings . . . the members of the Politburo drive up to the Kremlin in their big black cars [Chicago gangster style] and settle down for an all night discussion of the lands where they will strike next." [47] Less melodramatic but no less certain that they knew world-conquering conspirators when they saw them, the Alsop brothers took to the columns of *The Saturday Evening Post* to instruct the nation in the lessons it must learn from Korea: "Such is the first part of the lesson of Korea, that the Kremlin world strategy exists beyond question, that it is to be taken completely seriously, and that it must be checkmated at all costs. . . . Only all-out effort will save us now." [48]

Some of the myth-makers were more cautious, fearing the broadening and deepening of America's Asian involvement. But they did not suggest that the United States withdraw from the hopeless quagmire; they only "viewed with alarm." *U.S. News & World Report,* which never accepted the theory that China was a Russian puppet, was convinced that Russia wanted to entrap the United States in a war with China and that the United States, by its increasing involvement on the continent, was walking into the trap.[49] The liberal *New Republic* feared that the American undertaking to defend Formosa would lead to a renewal of the ruinous entanglement with Chiang Kai-shek's lost cause.[50] And the *Atlantic* was distressed about the failure to establish diplomatic relations with Red China, noting that "the internal attack from McCarthy," along with "the external attack from Russia" (this the mandatory bow to orthodoxy), had made the establishment of nor-

47. *Time,* July 12, 1950.

48. *The Saturday Evening Post,* September 2, 1950.

49. *U.S. News & World Report,* see particularly the issues of July 28, August 9, and August 11, 1950.

50. *New Republic,* August 21, August 28, 1950.

mal relations impossible.[51] But generally they all accepted the myth that Korea was an idealistic cause and not merely one aspect of a general pattern of military intervention in Asia. Even that enlightened journal of moral opinion *The Christian Century* approved the Korean intervention as a righteous crusade.[52]

Far more typical of the American press, in their refusal to consider long-range consequences, were Henry Luce's *Time* and *Life*. As could have been expected, they were ecstatic that America had at last plunged into the endless mire of the Asian continent. They were unhappy, however, that Far Eastern policy-making was not literally turned over to General MacArthur and that the cause of Chiang Kai-shek was not made the overriding concern of that policy. The whining, wheedling Generalissimo and his beaten, demoralized army were rapidly rehabilitated by the glowing words of *Life* and *Time* into a potent force, ready to be "unleashed." By August 7, *Time* was pleased to note that the administration was coming to see that Chiang's army was "the only anti-Red army with the will and size to fight." [53] *Time* did not explain how it had reached this fantastic conclusion.

The New York Times, which did not lag far behind *Time* in its enthusiasm for Asian adventures, saw the "Korean episode" not as a blunder but as an opportunity, "the first opportunity the West has had to prove to Asians its determination to fight against Communism." But the *Times* feared that the nation would not make the most of its "opportunities" and might fail to give adequate support to the French in Indochina. Although conceding that Ho Chi Minh was popular

51. *Atlantic Monthly,* October 1950.

52. *The Christian Century,* July 12, 1950.

53. *Time,* August 7, 1950; see also the issues of July 10 and July 24, 1950; see also *Life,* July 10, 1950.

in Vietnam and that the people of that country were mainly concerned with winning their independence from France, the *Times* was haunted by the specter of falling dominoes. It could not, therefore, permit the Vietnamese people to go their own way, for a "Communist Indo-China would be a major disaster. It would open the way to Thailand, Burma, Malaya, and Indonesia, and carry the hammer and sickle to the frontiers of India." [54]

While press and politicians, on that critical June 26, 1950, rushed to pledge their support to a war against overseas Communists, certain McCarthyite senators took the occasion to serve notice that there would be no truce in their war on the Truman Administration, for it was here, they believed, that the real enemy was to be found. Malone of Nevada saw no reason for surprise at what had happened in Korea, given the kind of men who had been making America's foreign policy. So that there would be no doubt as to what he meant, he renewed the old charge that General Marshall and others in the State Department had helped the Communists gain access to Japanese arms in Manchuria and then had cut off ammunition and supplies to Chiang Kai-shek.[55] "The Korean debacle," added Jenner of Indiana, "also reminds us that the same sellout-to-Stalin statesmen, who turned Russia loose, are still in the saddle, riding herd on the American people." [56]

If the Malones, the Jenners, and the McCarthys were not willing to give up their irresponsible activities, perhaps it would be possible to bury them, along with their cause, which is exactly what the Tydings subcommittee (a subcommittee of the Senate Foreign Relations Committee) attempted to do.

54. *The New York Times,* July 11, 1950.

55. *Congressional Record, op. cit.,* p. 9186.

56. *Ibid.,* p. 9188.

The Democratic majority of that subcommittee (Chairman Millard Tydings of Maryland, Brian McMahon of Connecticut, and Theodore Green of Rhode Island) declared on July 12 that the task for which it had been created—investigation of Senator McCarthy's Communists-in-government charges—had been completed. It dismissed the charges in the strongest language: "At a time when American blood is again being shed to preserve our dream of freedom, we are constrained fearlessly and frankly to call the charges . . . a fraud and a hoax perpetrated on the Senate of the United States and the American people." The main point of the report was this: "The result has been to confuse and divide the American people, at a time when they should be strong in their unity, to a degree far beyond the hopes of the Communists themselves, whose stock in trade is confusion and division." [57] The implication was clear: Domestic anti-Communism played the Kremlin's game and was thus un-American.

Although its assertions of "fraud and hoax" were doubtless true, the subcommittee majority appealed for public support through patriotic rabble-rousing, and its language was pure "McCarthyism." Senator McCarthy on home ground, replied in kind:

> The most loyal stooges of the Kremlin could not have done a better job of giving a clean bill of health to Stalin's Fifth Column in this country. At a time when American blood is staining the Korean valleys, the Tydings-McMahon report gives unlimited aid and comfort to the very enemies responsible for tying the hands and shooting the faces off some of our soldiers.[58]

McCarthy's conclusion was the exact opposite of that drawn

57. *The New York Times,* July 18, 1950.
58. *Ibid.*

by the subcommittee's majority report, but the implication was no less clear: The main enemy was within, and it was because of that enemy that Americans were dying in Korea.

The Republican minority on the Tydings subcommittee, Senators Henry Cabot Lodge of Massachusetts and Bourke Hickenlooper of Iowa, was caught in the no-man's land between. This position must have been particularly uncomfortable for the moderate Lodge, who could hardly have credited the McCarthy charges but revealed his dread of challenging the high priest of anti-Communism when he issued this innocuous demurer to the majority report: "The fact that many charges have been made which have not been proved does not in the slightest degree relieve the subcommittee of the responsibility for undertaking a relentlessly thorough investigation of its own." [59] This appeared to be a calm and judicious statement, but it was no such thing. Charges did not merit "thorough investigation" simply because they were made by a senator, especially since many of the accused had been repeatedly cleared through FBI investigations. McCarthy's old *bête noir* John Stewart Service, for example, had been cleared by four loyalty boards, the House Judiciary Committee, and a New York grand jury, on the evidence of seventeen FBI agents.[60] Thus, it did not logically follow, as Lodge implied, that accused persons should be subjected to repeated and "relentlessly thorough" investigations, presumably until they were finally convicted of something.

It seemed that the only men bold enough to do battle with McCarthy or any of his cohorts tended to do it on the latter's terms. In the very act of castigating McCarthyites for their unethical practices, Senator Tydings sounded like nothing so much as a McCarthyite. He and Senator Jenner, in an angry

59. *Ibid.*

60. *Congressional Record, op. cit.,* p. 10,715.

exchange, branded each other friends of the Kremlin. Tydings attacked Jenner's votes against the Marshall Plan and the Atlantic Pact, noting that "Joe Stalin and the *Daily Worker* and the Senator [Jenner] all vote the same way." He then wrapped himself in the flag with the boast that "General Pershing gave me the highest awards this Government has to give which I can wear on my breast." Tydings further asserted that he had voted for all of those anti-Communist measures (Marshall Plan and the like) which Jenner had joined Stalin in opposing.[61] The senator from Maryland apparently believed, as did the President, that those who pursued domestic Communists more vigorously than overseas Communists were playing the Kremlin's game.

Jenner insisted that it was the other way around and explained that he voted against such measures as the Marshall Plan because he did not believe that he was "obligated to squander our substance in a suicidal attempt to underwrite everybody else's interest and security but our own." [62] "What is happening . . . to America," he asked, "when the senator from Maryland charges that anyone who is determined to keep America sound, strong, and free is playing Stalin's game?" Who was really following the "commie line"? Jenner asked. Was it the senator from Maryland, "who has conducted the most scandalous and brazen whitewash of treasonable conspiracy in our history," or was it the senator from Indiana, "who would ferret out these rats [the traitors in government] and fumigate their State Department haven." As for Tydings' medals, Jenner confessed that he did not know that the senator from Maryland was "such a brave and heroic man until he told us from his own itsy-bitsy lips yesterday, but I do know that there is another medal which will probably come to him.

61. *Ibid.*, p. 10,714.
62. *Ibid.*, pp. 10,791–10,792.

It will be very large, and emblazoned with a single name: 'Thanks, from good old Joe, for a job well done.' " [63]

McCarthy himself returned to the fray a few days later (July 25), taking vicious swipes at those who had already been so thoroughly tarred by his brush that, in the minds of many Americans, their names were synonymous with treason. He was completely unrestrained in his denunciations of Acheson, Jessup, Service, and Lattimore, the latter being quoted as having urged the betrayal of Asian nations to Communism: "Let them fall, but do not let it appear that we pushed them." The "Red Dean," as he called Acheson, and others in the State Department were carrying out this policy of thrusting daggers into the backs of Asia's anti-Communists. "They either do not know what they are doing," said he, "—and I do not think that is possible—or else they are trying to create a Red Asia and a Red Pacific Ocean which will wash our shores." He broadened the charge to include the entire Democratic Party: "For the first time we saw the Democratic Party line up solidly [in support of the Tydings committee report] and effectively label itself as the party of betrayal and the party that protects Communists in Government." [64]

McCarthy knew that there was a strong tide running in his favor, which he sought to demonstrate by quoting at length from a cross section of the nation's press. Beginning with his hometown newspaper, the Appleton (Wis.) *Post-Crescent*, he spread on the pages of the *Congressional Record* favorable editorials from the Washington *Times-Herald*, the Shreveport (La.) *Times*, the Dallas *Morning News*, the St. Louis *Globe-Democrat*, the Cincinnati *Enquirer*, the Wheeling (W.Va.) *Intelligencer*, the *Arizona Daily Star*, the *Illinois State Journal*, the Indianapolis *Times*, and *Life* magazine. Not all of these

63. *Ibid.*, pp. 10,791–10,792.
64. *Ibid.*, pp. 10,923–10,924.

vere necessarily enthusiastic about the man McCarthy and
iis methods but all gave aid and comfort to his cause, de-
10uncing the Tydings committee's report and demanding a
horough purging of Communist influence from the govern-
nent. Most of them saw the senator as the people's champion,
he Wheeling *Intelligencer* commenting that "Senator Mc-
Carthy fought his battle almost single-handed and against ter-
ific odds." [65]

By August President Truman had come to the realization
hat the Korean War was not weakening the McCarthyite mad-
1ess but was actually intensifying it. And there was a possi-
)ility that the fanatical "commie-hunters" would enact one of
:he ferocious anti-subversive bills that had already been intro-
luced by McCarthyites or neo-McCarthyites, Karl Mundt and
Richard Nixon, Homer Ferguson and Olin Johnston, and Pat
McCarran. Fearing that the McCarran bill might pass, the
President proposed a milder bill of his own, which was more
solicitous of civil liberties. "By introducing a rival bill instead
of seeking to defeat McCarran's," says Athan Theoharis, "he
[the President] undermined his attempt to emphasize the importance of civil libertarian considerations. Indeed, his intro-
duction of an alternate bill only served to affirm an apparent
need for more effective legislation." [66] As the McCarthyites
saw it, this was a confession by the President that he had not
been doing a proper job of purging Communists from the government, which was exactly what they had been saying. The
President, obviously rattled by his critics, had blundered badly,
and he would pay dearly for it.

The McCarthyites, sensing victory even as the President
presented his moderate proposal on August 8, came snarling
to the attack two days later. Nothing had happened to shift

65. *Ibid.*, p. 10,934.

66. Athan Theoharis, *Seeds of Repression: Harry S. Truman and the
Origins of McCarthyism* (Chicago: Quadrangle Books, 1971), p. 117.

the focus of their attack from Washington to Korea, warned William Jenner, and they did not intend to be put off by the President's anti-subversive bill. "The only thing which has been added," he insisted, "is that our GI's are dying in Korea. However, the same treacherous gang in the State Department, who are trying to save face by trying to cover up their bloody tracks of treason, are still in the saddle, riding herd on the American people." [67] Ferguson of Michigan was less crude but more succinct, "He [the President] has recognized . . . that the mere fact that communism is moving into South Korea is no sign that it is not moving here in America through its agents and servants." [68] And Karl Mundt of South Dakota, feigning surprise, was obviously delighted that the President had admitted by implication that his previous anti-Communist measures had been inadequate: "I was surprised . . . because of his previous public utterances which had indicated that he did not feel that legislation of this type was essential." [69]

The attack continued on August 12 when Senator Ferguson denounced the "Achesonian policy," which had written off China, Formosa, and Korea, and about all of Asia: "That policy opened the door and spread the welcome mat for the communists to move in those areas." [70] And Acheson's old enemy Kenneth Wherry went completely berserk, as he demanded that the Democrats prove their patriotism by helping him and others (McCarthyites) "in trying to get rid of the alien-minded radicals and the moral perverts in the Truman Administration." [71] Two days later he asserted that Acheson had deliberately set South Korea up to be attacked and, in one

67. *Congressional Record, op. cit.,* p. 12,186.
68. *Ibid.,* p. 12,187.
69. *Ibid.,* p. 12,188.
70. *Ibid.,* p. 12,414.
71. *Ibid.,* p. 12,419.

of the lowest charges yet made, concluded: "The blood of our boys today is on his shoulders and not on the shoulders of anyone else." [72]

Kenneth Wherry and the Asialationists were enraged that they should have been trapped into supporting a war that the Administration might use to get itself off the hook on the Communists-in-government issue. The Korean War, so far as they were concerned, was just another harebrained overseas adventure of the Eastern internationalists and the deficit-spending New Dealers. The contempt they felt toward Korea as an anti-Communist battleground is betrayed in Ferguson's reference to "the *mere* fact that communism is moving into Korea" and in Jenner's observation that "the *only thing* which has been added" is the Korean War (italics added). They dared not oppose the war outright, since American blood was being shed there in the killing of Communists, but they had no intention of relenting in their attacks upon the Truman Administration's alleged "commie-coddling." How completely they had swept all before them on this issue was made abundantly clear when the McCarran subversives-control bill passed Congress on September 17 by whopping majorities of 354–20 in the House and 70–7 in the Senate. Adding insult to injury, the bill was ridden roughshod over the President's veto a few days later (286–48 in the House and 57–10 in the Senate).

The President had maneuvered himself into this predicament when he transformed the power struggle with Russia into a moral-ideological crusade against Communism. The Mc-Carthyites, taking him at his word, had forced him to drive his own logic to its ultimate conclusion in the Far East. And the McCarthyite lunacy that had made it impossible to avoid

72. *Ibid.*, p. 12,591.

a fight in Korea had, at the same time, made it almost impossible to carry on that fight. Nonetheless, once the President had decreed that "stopping the Communists" was the nation's supreme mission, it was neither logical nor fair of him to ask the McCarthyites to modify or abandon their crusade against "the Communists" within. After all, it was the President himself who had said "We've got to stop the sons-of-bitches, no matter what." The McCarthyites echoed that cry and added "no matter where."

While the latter made good headway in winning public support for their fight against the alleged Communists within, the President was finding it difficult to sustain enthusiasm for the fight against Communists in Korea. Of course, the American people gave nominal support to the war, for, in the "McCarthy era," few men were bold enough to oppose an anti-Communist war. Not being fully convinced that Korea really mattered, however, their support was given in an increasingly rancorous and resentful spirit. Senator Ferguson thus spoke truly when he suggested "that our people are confused and . . . our boys are bewildered about what they are fighting for" and when he quoted the bitter complaint of an American soldier in Korea, "I'll be damned if I see why I'm fighting to save this hellhole." [73]

As the war dragged on, it became clear that it was, on the one side, strictly an American operation on behalf of South Korea. What little assistance came from other members of the United Nations was of a token nature, and it came mainly from nations who had the most compelling reasons for keeping the United States a friendly and generous ally. On the other side, there were only North Koreans, although the Russians did supply war matériels and a great deal of anti-Ameri-

73. *Ibid.*, p. 12,414.

can propaganda. But, as General MacArthur would later testify, "the linking of the Soviet to this Korean War has paled out as the events have progressed." [74] No matter how desperately America's political commentators searched and hypothesized, the Russian presence would not materialize.

No Russian soldiers were being killed; no Russian armies were being defeated; and Russian power was not being diminished in the slightest degree. Nor was the power and majesty of the United Nations being enhanced by one iota. For all the grandiloquent statements of the war's aims, there was only one thing that it seemed clearly to be accomplishing: The United States was preventing the North Koreans from uniting their country by force of arms. This was a war that had to provide its own justification, as the spilling of American blood cried out for more blood. And while this horrendous circumstance would heat up emotions, it would not sustain vigorous, ungrudging support for a dubious cause, and it would not prevent the nation from rending itself in angry debate over a war that was never fully understood.

Most confusing was the enigmatic role of the Russians. It should be recalled that George F. Kennan's "containment theory" had assumed, as a basic premise, that Russian expansionist aims would never be pressed in a reckless manner. And one cannot conceive of a more reckless undertaking than for Russia, not yet recovered from World War II, to have risked a confrontation with the awesome military might of the United States. As Acheson said, "Korea was too near major forces and bases of ours in Japan and too far from any of theirs to offer a tempting target. . . ." [75] The Joint Chiefs of Staff were also of the opinion that Russia was not prepared for a showdown with the United States over Korea, "since the military

74. *Military Situation in the Far East,* p. 250.
75. Acheson, *op. cit.,* p. 405.

balance was more favorable to the United States and unfavorable to the Soviet Union than it was likely to continue in the longer run." [76]

Moreover, Kennan and the State Department's other distinguished Russia expert Charles Bohlen predicted at the outset of the crisis that Russia would not intervene diplomatically by rushing back to the U.N. Security Council for the purpose of vetoing action on Korea. They explained that "the cumbersome Soviet bureaucracy was simply not equipped to make quick decisions. It would take some time . . . for Moscow to figure out the correlation of forces involved." [77] This could only mean that, in the view of Kennan and Bohlen, Moscow had been taken by surprise and would need time to figure out what had happened, for it is inconceivable that the Kremlin had ordered an attack without giving a great deal of prior consideration to "the correlation of forces involved." In any case, things turned out as Kennan and Bohlen predicted: The Russians did not return to the Security Council to veto its actions on Korea, and, in fact, did not return for over a month. It was almost as though they were hoping that the United Nations would restrain their unruly little satellite.

Not many people were prepared to argue that Russia was innocent of all responsibility for the Korean War, and, if they did, they were not likely to be heard. One very persuasive case was presented, however, in the March 1951 issue of *Current History,* and its author was Wilbur Hitchcock, a former official of the American military government in Korea. He pointed out that, as a result of the attack, Russia lost certain inestimable advantages: The United States was forced into a vigorous program of rearmament, which would make it impossible for Russia to gain a decisive military advantage; a

76. *Ibid.,* p. 407.
77. *Ibid.,* p. 408.

number of nations were frightened away from a position of neutrality; the element of surprise had been squandered, in the event more important attacks were contemplated elsewhere; and finally, all possibility that Red China would replace Nationalist China in the United Nations was lost. In view of these strong arguments against the attack, and in the absence of any persuasive explanation for a Russian adventure in Korea, Hitchcock concluded that Kim Il-sung of North Korea had ordered the attack and that he had done it without the knowledge of Moscow.[78]

Nothing went so far to acquit the Russians of complicity in the Korean War as the fact that men sought the proof of it, not by gathering evidence, but by a process of pure reason. In ivory towers and editorial offices all over the land, as well as in the White House and in the halls of Congress, America's keenest minds grappled with this exercise in logic. They came up with some extraordinary theories: (1) the "diversionary move" theory, which argued that the Korean attack was for no other purpose than to divert American attention from more important attacks elsewhere; (2) the "soft-spot probing" theory, which saw the Russians as probing for areas of the world that could be taken with ease; (3) the "will-testing" theory, which held that Stalin, in Hitlerite fashion, was trying to find out if the West had the will to resist acts of aggression; (4) the "demonstration" theory, in which Soviet strength and American weakness was to be demonstrated to the nations of the world; and finally (5) the "threat to Japan" theory, according to which Russia intended to prevent the resurgence of a powerful, industrial Japan on the side of the West.[79]

Any theory that implicated Russia in Korea, no matter how

78. Wilbur Hitchcock, "North Korea Jumps the Gun," *Current History,* March 1950, pp. 136–144.

79. Summarized in Alexander L. George, "American Policy Making and the Korean Aggression," *World Politics,* January 1955, pp. 209–232.

bizarre, was surely preferable to one that exonerated that arch-manipulator of puppets. The American people had rallied strongly to the war in Korea for one reason only: They believed that, somehow or other, they were thwarting "the Communists' "—that is, Russia's—world-conquering ambitions. To accept the proposition that Russia had had nothing to do with launching North Korean armies across the 38th parallel would have been to raise the possibility that the nation was throwing away the lives of its sons for no good reason. Needless to say, such a heretical idea was not going to be entertained for an instant by America's publicists, scholars, and politicians. As already shown, they directed themselves, not to the question of *whether* Russia had done it, but of *why* Russia had done it. And, until they found the answer, Americans would go on fighting in Korea without being sure exactly what it was they were stopping the Russians from doing and, in fact, without even being absolutely certain that it was the Russians they were stopping.

It is doubtful that any aspect of the Korean War caused the Truman Administration so much worry during the summer of 1950 as the fear that the Russian role in that war would, as General MacArthur put it, "pale out" altogether. Since this could not be permitted to happen, under any circumstances, the administration's main task in public relations (propaganda) was to keep the people convinced that the attack upon South Korea was really an act of Russian aggression, the ultimate objective of which was the total destruction of the United States, along with freedom and all good things. While the United States was never prepared to make such charges in an official way, its spokesmen never ceased to make them in the most reckless, if unofficial, way.

One such spokesman who served the administration exceedingly well was the prestigious Republican John Foster Dulles, a man strongly committed to bipartisanship and to the "containment of Russia" policy. This future secretary of state had long advocated rabble-rousing the people to secure support for expansive foreign policies. "Mass emotion on a substantial scale is a prerequisite," he had said in 1939. "A sense of peril from abroad must be created." [80] More recently he had urged the use of this same device as a means of restoring the national unity that had been shattered by McCarthyism. It was a sort of poetic justice that Mr. Dulles, more the Presbyterian elder than the Machiavellian statesman, should have been hooked by his own trickery. In the end, probably no one in America would become so thoroughly convinced of the reality of the "world Communist conspiracy" or more terrified of it than he.

Dulles had not a single doubt as to Russia's role in the Korean War. He was convinced that Russia had planned, mounted, and ordered the North Korean attack and that this was part of a general plan for the conquest of the world. As one of America's leading "hardheaded realists" who needed no proof for the obvious, Mr. Dulles did not even bother with theories of "puppetry" to explain the Russian action. He saw it as the most blatant aggression: "No doubt this dangerous moment had to come. There would be a time when the leaders of Bolshevik communism would judge that they had largely exhausted the possibilities of indirect aggression and would explore the possibilities of direct aggression. That, they are doing now." [81]

Another distinguished Republican whose prestigious voice was brought into the service of the administration point of view was Warren R. Austin, the United States representative in the U.N. Security Council. A favorite device of his for convicting the Soviet Union of aggression was to propound a series

80. See p. 36, fn. 13.

81. S.D. *Bulletin*, XXIII, August 7, 1950, p. 207.

of leading questions, to which he then provided the answers. In a speech before the Security Council on August 10, he repeated the catechism of an earlier speech, selected questions from which follow:

> Whose troops are attacking deep in somebody else's territory? The North Koreans.
>
> Who has the influence and the power to call off the invading North Korean Army? The Soviet Union.
>
> What member of the Security Council is supporting the North Korean regime in the Security Council? The Soviet Union.
>
> What kind of a "peace settlement" had the Soviet Union proposed? The kind of settlement that would send the United Nations police away and leave the bandits to plunder Korea at will.[82]

This cool logic is a great deal less impressive when one notices that it only proves that Russia, like other great powers, gives moral and material support to its satellites. Nevertheless, it was used to convict the Soviet Union of aggression, without a single piece of hard evidence being adduced to prove that Russia had mounted, or directed, or participated in the attack on South Korea, or that it had any reason for desiring such an attack.

Secretary of State Acheson was so impressed by Austin's catechism that he recited a bit of it for the press on August 11 and drew the following moral: "It [Russia] has clearly shown, in demanding the withdrawal of United Nations forces from Korea, that the settlement it desires in Korea is abject submission to Communist control." [83] That this endlessly grasping Russia was the real enemy was a fact that Americans must never forget, warned Ambassador Philip Jessup in a CBS radio interview of August 27: "It is of utmost importance that

82. *Ibid.*, August 28, 1950, p. 328.
83. *Ibid.*, August 21, 1950, p. 286.

Americans see clearly who and what are responsible for the dangers we face. Above all, the force of world communism and its leaders—the men in the Kremlin—are responsible. They are the culprits." It is not surprising that Jessup, thought by many to be himself a "culprit," should have ended the interview with a plea for unity against the *Russian* culprits: "Not at this point can we afford to be divided, to waste our energies in recriminations among ourselves." [84]

In a radio-television address of September 1, the President himself went after the Russian "culprits." Although his subject was "The Situation in Korea," he did not even mention the one known aggressor, North Korea, but excoriated the Soviet Union for its obstructionism in the United Nations and for its violation of "pledges of international cooperation." And while the President could not be explicit in charging the Soviets with aggression, he accomplished the same purpose with thinly veiled allusions. There could be no mistaking his meaning when he spoke of "Communist aggressors," "Communist imperialism," and "Communist dictatorships," or when he said, "Two months ago Communist imperialism turned from the familiar tactics of infiltration and subversion to a brutal attack on the small Republic of Korea." [85]

The theme of "Soviet world conquest" was strongly emphasized by the American deputy representative in the U.N. Security Council John C. Ross when he asked, "Can there be any doubt that the armed attack upon the Republic of Korea is part of a Soviet Communist plan of world domination?" This was a rhetorical question, which, of course, required no answer, but "hardheaded realists" were expected to draw the proper inferences. The administration was creating a national

84. *Ibid.,* September 4, 1950, p. 378.
85. *Presidential Papers: Truman* (1950), p. 609.

mood that would tolerate no questions as to Russian guilt, unless, like Mr. Ross's question, they carried their own built-in answers.

But the administration need not have worried overmuch about this problem. Certainly America's conservatives and reactionaries were not going to oppose a war against "the Communists," having staked their whole claim to political preferment on the issue of anti-Communism. The liberals were likely to be even more dependable in their support of the administration view, for they had found the one issue that would make it possible for them to stick to their liberal guns. So long as they proved their anti-Communism by parroting the orthodox view that America was repelling Russian (Communist) aggression in Korea, they would be free to go on battling McCarthyism at home.

How little the liberal position differed from that of the most arch-reactionary was indicated in resolutions adopted in late September by the national council of the Americans for Democratic Action. These liberal gentlemen would withdraw recognition from Chiang Kai-shek's Nationalist government of China but would grant it *de facto* recognition as the government of Formosa. They would recognize Red China and vote for its seating in the United Nations but not until they received "concrete assurances" that it would not intervene in Korea or attack Formosa. And, although they attacked American reactionaries for recommending an Asian policy that "would rely on brute force and on alliances with discredited reactionaries," this very policy was implicit in their own resolutions.

"Brute force" was accepted quite explicitly, as a matter of fact, in their recommendation that Korea be united by a United Nations army (actually a United States army, as they well knew), and it was implicitly accepted in their strong recommendations on Formosa, which amounted to unilateral

American intervention in China's civil war. Moreover, while they urged liberal reforms for Korea, their support for strong interventionist policies around the periphery of China was not made contingent upon the removal of "discredited reactionaries" Syngman Rhee of Korea and Chiang Kai-shek of Formosa.[86] Liberals, like others, were learning to "rely on brute force and on alliances with discredited reactionaries."

The administration thus got a great deal of help in contriving explanations for its Korean adventure. Both official and unofficial "propagandists" devoted their main energies to keeping the people convinced that they were fighting for the purpose of "stopping the Communists," that is, the Russians. But while publicists worked hard to maintain the illusion of a Russian presence in Korea, the administration was very careful to avoid provoking that nation into interjecting an actual presence there, for, as General Omar Bradley later testified, Russian intervention would have made the American position so difficult that we did not "wish to take that risk." [87] It was indeed a strange war that required the United States to take every precaution to avoid confrontation with the nation it was presumably stopping.

Clearly, this was a symbolic war. As President Truman himself said, "we considered the Korean situation vital as a symbol of the strength and determination of the West." [88] But for whom was it a symbol? David Rees, in his *Korea: the Limited War,* saw it as important in bolstering the morale of Europe: "It followed then that the defense of South Korea would reassure NATO allies that the U.S. would defend the alliance at all costs. . . ." [89] Others, like *The New York Times,* thought

---

86. *The New York Times,* September 25, 1950.

87. *Military Situation in the Far East,* p. 891.

88. Truman, *Years of Trial and Hope,* p. 339.

89. David Rees, *Korea: the Limited War* (Baltimore: Penguin Books, 1964), p. 31.

the United States must fight in Korea "if we expect to be taken seriously in the Pacific." [90] But one would doubt that Europe, after the experiences of World War II, the Marshall Plan, and NATO, required an additional demonstration of American good faith. As for the Far East, the spectacle of Westerners killing Asians was not good symbolism; they had seen all too much of that.

The war was a symbol for the American people and for no one else. After all, it was only in America, at the very source of its power, that the administration's anti-Communist faith was in doubt. The matter was put very well by a senator, said to be close to the President and the secretary of state, who was quoted in Holmes Alexander's nationally syndicated column as saying, "if the Republicans hadn't been hammering on Harry Truman, he'd never have gone into Korea." [91] Bearing strongly on the same point was James Reston's observation in January that the State Department was devising assistance programs for Asia in an effort to demonstrate that it was as determined to resist Communism in Asia as in Europe. And it has been shown how the administration, under the "hammering" of the McCarthyites, had for some months been moving steadily in the direction of renewed Asian involvement through its "harassment of China" policy. When the Korean attack came, it dared not refuse to fight. To back away would seem to validate the McCarthy charges that the administration was "soft on Communism," whereas, to accept the fight would surely prove that the administration was wholly devoted, as Secretary Acheson had said, "to doing everything within our power to prevent the further spread of Communism."

90. *The New York Times,* June 27, 1950.
91. Quoted in Fleming, *The Cold War,* p. 658.

CHAPTER NINE

**The Truman-MacArthur Controversy over China
Harassment: From Continental Beachheads or
from Offshore Positions? (1950–1951)**

The Truman Administration needed to win in Korea
and get out quickly, for, with every passing day, the
myth of a United Nations war was becoming more
transparent, the theory of Russian puppeteering more
difficult to sustain, and the possibility of a broadening involvement in Asia more likely. What was
needed was a miracle, and it appeared that one had
been provided when, in mid-September, General
Douglas MacArthur landed his forces behind the
North Koreans at Inchon and swiftly destroyed their
capacity to make war on the South. There was nothing now to prevent MacArthur from marching into
North Korea to unite the country by force of arms,
and he had a United Nations mandate to do just that.
This was an extremely reckless thing to do, for the
Chinese were certain to be alarmed at this approach
to their border by so powerful and unfriendly a force.
And they knew perfectly well that this was not the
army of an impartial peace-keeping body but rather
an army of the United States and its allies. Thus, the
Chinese government issued warnings, through the
Indian and other ambassadors, against an approach

to its border by any but Korean troops and, in late October, as an added warning, made a brief but vicious foray against advance elements of the American force.

General MacArthur chose to ignore the warnings, and on November 24 launched his "home by Christmas" offensive from deep inside North Korea. Three days later the Chinese struck the thinly spread Americans with devastating force and sent them reeling back down the Korean peninsula. In the face of what was to become the longest retreat in American military history, President Truman began to prepare the people for the worst. In a frantic speech on December 15 he warned them that "Our homes, our nation, all the things we believe in are in great danger." Against the Western world's efforts to build a just peace, he continued, "the rulers of the Soviet Union have been waging a relentless attack. They have tried to undermine or overwhelm the free nations one by one. They have used threats and treachery and violence." [1] These words sent Governor Thomas E. Dewey of New York rushing to his legislature to ask it to place the state on a war footing, explaining, "For the first time since the very early days of our nation we face the genuine possibility of an attack upon our homeland by a foreign enemy." [2]

Governor Dewey's behavior was not so strange in view of the President's speech. It was indeed a wildly alarmist speech, but that fact had hardly been noticed by a people in the grip of the "commie-fear." Neither had they yet noticed the astonishing incongruities of a Korean policy that sent Americans to fight North Koreans on the grounds that they were "stopping the Russians"; and which insisted that Russia was out to conquer the world, while that nation failed to raise a hand to prevent the annihilation of its North Korean neighbor; and

1. *Presidential Papers: Truman* (1950), p. 741.
2. *The New York Times*, January 4, 1951.

which villified China unceasingly and ringed it about with military power, although it had been little, if at all, implicated in the Korean affair. None of this made much sense, but now that China had intervened, perhaps things would begin to sort themselves out.

At least the encirclement of China might prove to have its strategic uses. Since China had now apparently identified itself as America's main enemy in the Far East, the positions around its periphery (Korea, Formosa, and Indochina) could be used as the staging areas from which to attack it. And if China was deserving of all the fury it had aroused in the United States and if its overriding obsession was the ultimate destruction or conquest of the United States, as was assumed, then surely good sense demanded that China be invaded and its power destroyed before it grew any larger. There was no other good reason for holding beachheads around that country's periphery. Still, the Truman Administration was not prepared to attack China and would not even persist in its former object of reunifying Korea. It would, however, cling tenaciously to South Korea and, through the inexorable extension of logic, to all the other pathetic little appendages of China.

But why not attack China? According to the administration, it was only the puppet of Russia. To attack it, said Chief of Staff Omar Bradley, would be to fight the wrong war with the wrong country: Chinese territory must be held inviolate. All this was just too much for some Americans to grasp, and so it is not surprising that a great many of them should have been attracted to the simpler, and seemingly more decisive, strategy recommended by General Douglas MacArthur. His strategy did not offer a definitive solution to America's Asian dilemma, as was widely believed, but it did seem to strike nearer to the heart of the problem, that is, toward China itself.

Its main points were these: (1) that the United States concentrate its efforts more on China than on its small "puppets" like Korea; (2) that it contain China from President Truman's own offshore line, although with the line pushed forward to include the island of Formosa; and finally (3) that the United States employ, in this operation, those air and naval weapons in which it enjoyed an overwhelming superiority and in the use of which it would suffer fewer casualties.

MacArthur did not make it perfectly clear what was to be done with the troops still fighting in Korea, and he could not publicly propose the abandonment of Korea, for this would have dealt too heavy a blow to his reputation as a "fighting general." But he had, shortly after China's intervention, suggested this to the Joint Chiefs of Staff as one possible course of action and as an unavoidable course if stronger measures were not taken against China.[3] This fact, in view of his known opposition to American involvement in a land war on the Asian continent, and of the fact that his political allies Herbert Hoover and Robert A. Taft recommended withdrawal, leads one to conclude that these men were disposed to remove all American ground forces from the continent.

To avoid further ground war in Asia, while building America's Pacific defenses along an offshore line, was sound strategy. But General MacArthur was on shaky ground in his recommendation that the United States undertake direct air and naval strikes against China. Such strikes were not likely to seriously damage so large and unindustrialized a nation as China, whereas, they opened up the possibility of a broadened war. Nonetheless, the proposition made a strong appeal to simple logic, since it insisted that the United States stop frittering away its energies on the fringe of Asia and strike directly at China, which was presumably the main enemy and the

3. *Military Situation in the Far East*, p. 906.

chief disturber of the peace in Asia. Certainly this seemed to make more sense than the Truman strategy of converting the small countries around China's border into military beach-heads, without expanding them in offensive operations against China and without destroying China's capacity to keep the beachhead nations in a perpetual state of agitation.

It was precisely this dilemma, always implicit in the "limited war" strategy of the Truman and subsequent administrations, that made General MacArthur's alternative plan so appealing to many Americans who were attracted by the suggestion that they could "eat their cake and have it too." They got the impression that the general was proposing to put an end to the cruel dilemma, once and for all, by eliminating China as a potential threat to the United States. But MacArthur came no nearer to cutting this Gordian knot than had the administration. From secure island bastions, he proposed to make war on China from the relative safety of planes and ships. This was not good military strategy, but, since it promised relatively few casualties, it was good politics, and this was a consideration that was probably never farther from Douglas Mac-Arthur's mind than from Harry Truman's.

It was, in fact, as politician and would-be world statesman that General MacArthur had begun to make his own Far Eastern policy in late July when he visited Chiang Kai-shek on Formosa. It is possible but not at all probable that the general was unaware of all the political implications of his visit and that he was genuinely astonished that it should have been greeted, as he said, "by a great furor." In any case, he was entitled to feign astonishment, for he did have legitimate business in Formosa. He had been given responsibility for the island's defense when, in concert with the Korean intervention, President Truman dispatched the Seventh Fleet to the Formosa Strait with the statement that "the occupation of

Formosa by Communist forces would be a direct threat to the security of the Pacific area and to the United States forces performing their lawful and necessary functions in that area." [4]

The President had subsequently authorized additional measures on behalf of Formosa: "extensive military aid to Nationalist China; and a military survey by MacArthur's headquarters of the requirements of Chiang Kai-shek's forces; and the plan to carry out reconnaissance flights along the China coast to determine the imminence of attacks against Formosa." [5] Clearly the January 5 policy of non-intervention in China's civil war had been reversed, and the United States was now committed to the defense of Formosa, which, for the time being, was MacArthur's responsibility.

Despite all this, however, the administration insisted that its only desire was to neutralize Formosa and to submit the question of the island's legal status to the United Nations. The President was particularly anxious to avoid giving the impression that he had entered into a new alliance with Chiang Kai-shek or that he would, in any way, encourage or assist him in an attempt to return to the mainland. But exactly this impression was conveyed when MacArthur visited the island, kissed Madame Chiang's hand, and stood contentedly by while Chiang gleefully announced that victory (presumably victory over Red China) was assured, "now that we can again work closely together with our old comrade in arms" General MacArthur.[6]

Certainly the spirit, if not the letter, of the Truman Far Eastern policy had been violated, and Averell Harriman was hurried off to Tokyo to try to persuade the general to accept the policy of his commander-in-chief. But, as Harriman sus-

4. *Presidential Papers: Truman* (1950), p. 492.

5. Truman, *Years of Trial and Hope*, p. 349.

6. Dean Acheson, *Present at the Creation* (New York: Norton, 1969), p. 322.

pected, the mission was a failure. MacArthur had been persuaded of nothing, and by the end of August he was again making public policy pronouncements. In a message to the Veterans of Foreign Wars, the general called for "aggressive, resolute and dynamic leadership" in Asia in such aggressive, resolute terms that the President had no choice but to order him to withdraw the message.[7] In early October President Truman met General MacArthur at Wake Island and tried to persuade him to accept administration policy or, at least, not to oppose it in public. The mission appeared to have been a great success; MacArthur stopped making public pronouncements.

Indeed, MacArthur fell silent for a time but only because he had turned to the battlefield as his policy-making arena. Operating in a field where even the President would hesitate to restrain him, he dispatched his forces across the 38th parallel at the beginning of October. The President and the Joint Chiefs of Staff had approved this action, but they grew extremely apprehensive over the speed and recklessness of MacArthur's advance and over the increasing threat of Chinese intervention. They urged the general to proceed with greater caution and to halt his troops on the high ground below the Yalu. But MacArthur had thrown caution to the winds, and in late November he hurled his armies forward in their mad dash to the Yalu River, with the Americans leading the way despite the fact that the Joint Chiefs had forbidden their use in the northernmost provinces of Korea.

Of the disaster thus precipitated, MacArthur later said, "I myself felt that we had reached up, sprung the Red trap, and escaped it." [8] If it had been MacArthur's intention to provide the Chinese with a tempting prey, he had proceeded in exactly

7. *Military Situation in the Far East,* pp. 3479–3480.

8. Douglas MacArthur, *Reminiscences* (New York: McGraw-Hill, 1964), p. 377.

the right way. In sending his troops to the Yalu, he had exposed them to the most dangerous and unnecessary risks, as though inviting the Chinese to prepare a trap. This is exactly what they did, the trap being sprung with stunning force at the end of November. And, during the bitter days of December, while American and South Korean troops fought desperately to save themselves from the trap into which they had been thrust, their commanding general found the time to grant interviews to newsmen, and through them, to publicly carp at the President for not permitting him to carry on aerial warfare against China, calling this restriction an "enormous handicap, unprecedented in military history." [9] That General MacArthur sought war with China can hardly be doubted.

Joyce and Gabriel Kolko have charged that, from the beginning of the Korean War, MacArthur and President Syngman Rhee of South Korea had been plotting toward this end through a deliberate strategy of continuous retreat, which would force the buildup of American forces in the Far East to the point where they could challenge Red China.[10] The evidence for such a conspiracy is, by no means, conclusive. What is certain, however, is that after Red China's intervention MacArthur conceived an inordinate desire to attack that country. In a memorandum of December 30 to the Joint Chiefs of Staff he recommended the following acts of war:

(1) blockade the coast of China; (2) destroy through naval gunfire and air bombardment China's industrial capacity to wage war; (3) secure reinforcements from the Nationalist garrison on Formosa to strengthen our position in Korea if we decide to continue the fight for that peninsula; and (4) release existing restrictions upon the Formosan garrison for diversionary action, possibly lead-

9. *The New York Times,* December 1, 1950.

10. Joyce and Gabriel Kolko, *The Limits of Power: the World and United States Foreign Policy, 1945–1954* (New York: Harper & Row, 1972), p. 592.

ing to counter invasion against vulnerable areas of the Chinese mainland.[11]

MacArthur later told the Armed Services and Foreign Affairs committees of the Senate that he had only intended to use these tactics to force China out of Korea, thus avoiding the heavy casualties that would result from ground fighting. But so innocent an explanation for such massive attacks upon China is not convincing.

MacArthur had clearly had more in mind than this when he told Harriman in August that "we should fight the Communists every place—fight them like hell," and when he cautioned the V.F.W. against "defeatism and appeasement in the Pacific" on the grounds that Asians only respect "aggressive, resolute and dynamic leadership." Although this was somewhat vague, MacArthur had made what he wanted to accomplish reasonably clear in his December 30 memorandum to the Joint Chiefs: "I believe that by the foregoing measures we could severely cripple and largely neutralize China's capability to wage aggressive war and thus save Asia from the engulfment otherwise facing it." [12]

To accomplish all this someone would have had to enter China and lay violent hands upon that country's Red government. MacArthur knew this, of course, but the only thing he had to suggest was the "unleashing of Chiang." With this proposition, MacArthur's strategic concepts degenerated into what can only be termed sinister or silly. Fortunately his proposals were not taken seriously by anyone in a post of responsibility, least of all by the Joint Chiefs of Staff. Nor did anyone take seriously his contention that the United States could arm and supply Chiang for an assault upon the main-

11. MacArthur, *op. cit.,* p. 379.
12. *Ibid.*

land without thereby incurring the responsibility of going to
his rescue when he ran into difficulties, as he surely would.[13]
President Truman and his military advisers had already
learned, through bitter experience, how difficult it was to get
rid of the terrible burden of Chiang Kai-shek. They also knew
that it would be they and not the general who would face the
angry cries of sellout if they sent Chiang to the continent and
then abandoned him to the fury of the "Communists."

Angry cries had already begun to be heard during the
previous summer, at the time of MacArthur's first essay at
policy-making by rabble-rousing. Henry Luce's *Life* and *Time*
kept themselves in a perpetual state of rage because America
was not prepared for endless sacrifice on behalf of Chiang
Kai-shek. These journals—more propaganda sheets than newsmagazines—had difficulty deciding whether MacArthur or
Chiang Kai-shek was the greatest and wisest defender of
Western civilization. *Life* praised MacArthur for never having
lost faith in Chiang, and *Time* thought that the only person
who talked sense about the Far East was MacArthur and
that he should be given full charge of the nation's Formosa
policy, presumably because he believed that Americans should
again learn to love Chiang.[14] Determined to rehabilitate the
reputation of Chiang, *Time,* as already noted, came to the
conclusion that this eternally whining warlord, with the near-
perfect no-win record, was a great world leader with the only
"anti-Red army with the will and size to fight." [15]

In September *Time* unearthed the startling news that Mao's
regime was in serious trouble and that the people in mainland
China were excited by the prospects of a return of the Kuomintang.[16] By December *Life* had discovered that Mao was

13. *Military Situation in the Far East,* p. 108.
14. *Life,* July 10, 1950; *Time,* July 17, 24, 1950.
15. *Time,* August 7, 1950.
16. *Ibid.,* September 4, 1950.

no more than a Kremlin puppet who mouthed Russian propaganda.[17] Then came the heartening word from the other side of the Formosa Strait that the natives of that island were growing happier daily because of the marvelous job of economic reconstruction being done by Chiang. Indeed, it appeared that the only cloud in the sky of Nationalist China's leaders, now that America seemed again ready to do their bidding, was their feeling that Dean Acheson "does not want us to live." [18] Very well, the gentlemen of America's conservative press would take care of that fellow in striped pants. A great many of them were already mouthing the Luce-MacArthur line or some variation of it. And after their hero MacArthur had gotten both his command and his reputation crumpled up in North Korea, they grew quite shrill in their demands that those aging "warlords" Chiang and MacArthur and their battered armies be "unleashed."

Clearly, the administration had the task, not only of keeping General MacArthur from enlarging the war, but of preventing him from destroying the myth by which that war was justified. He had never put much credence in the administration's explanation of North Korea's aggression as an act of Russian puppetry and was, in fact, convinced that Russia had had little, if anything, to do with North Korea's action, as he later made clear in testimony before Senate committees. But MacArthur posed his most serious threat to the administration's policy rationale in the fact that his own policy *seemed* to make more sense. At least, it did not so obviously pull in opposite directions as did administration policy, and it proposed to go directly after China whose troops were killing American boys. There was a potent appeal in this.

But the Truman Administration had always insisted—almost

17. *Life,* December 4, 1950.
18. *Time,* September 11, October 2, 1950.

frantically, as has been noted—that Russia was the real villain and North Korea only a puppet. Red China's intervention had forced a reorientation of administration thinking, along the following lines: The small North Korean puppet had not been able to conquer South Korea, and so Russia had called on its large Chinese puppet to do the job. The theory originated in fantasy and grew more fantastic in application. The United States was threatened, the administration insisted, by puppet armies manipulated by the Soviet Union. And yet the United States would strike neither at the puppeteer Russia nor at the puppet China. It would only strike the puppet's arm, which was thrust into Korea.

Fantastic or not, the administration was stuck with the theory. Although President Truman had once tried hard to prevent the "Communist conspiracy" theory from being applied to Far Eastern policy, he had now applied it to the whole world, along with the myth of the puppets: "I said to [Prime Minister Clement Atlee of Great Britain] that in my opinion the Chinese Communists were Russian satellites. The problem we were facing was part of a pattern. After Korea, it would be Indo-China, then Hong Kong, then Malaya." [19] Even that tough "realist" and myth-debunker Dean Acheson had decided to believe it, although he was not willing to state the matter so baldly, particularly in public. But his views have been recorded by Truman: "He [Acheson] said that we needed to bear in mind that the Soviet Union was behind every one of the Chinese and North Korean moves and that we had to think of all that happened in Korea as world matters. We should never lose sight of the fact that we were facing the Soviet Union all around the world." [20]

19. Truman, *Years of Trial and Hope,* p. 399.
20. *Ibid.,* p. 386.

Those of moderate or liberal view generally followed the President into this never-never-land where it was necessary to virtually turn loose one's grip upon reality. No one ever demonstrated this so well as *The New York Times'* military analyst Hanson Baldwin who admitted that "we are involved in precisely the type of war which we can never win, a land struggle on the Asiatic continent in a theatre where no decision is possible against the hordes of Asia." Nonetheless, Baldwin concluded that if the Korean War were ended by giving up Formosa or letting the Red Chinese into the United Nations, under the pressure of defeat, "our entire position in the Western Pacific will be imperiled and in this correspondent's opinion much of Asia will fall like a house of cards to Communism." [21] Baldwin did not show that this was the case, but he did not need to; he was fighting "commies." The *Times'* editorialist had no more difficulty than its military analyst in projecting the nation to the very brink of doom. If any concessions at all were made to China, said he, it would "clear the path for further Communist aggression in Asia, which might engulf Japan and, as President Truman pointed out, spread swiftly to Europe and the Western Hemisphere." [22]

A small voice of sanity was raised by *U.S. News & World Report,* which warned that the United States was taking "unjustifiable risks of becoming involved in a costly and almost hopeless land war on the [Asian] mainland." [23] But not many voices were raised in opposition to a war against "the Communists." Even such liberal journals as the *New Republic* and *The Nation* were quite content with Truman interventionism so long as it was covered with moral cant—Korea seen as a United Nations crusade, Formosa as a neutralizing act, and assistance

21. *The New York Times, op. cit.*
22. *Ibid.,* December 4, 1950.
23. *U.S. News & World Report,* August 11, 1950.

to the French in Indochina as a struggle for liberal government free of French rule.[24] It seemed that just about every
publicist who touched the Korean tar-baby got caught by it,
for they dared not tell hardheaded Americans that they were
fighting to save "the Gooks" (as G.I.'s called their Korean
allies) or the United Nations unless this salvationist crusade
was closely bound up with American security. And once
Korea was made vital to American security, simple logic demanded that defensive bulwarks be manned in other, similar
positions around the periphery of China.

But the arguments presented to justify adventures around
China's border were usually based more upon theory than
fact. Was China the puppeteer, as MacArthur contended, or
was it simply a larger and more dangerous puppet, as the
administration contended? The one view was as simplistic as
the other, and neither was conspicuous for logic. Both Mac-
Arthurites and Trumanites insisted that China posed a grave
threat to American security, but neither ever proved that this
was so, and neither ever put forward a realistic proposal for
dealing with it. Attack the menace directly by sea and air,
said MacArthur; no, said the administration, harass it by
building beachheads around its periphery.

MacArthur was in a position to go on pressing his reckless
demands for an attack upon China from afar. But the administration, being saddled with the responsibility for policy,
would have to do better than this. It had the task of soothing
the minds of that large body of intelligent people who had
rushed to the support of the Korean War out of an urgent
necessity to prove themselves dedicated "anti-Communists."
They could never admit that they supported a war that was
undertaken for no other reason than to cater to the ideological
compulsion (created by the McCarthyite hysteria) to fight

24. See *New Republic*, August 21, 28, and September 4, 11, 1950; also
The Nation, November 11, December 2, 1950.

"commies." On the other hand, they would not be comfortable for long with the bare bones of the "puppet theory."

What was needed was a pseudo-scholarly rationale that was abstruse enough to be sustained without too-blatant an appeal to "external McCarthyism"—that is, simply opposing Communism. The need was supplied by the "limited war" theory, which John Spanier, a leading proponent of the theory, has explained this way:

> If the United States can ensure that neither the Soviets nor the Chinese will seek to transform the *status quo* into a *status quo minus* by means of total war, it cannot prevent such a transformation by threatening to respond to limited challenges with strikes against Moscow and Peking. Unless the United States is able to react to such challenges—which are at the very heart of Communist strategy—with equally limited responses, it will confront a truly agonizing dilemma: total war with its suicidal risks, or inaction and surrender.[25]

This analysis is concerned with a change in the *status quo,* but, in actual fact, a change in the *status quo* would matter only if it gave the Soviet Union (or any other powerful nation) a strategic position that would seriously menace a *vital American interest*. And it should be kept in mind that American military action around the periphery of China over the next twenty years (Korea, Vietnam, Laos, Cambodia, Formosa) never really involved such interests, for certainly no government tosses off theories of "limited war" to justify its defense of legitimate national interests. It is for this reason, contradictory as it seems, that those Asian wars could not truly be "limited wars": The government could never admit— for at least twenty years—that it had asked its young men to die for a cause that did not involve a vital national interest.

Actually, the concept of "limited war" added nothing new

25. John W. Spanier, *The Truman-MacArthur Controversy and the Korean War* (New York: W. W. Norton, 1965), p. 3.

to the theory and practice of war—neither of why, nor of where, nor of how to conduct it. In carrying on war in the Far East, the United States would conduct itself very much as imperial powers had always done, that is, having decided to take or hold a given piece of territory, it would try to accomplish that purpose with the least possible expenditure of men and money and without provoking the intervention of other great powers. According to the "limited war" theory the United States would avoid the big war with Russia and/or China by attacking not these great powers but only their alleged world-conquering puppets. What it meant in practice was that the United States would use the threat of unlimited war (always strongly implied) against Russia and China in order to gain the privilege of intervening anywhere in the world, outside those powers' very restricted baliwicks, on behalf of rightist governments.

It accomplished its dual purpose wonderfully well. America's liberals and intellectuals were calmed by a theory so rational in concept and so noble in purpose. And Russia and China, understanding the theory in its old-fashioned terms, were properly alarmed, as they indicated in their reactions to the United Nations' (American) crossing of the 38th parallel. Russia hastily removed its military mission from North Korea and stood with arms folded while its North Korean neighbor was crushed. And China intervened only after repeated warnings against an approach to its border by non-Korean troops and, even then, under the pretense that it was being done by volunteers and not by the Chinese government.

In this instance, the United States would grant China immunity from attack, for it was the United States, after all, and not China that had violated the rules of the international power game, when its troops, inadequately covered by a United Nations camouflage, pressed threateningly close to the Chinese border. But the rules of the game that China and the United

States were playing along the rim of Asia were defined with nice precision by the events that followed China's intervention in Korea, and they may be stated as follows: The United States would not encroach upon China's sovereignty and would not again press its military forces up to China's border, but, in return, China would be expected to restrict itself within a very narrowly defined defensive zone—its own and immediately contiguous territory—and refrain from interference with American power in any other part of Asia.

Moreover, the United States made it clear that once it had extended its protection over an area it would use all the force necessary to hold it, accepting even the risk of total war. That this was true is borne out by the fact that the Truman Administration, in pursuing its "limited war" strategy, refrained from acts of war directly against China on the grounds that they might precipitate Russian intervention and that this would bring on World War III. But, as General MacArthur noted, the risks were present from the moment of the original decision to intervene in Korea: "All the risks inherent in this decision—including the possibility of Chinese and Russian involvement—applied then just as much as they applied later." [26] And so it is clear that the United States, while it would not commit provocative acts directly against China, would not curtail its activities along China's borders by one iota in order to decrease the risks of all-out war.

If the theory of "limited war" imposed any real limits on the use of American military power, it has never been clear what they were, other than to refrain from attacking Russia and China so long as they remained strictly neutral. Even nuclear war, the threat of which, one would suppose, had been chiefly responsible for the emergence of the "limited war" concept, was not forsworn, and that threat was actually used

26. MacArthur, *op. cit.*, p. 331.

against China—in November 1950 by the Truman Administration and in the mid-1950s by the Eisenhower Administration. And, during the following two decades, every other form
of power would be used without stint against China's neighbors in Indochina. Indeed, there is no evidence that America's
politicians have ever set any limits to their own use of power.
Thus, every administration from 1950 through the early 1970s
has been guilty of the greatest hypocrisy or self-deception in
claiming that it was pursuing a policy of "limited war" when
virtually the entire responsibility for keeping it limited was
placed on the other side. This was "limited war," which depended for its success on the threat of "unlimited war," even
to the point of nuclear holocaust, held over the heads of the
enemy.

Needless to say, the theory of "limited war" has never
gained wide acceptance among the American people. Perhaps
it is true, as John Spanier has said, that the American people
mistrust the concept of "limited war" because they believe that
American power is "righteous power" and that "only its full
exercise can assure salvation or an absolution of sin." [27] But
it is possible that this was simply the people's way of stating—
if, indeed, it was ever stated—their repugnance to giving up
their sons to wars that are not absolutely essential to the well-
being of their nation. And certainly they have not found it
easy to understand how this can be the case when they fight
against remote and insignificant little states on behalf of other
remote and insignificant little states to no better purpose than
the *status quo ante*.

Even more difficult to understand has been the fact that
China, the presumed enemy and the one Far Eastern nation
thought to be a potential threat to the United States, has always been allowed the status of a "privileged sanctuary," from

27. Spanier, *op. cit.*, p. 5.

which to provide its neighbors the means and encouragement
to wage endless war. And, since China has been permitted to
continue building its own power unmolested, it will one day
be in a position to force the United States to abandon the
beachhead and island positions around its periphery. It should
thus be obvious that the beachheads maintained by "limited
war" have never contained anything that actually needed to be
contained; a China grown powerful enough to require containing can easily make the "containing beachheads" untenable. For only a very limited time then—ten to twenty years—
would it be possible for American presidents to vent their fury
against Communism through the desperate, sanguinary policy
of "limited warfare" around the periphery of China.

Like other cold war rationalizations, the "limited war"
theory could not be sustained by simple exposition. Sweeping
analogies were needed to give it clarity, as in Spanier's use of
the "salami tactic" explanation: "This tactic seeks to slice off
one piece at a time; no one piece is so large that it will be
missed particularly. But in the end the salami will nevertheless
have disappeared." [28] The analogy does not hold up very well
when examined in all its ramifications. It begins with the assumption that the Asian salami belongs to the United States,
or, at least, that the United States has preeminent salami-
slicing rights there. It further assumes that any salami-slicing
done by Communists is always illegitimate, because the butcher
is bound to be standing with his feet in Moscow. Finally, it
ignores the fact that China, the only cut of salami on the
Asian continent that really mattered, had already been sliced
off, in a self-slicing operation, and that what the United States

28. *Ibid.,* p. 3. As late as 1972, General Maxwell Taylor was still using
the "salami tactics" rationale to justify limited wars: "On the other hand,
giving up the option [of limited war] would mean never defending our interests except by general nuclear war, or submitting to "salami" tactics
which someday might goad us into an impatient, irrational action." See
U.S. News & World Report, November 27, 1972.

was defending in Asia was not choice new cuts of salami but only bits and pieces of the rind from the China cut.

America's liberals and intellectuals embraced the "theory" as eagerly as they had embraced the "fact" of "limited war." It helped them explain why they had suddenly come to favor interventionist policies which, for three years, they had denounced as the height of folly, and it gave an apparent intellectual respectability to their strange reversal of position. But the theory attained credibility only in the fact that others recommended stronger measures. In the light of General MacArthur's call for more aggressive action, the President and his supporters seemed the most moderate and rational of men, struggling to prevent their nation from becoming involved in what General Omar Bradley had said would be "the wrong war, at the wrong time, and with the wrong enemy."

But if the big war with China would have been the wrong war with the wrong enemy, then obviously the original intervention had been the wrong intervention against the wrong enemy, for it must be remembered that the Russian presence in Korea (and presumably Russia was the right enemy) had never been established and had, as General MacArthur said, "paled out as the events progressed." Because of the danger of Russian involvement, General Bradley had no enthusiasm for the Korean adventure: "Korea is a poor place to fight a war, and a lot of military implications are involved in extending the war." The President and most of his advisers were as worried as Bradley about the "military implications" of "extending the war." Even if Korea were the "wrong little war," which they did not admit, they saw this as no reason for allowing themselves to be pushed into the "wrong big war," which is exactly what MacArthur was threatening to do. The big question for the administration then was whether or not it could summon up the courage to put a halter on the headstrong general.

The critical period, which would determine whether or not the administration would take firm control of its Far Eastern policy, was the fall of 1950, but this was the very period when no one was likely to attempt to put a halter on "commie-fighter" Douglas MacArthur. A congressional election campaign was in progress, and America's high priest of "anti-Communism," the junior senator from Wisconsin, was out on the hustings. "Joe McCarthy moved into this thicket of doubt and anxiety with the confident stealth of a wolf invading a sheepfold," said Cabell Phillips. "He flayed the democrats for obstructing his holy war against communists and branded Truman and Acheson as traitors." [29] Although stunned by the spreading reach of the McCarthy influence, the President and Democratic leaders had no idea how to counter the phenomenon: "The President used his press conferences and occasional speeches to rebuke McCarthy, but he could not say in public what he so frankly said in private about 'that s.o.b.' " [30]

The elections were generally conceded to be a McCarthyite victory. Although the Republicans failed to gain control of Congress, they picked up five seats in the Senate and twenty-eight in the House, most of them by McCarthyites or McCarthyite "fellow travelers." Particularly pleasing to McCarthy were the senatorial victories of anti-Communist stalwarts Everett Dirksen over Senate Majority Leader Scott Lucas in Illinois and Richard Nixon over Helen Gahagan Douglas in California. But sweetest of all to the senator from Wisconsin was the victory that he personally engineered for nonentity John Marshall Butler over thirty-year congressional veteran Millard Tydings in Maryland. In a bitter campaign of lies and innuendoes, climaxed by a faked photograph that showed Tydings happily conversing with Communist leader Earl

29. Cabell Phillips, *The Truman Presidency* (New York: Macmillan, 1966), p. 390.

30. *Ibid.*, p. 392.

Browder, the Maryland senator was demolished. This was Mc-Carthy's personal vengeance against the man whose Senate Investigating subcommittee had dared to call his Communists-in-government charges "false and vicious." Nothing could have been better calculated to strike terror into the hearts of politicians all over the land, and not least, in the White House.

Since the early spring, the administration had been in pell-mell retreat before these McCarthyites who, in their increasing sway over public opinion, were acquiring an almost unlimited capacity for mischief. And they had every intention of carrying on their activities in league with mischief-making General MacArthur who apparently had no objections to being used in this way. In fact, he indicated that he would do some "using" of his own, for so long as the McCarthyites tied the hands of the President, he would be free to do virtually as he pleased in the Far East. But the McCarthyites had other ideas. They preferred to see the President tie the general's hands, thus presenting them with a hero (and in time, a martyr) of gigantic stature whose cause meshed perfectly with their own. It seemed to prove everything they had ever said about the Truman "sellout" in Asia and gave them a well-nigh irresistible new line: The administration "softies on Communism" were now trying to prevent MacArthur from putting the "commies" to flight.

There was never any sort of formal alliance between Mc-Carthyites and MacArthurites, and it is doubtful that the senator and the general had any great fondness for each other, but their respective crusades came into perfect conjunction in the latter months of 1950, forming one of the most destructively potent combinations any American President had ever faced. President Truman was aware of the connection between these forces and of their great menace, as he revealed when he defended his secretary of state against their vicious assaults:

These men kept repeating the completely baseless charge that some-how Acheson had brought about the Communist victory in China, and they now charged that it was Acheson who was depriving General MacArthur of the means of gaining victory.

With his Formosa statement to the Veterans of Foreign Wars and with his more recent public utterances, General MacArthur had given these Acheson-haters an argument behind which they could gather their forces for the attack.[31]

What the President could not see—or admit—was the extent to which this evil force had come to dominate his foreign policy and how near it had come to taking away from him all control over his Far Eastern policy.

The logic of the latter assertion is readily understood when one contemplates the incredible lengths to which General MacArthur had been allowed to go in Korea, dragging the nation with him to the very brink of war with China. In sending his U.N. forces to the Yalu River, MacArthur had ignored the sound advice of his superiors, violated their explicit instructions, and assumed, against their wishes, the most unacceptable risks. He had allowed the Eighth Army and the Tenth Corps to become widely separated as they advanced, despite serious concerns expressed by the Joint Chiefs of Staff. He had rebuffed the Chiefs' suggestion that he halt his forces on the defensible high ground below the Yalu. And he had contemptuously ignored their instructions that only South Korean troops be permitted to advance into the area next to the China border. Finally, he had sent his thinly spread troops into the danger zone, knowing that the Chinese Communists had repeatedly warned against it and that they had massed large concentrations of troops north of the Yalu. Had a lesser general courted disaster so recklessly, or had he been less connived at by the Joint Chiefs, it is probable that he would have been summarily relieved of his command and possibly

31. Truman, *Years of Trial and Hope*, p. 430.

court-martialed. But General MacArthur would be allowed to continue in his course of insubordination for another five months, repeatedly and publicly denouncing his commander-in-chief's policies—the very policies it was his duty to carry out.

"Prophet of containment" George Kennan was appalled by this dangerous state of affairs: "It seemed to me that official Washington had in effect, for domestic political reasons, consigned the fortunes of our country and of world peace to an agency, namely General MacArthur's headquarters, over which it had no effective authority." [32] And Kennan fully understood the "domestic political reasons" that explained the administration's failure to restrain General MacArthur or to take a firm grasp of its Far Eastern policy:

> This was at the height of the McCarthyist hysteria. The China lobby, in particular, was in full cry. There were violent differences in Congress over Far Eastern policy. No attempt could be made to give any final definition to that policy, and especially to discuss it with the Russians, without blowing the domestic political situation sky-high.[33]

The failure to retain control of policy in the Far East also gave pause to Dean Acheson when he came to write his memoirs: "All the President's advisers in this matter [the MacArthur matter], civilian and military, knew that something was badly wrong, though what it was, how to find out and what to do about it they muffed. . . . I have an unhappy conviction that none of us, myself prominently included, served him as he was entitled to be served." [34] But Acheson was not as eager as Kennan to probe the reasons for the failure. He could not afford to be, for his had been a larger responsibility

32. George F. Kennan, *Memoirs, 1925–1950*, II (Boston: Little, Brown, 1967), pp. 24–25.

33. *Ibid.*, p. 28.

34. Acheson, *op. cit.*, p. 466.

for the formation of policy, and so he had been more deeply implicated in the administration's surrender to its critics.

During that December of muffed opportunities, while the administration was reeling from the McCarthyite blows and veering toward panic over MacArthur's continuing retreat in Korea, British Prime Minister Clement Atlee requested a conference with President Truman. The Prime Minister apparently wanted to see if he could find out what had gone wrong with America's Far Eastern policy, which is exactly what American policy-makers did not want him to find out. Since, however, the confrontation could not be avoided, Mr. Acheson and his associates had an excellent opportunity to find out what had gone "so badly wrong" and "what to do about it," but they went on "muffing" their opportunities. They paid scant heed to the Britishers who tried to show them what had gone wrong and to talk them back in the direction of their former, sensible course. Rather, they used the theories of "limited war" and "puppetry" in a desperate effort to cover the fact that they had gone over completely to the position of their bitterest congressional foes. Although they had not yielded to the MacArthur demand for attacks upon China (neither had many of their congressional foes), they had adopted just about every other measure of "hate and harassment" of China that had been proposed by Judd, Knowland, Taft, McCarthy, and others.

The congressional opposition was, if anything, more unhappy about Mr. Atlee's visit than the administration. A great many congressmen, some of whom believed England's socialist Prime Minister to be no better than a "commie," were already snarling over the fact that the British recognized the Peking government and traded with it, whereas they gave little more than nominal support to the United Nations in Korea. Now this "fellow-traveling Limey" was coming to America, probably for the purpose of subverting the President into a policy of "appeasing commies." Thus, twenty-four senators, mostly Republicans of McCarthyite persuasion, sought passage of a resolution that would attempt to require the President to submit any agreement made with the British to the Senate in the form of a treaty.[35]

Whatever Congress and the administration thought of the visit, there were good reasons for Mr. Atlee to wonder if the Americans had not taken leave of their senses. In August Secretary of the Navy Francis P. Matthews had called for preventive war against Russia, and General Orville Anderson of the War College had announced that the Air Force was equipped and ready to do the job. This saber-rattling had taken on ominous meaning when the President, at a press conference on November 30, admitted that the use of "the bomb" in Korea was being considered.[36] When, in addition to these frightening statements, one notes the administration's continued retreat before the McCarthyites and its utter impotence in the face of the swashbuckling MacArthur, one has no difficulty in understanding why Mr. Atlee should have concluded that panic-time had arrived.

Even before the December crisis, Prime Minister Atlee had been growing uneasy about the general drift of American foreign policy. And he had received another jolt when President Truman announced, at the time of the Korean intervention, a renewed American commitment to defend the island of Formosa and to increase assistance to the French in Indochina. The fact that these actions were taken simultaneously caused some concern to the British, as James Reston of *The New York Times* reported in August: "This seemed

---

35. *Congressional Record*, XCVI, 81st Cong., 2nd Sess. (1950), p. 16,565.
36. *Presidential Papers: Truman* (1950), p. 727.

to link the three things together, and while there was overwhelming support for the Korean action . . . , there was no such general support for the additional aid to Generalissimo Chiang in Formosa and the French and Bao Dai in Indo-China." [37]

The British Prime Minister would have been alarmed indeed if he had realized that this sweeping action was the fulfillment of the dreadful terms of the administration's surrender to anti-Communist fanaticism. The surrender had been signaled at least as early as May when Dean Acheson announced that America's mission in the world was to "stop the spread of Communism"; that it was total and irrevocable had been confirmed by the administration's three-pronged lunge at the periphery of China in June. America was no longer reacting in a rational manner against threats to the security of itself and the Atlantic community; it was reacting emotionally against "the commies" who must be furiously smitten wherever they raised their heads anew.

Mr. Atlee could not accept such a heavily ideologized view of foreign affairs and probably could not believe that anyone else had. But, during his visit to America, he must have gotten a frightening glimpse of how completely it had taken possession of his American counterparts. While the Americans professed to be open-minded on Far Eastern matters and emphasized the wide area of agreement between the British and themselves, their persistently censorious attitude toward China was most disturbing, for it could only complicate matters. They condemned China in the strongest moral terms, without even considering the possibility that its intervention in Korea might have been a very natural and legitimate act of self-defense. Their own intervention in that faraway country, on

37. *The New York Times,* August 11, 1950.

the other hand, was seen as a great moral act on behalf of the world's peace-keeping body against a brutal act of aggression. As President Truman phrased it: "The purpose of our action [in Korea] was to protect a little country from the result of aggression, and we had been on the verge of succeeding when a viciously hostile country intervened." [38] Behind such moral cant, America's statesmen could retreat from sensible statesmanship, while obscuring the real reason for it.

The visiting British statesmen discovered that the Americans, despite all their talk about wanting to maintain solidarity with Great Britain and to avoid a general war, were not willing to make appreciable concessions toward either of these ends. They would refrain from direct attacks on China but, beyond that, would yield nothing whatsoever and, instead of looking for ways to open negotiations with China, seemed to be seeking out every possible means of harassing it. Thus, the Prime Minister found the going rough when he suggested that the Anglo-American position in Korea was extremely precarious and that they would have to pay a price to extricate themselves. "He thought," recalled Acheson, "that withdrawal from Korea and Formosa and the Chinese seat in the United Nations would not be too high a price." [39]

The withdrawal from Korea was suggested as the proper course of action if it turned out that the country could be held only through the use of atomic weapons or any of the other drastic measures being recommended by General MacArthur. The longer range question of the withdrawal of all foreign troops (American as well as Chinese) from Korea, however, was a question that would have to be open for discussion if the Chinese were to be brought to the negotiating

38. Truman, *Years of Trial and Hope*, p. 408.
39. Acheson, *op. cit.*, p. 481.

table at an early date. But the Americans were determined in this matter, the President stating quite bluntly, as Acheson recorded, "that we would stay in Korea and fight. If we had support from others, fine; if not, we would stay on anyway." [40]

Very well, Korea was not negotiable. But Formosa, the British thought, was surely an area in which the United States could reduce the scope of its military encirclement of China. This would have required the United States to do no more than return to its offshore policy as proclaimed on January 12, and to its policy of non-involvement in China's civil war (Formosa), which was announced as irrevocable policy on January 5. This could have been implemented by simply refusing to renew the ruinous entanglement with the Chiang Kai-shek regime and by gradually withdrawing the Seventh Fleet from the Formosa Strait. And it was inconceivable, from the British point of view, that the United States would re-commit itself to Chiang after its own thousand-page *White Paper* had proven conclusively that the "incompetent bunglers of the Kuomintang" (Acheson's phrase) were not only incapable of serving any important American interest but actually constituted a dangerous and expensive liability.

But the Americans were wholly adamant on this question. The mere discussion of it made them irritable, for they could find no moral cover for a policy that they had never thought particularly righteous or very smart. Domestic political pressures, however, required the defense of Formosa, which, in turn, required a reversal of strategic concepts. Dean Acheson explained it very much as Senator Knowland might have done: "If . . . we permitted Formosa to be attacked and fall, we would raise the gravest dangers in Japan and the Philippines which were the bases from which our operations were

40. *Ibid.,* p. 484.

being conducted and upon which our whole Pacific position rested." [41] Generals Marshall and Bradley argued that "we could not have our chain of island outposts split by a Formosa in hostile possession." [42] And Mr. Truman, once again referring to China as a "viciously hostile" nation, said, "We can't open our flank now by giving up Formosa to that country. . . ." [43] These men had not believed such things when they announced in January that "our chain of island outposts" included the Philippines, the Ryukyus, and Japan, and when Dean Acheson called Senator Taft's demand for the defense of Formosa a "silly venture."

Finally, there was the question of the China seat in the United Nations. Elementary logic argued strongly for a speedy normalization of China's relations with the rest of the world as an essential step toward settling the Korean War and other outstanding problems in the Far East. And simple justice demanded that the world's largest nation be a member of the United Nations and that it be represented by the actual government of its 500 million people and not by an island of 13 million inhabitants. But again the Americans retreated behind a façade of meaningless moralisms. According to President Truman, "Acheson took the position that we should not even consider it [giving Red China its seat in the U.N.]. If we did . . . it would be like offering a reward for aggression. For that reason, if for no other, Acheson preferred that there be no negotiations at all, even if the Communists won and forced us out of Korea." [44] Another rising moralist, the assistant secretary of state for Far Eastern affairs, Dean Rusk, offered the opinion that the United States had already demon-

41. Truman, *Years of Trial and Hope,* p. 403.
42. *Ibid.,* p. 404.
43. *Ibid.,* p. 408.
44. *Ibid.,* p. 404.

strated its peaceful intentions, and so he "could see no reason why we should have to prove our goodwill by agreeing to the seating of the Chinese Reds in the U.N. in order to get a settlement." [45]

All of this must have been very mystifying for the Britishers. The American leaders seemed to genuinely want peace and, with all their problems, they needed to get the earliest settlement possible. But they were absolutely intransigent on those very issues where concessions would have to be made before there would be any hope of fruitful negotiations with China. One could, of course, understand their desire to preserve the independence of South Korea, having expended so much of their prestige and blood in that undertaking. But, once a line had been stabilized in the vicinity of the 38th parallel, thus proving their point, there was no reason why the other issues should not have been negotiated—at least, so the British saw it. After all, disengagement from China's civil war and from the Asian continent (Korea, Indochina, Formosa) had been the main goal of America's Far Eastern policy since 1947, and certainly it would have been to America's advantage to disencumber itself of liabilities that offered only endless sacrifice without any compensating advantage whatsoever.

The Americans were greatly embarrassed by these talks—no one so much as Secretary of State Dean Acheson. He tried to cover up the extreme weakness—and downright foolishness—of the American position by taking a condescending attitude toward the visiting Englishmen, later commenting in his memoirs: "Our five days of talks are not worth a day-by-day, play-by-play account." [46] He even affected to believe that Atlee and his compatriots had lost touch with reality, for,

45. *Ibid.*, pp. 407–408.

46. Acheson, *op. cit.*, p. 480.

within a month of the meetings he was breathing a sigh of relief over their apparent "return to sanity." [47]

On the question of "comparative sanity," one feels constrained to point out that Acheson never seemed to have noticed that his English guests had used the very arguments that, less than a year earlier, he and the President had advanced with total fervor and conviction on behalf of a policy of disengagement from the Asian continent. Neither did Acheson the ironist call attention to that cruel irony of fate that forced him and his colleagues to employ the arguments of Knowland, Judd, and Taft. So painful was this to Acheson that he avoided a detailed discussion of the Formosa problem in his own memoirs, and so one must go to those of Mr. Truman to find the secretary's explanation to Atlee that the fall of Formosa would "raise the greatest dangers to Japan and the Philippines which were the bases from which our operations were being conducted and upon which our Pacific position rested."

The cruel predicament of the President and his secretary of state could be partially explained—as they did repeatedly explain it to Mr. Atlee—by the limits imposed upon them by public opinion. Acheson observed that the American people would not follow a leadership "that proposed a vigorous policy of action against aggression on one ocean front while accepting defeat on the other." [48] And when the President was on the point of agreeing to make no decision on the use of atomic weapons without consulting the British, Acheson reminded him of congressional opposition: "The resolution of the twenty-four Republican senators gave fair warning of the temper of Congress." [49] The President betrayed his own ex-

47. *Ibid.*, p. 513.
48. *Ibid.*, p. 482.
49. *Ibid.*

treme sensitivity to the public mood when he commented: "We would face terrible divisions among our people here at home if the Chinese Communists were admitted to the United Nations, and I could not see what we could gain that would offset the loss in public morale." [50]

But the administration could not openly blame public opinion; the public was listening. Moreover, it would have been the most damning self-indictment to have claimed that a mercurial public opinion had forced the adoption of an interventionist policy of such vast and tragic proportions as that being carried out in the Far East. On the other hand, to plead public pressures of an unusual ferocity would have been even less admissible, for this would have raised the question of "McCarthyism." And that, because it struck at the very heart of the matter, could not have been endured.

It simply would not have been possible for America's political leaders to carry through their ideologized policy for Asia as cynical practitioners of "politics as usual." They had to become "true believers," and it has been shown how, under the goading of Senator Joe McCarthy, they had been moving swiftly along the road of self-conversion. That they had indeed arrived at the door of the "one true church" is revealed in President Truman's rebuke of Prime Minister Atlee for daring to doubt that the Chinese Communists were Russian satellites: "I said that in my opinion the Chinese Communists were Russian satellites. . . . I said that I did not want war with China or any nation but that the situation looked very dark to me. The Chinese Communists, in my belief, had made up their minds what they wanted to get, including a U.N. seat and Formosa—or war." [51] Apparently the President had ac-

50. Truman, *Years of Trial and Hope*, p. 407.
51. *Ibid.*, p. 399.

cepted these terms: He was prepared to fight a major war over Formosa and the China seat in the United Nations, despite the fact that his own administration had asserted, just a few months earlier, that neither of these matters involved an important American interest.

CHAPTER TEN

Chiang and McCarthy Win: Disengagement from Asia Is Un-American (1950–1951)

The visiting British statesmen failed to persuade the Americans to return to their former sensible course in the Far East or to convince them to modify, in the smallest degree, the frenzy that had taken possession of them. It was only about a week after the departure of these "visiting firemen" that President Truman went on national radio and television to deliver that incredible speech in which he warned the American people of a grave threat to their very existence: "Our homes, our nation, all the things we believe in are in great danger." [1] The idea that China, or Russia and China combined, posed so serious a threat to the United States in 1950–1951 did not make a great deal of sense. And that Mr. Truman was not at all proud of his alarmist statements of that time is pointed up in the fact that, although he quoted at length from the "national emergency" speech in his memoirs, he did not persist in the view that all the things we believed in had been "in great danger."

There is no way of knowing for certain why the President chose to speak in such extravagant terms.

1. See p. 234.

What is known for certain is that, during that period, administration leaders, like all other Americans in public life, were going to almost any extreme to establish the absolute purity of their anti-Communist faith. It is also a known fact that, whereas there had been no increased threat to America from Communist states, there had been a very substantial increase in the threat to the administration from the McCarthyites. The fight with the latter was essentially rhetorical, and it is only in that context—as an answer to McCarthyites—that Mr. Truman's rhetorical excesses of 1950 make any sense at all.

The President was no longer making any effort to keep his rhetoric within reasonable bounds, not even in official statements. In proclaiming a state of national emergency on December 16, he asserted that "world conquest by communist imperialism is the goal of the forces of aggression that have been loosed upon the world" and went on to warn that if it were successful,

> . . . the people of this country would no longer enjoy the full and rich life they have with God's help built for themselves and their children; they would no longer enjoy the blessings of the freedom of worshipping as they severally choose, the freedom of reading and listening to what they choose, the right of free speech . . . the right to choose those who conduct their government. . . .[2]

Mr. Truman thus demonstrated that America had things of value to defend, but he did not thereby prove that these things were more threatened by the "commies without" than by the "commies within." After all, the Korean and Chinese Communists were thousands of miles from America, whereas those alleged Communists Joe McCarthy was chasing were presumably working at the top echelons of the American government.

Any direction he turned, the President ended up playing

---

2. *Presidential Papers: Truman* (1950), p. 746.

the "McCarthyite game," and it could not have been otherwise, for the game was "anti-Communism," and Senator
Joseph McCarthy had made it *his* game. Thus, Mr. Truman,
having become as shrill in his anti-Communism as anyone in
the land, discovered that he, like everyone else in the land,
had to take his cue from the senator. It was McCarthyism that
had driven the President to seek a stronger anti-subversives
bill in the summer of 1950 and then, in early 1951, to establish a commission of distinguished citizens to investigate the
whole question of internal subversion. And it was McCarthyism that had goaded the administration into seeking anti-
Communist laurels for itself by intensifying its anti-Communism in the Far East.

With the administration everywhere on the defensive, the
McCarthyites pressed their advantage relentlessly during the
crisis weeks of December, rallying their forces behind that
great "commie fighter" General Douglas MacArthur. And in
the role of villian they shrewdly cast Dean Acheson, the effete
easterner who was not to be trusted, if for no other reason
than because his speech was too elegant and his mustache too
thin. Personified in these strong personalities, America's Far
Eastern problems were given fleshly reality and reduced to
simple moral terms. To a great many people, the solution
seemed obvious: Kick Acheson out of the State Department
and unleash MacArthur on the "commies."

Conservatives in the Senate raised a great clamor on behalf
of what seemed to them so simple and obvious a "blueprint
for victory." Enraged that the administration did not "give
MacArthur and his gallant troops a free hand," Senator
James P. Kem of Missouri warned that "if Mr. Acheson does
not resign or is not removed, drastic steps to force his removal
will be in order." The people of Missouri were fed up, said
he, none of them ever writing letters in defense of the secretary
of state, while many wrote in the vein of a lady from Kansas

City: "In the name of God, do something to get Acheson and his Communist clique out of our government." [3] Senator Malone of Nevada echoed the cry: "Public opinion mounts up demanding that there be a cleanup of the State Department —that the gang of pro-Communists there who have been protected and coddled and defended and covered up be swept out from top to bottom." [4]

Senator McCarthy, doubting that the President would be able to remove his secretary of state even if he wanted to, posed this question: "Will you act before it is too late, or are your hands so firmly tied by the Red masters of your administration that you cannot do what . . . patriotic Americans are demanding?" As to what patriotic Americans were demanding, McCarthy had not a single doubt: Acheson must go, and more than that, "General Douglas MacArthur should be immediately given the authority to hit the Chinese Communists wherever, whenever, and however he thinks it necessary so long as they are killing American men." [5]

This was the refrain heard endlessly across the land, "fire Acheson and unleash MacArthur." It was heard almost daily in the Senate, and no one offered it vigorous rebuttal. By January *The New York Times'* William S. White had reached this gloomy conclusion:

"McCarthyism," be it an incomparable epithet, is simply today a very considerable force in the Congress of the United States.

In sum, the air of Congress may be assumed to be at least latently full of "McCarthyism," however defined, all through the life of this Congress—in a spectacular way, if foreign events permit, and, in any case, in a pervasive way.[6]

3. *Congressional Record*, XCVI, 81st Cong., 2nd Sess. (1950), pp. 16,057–16,058.

4. *Ibid.*, p. 16,558.

5. *Ibid.*, pp. 16,178–16,181.

6. *The New York Times*, January 7, 1951.

White was one of a number of writers who noticed the connection between "foreign events" and McCarthyism, but he, like the others, never seemed to have noticed how strong and direct was that connection. Well, the President had noticed it. Since May 1950, he had been consciously pursuing a course designed "to turn the tables on the Communist witch-hunters in Congress" by a vigorous foreign policy "which would frustrate communism's dream of world conquest and guarantee a century of world peace in the bargain." [7]

But things were not working out well. General MacArthur, by his demand for victory over China, was making it virtually impossible for the administration to maintain its place as even the "number one commie-fighter overseas." Nonetheless, Mr. Truman made a valiant effort to win that title for his secretary of state in a news conference on December 19:

> Mr. Acheson has helped shape and carry out our policy of resistance to Communist imperialism. From the time of our sharing of arms with Greece and Turkey nearly 4 years ago, and coming down to the recent moment when he advised me to resist the Communist invasion of South Korea, no official in our Government has been more alive to communism's threat to freedom or more forceful in resisting it. . . .
>
> If I did anything else [but keep Acheson], it would weaken the firm and vigorous position this country has taken against Communist aggression.[8]

The President had no intention of firing his secretary of state, for "Communism—not our own country—would be served if we lost Mr. Acheson." [9]

But Mr. Acheson had a long way to go before he would be accepted as America's number one "commie-fighter," and there were many pitfalls along the way. First off, there was the

7. See p. 174.

8. *Presidential Papers: Truman* (1950), pp. 751–752.

9. *Ibid.*, p. 752.

dread possibility that he might be trapped into negotiating with Communists (the Chinese) who were proposing not unreasonable terms for negotiations: immediate acceptance of the Chinese Communist government as China's only representative in the United Nations and then negotiations on the removal of all foreign forces from Korea and of American forces from Formosa.[10] The irony of it is that this was in line with the American position of early 1950. But by 1951, negotiations with Communists on any subject other than a cease-fire along the lines of America's choosing (roughly the 38th parallel) would have been considered an intolerable softness on Communism. And the admission of Communist China to the United Nations would have amounted to "rewarding aggression," or as America's U.N. representative Warren Austin put it, in one of his irrelevant moral queries: "If the Communists are not seated as the representative of China before cease-fire and before negotiations, will they then break into the United Nations with mortars and grenades?"[11]

The secretary and his colleagues could moralize their way out of negotiations on "commie" terms, but they could not brush off the peace efforts of their friends. It was thus a great embarrassment to the State Department when the British, Canadians, Indians, and other allies and dependents of the United States introduced in the United Nations a resolution that called for the cessation of hostilities and withdrawal of all foreign troops from Korea, to be followed by a peace conference that would deal with the questions of Formosa's status and of China's seat in the United Nations.[12] "The choice whether to support or oppose the plan was a murderous one," said Acheson, "threatening, on one side, the loss of the Koreans and the fury of Congress and press and, on the other,

---

10. S.D. *Bulletin*, XXIV, January 15, 1951, pp. 113–116.

11. *Ibid.*, p. 167.

12. *Ibid.*, pp. 163–166.

the loss of our majority and support in the United Nations." But there was no way out, and so Mr. Acheson went along with the peace plan—for this most extraordinary of reasons, "We did so in the fervent hope and belief that the Chinese would reject it (as they did) and that our allies would return (as they did) to comparative sanity and follow us in censuring the Chinese as aggressors." [13] The peace proposal was adopted by the United Nations on January 11 but swiftly rejected by the Chinese government.

With the Chinese rejection of the proposal, Acheson was off the hook: He would not have to sit down with Communists to negotiate peace. He was much relieved to note that "the fury of Congress and press [about this latest "coddling of Communists"] soon abated." [14] It was now possible for him to press the United Nations to censure China as an aggressor, and this was accomplished in a resolution of February 1, 1951.[15] It was a costly victory, for America's allies went along "rather grudgingly," as Acheson confessed.[16] They knew that this was no more than moral posturing on the part of the United States and that, far from advancing the cause of peace, it would actually make peace more difficult to achieve. But it was not primarily peace Mr. Acheson was seeking at this time; he was building the administration's image as "commie fighter."

Indeed, during the early months of 1951 administration spokesmen busied themselves more with this endeavor than with seeking peace. They were untiring in their denunciations of China, "that viciously hostile country," as President Truman had called it. Even America's "ambassador of peace,"

13. Dean Acheson, *Present at the Creation* (New York: Norton, 1969), p. 513.

14. *Ibid.*

15. S.D. *Bulletin, op. cit.,* pp. 166–168.

16. Acheson, *op. cit.,* p. 513.

U.N. delegate Warren Austin, seemed to think that he could best serve the cause of peace by frequent verbal assaults upon the Chinese. He was particularly fond of hurling at them that much-treasured cliché of the period, "You can't shoot your way into the United Nations." [17] But Austin had difficulty deciding whether this "viciously hostile country" was a dangerous aggressor or only a contemptible puppet: "Unfaithful to the characteristics, traditions and interests of the Chinese people, the Chinese Communists have put their necks into the Soviet collar. . . . Really, this response [to the U.N. peace proposal of January 11] is not Chinese. It is their masters' response; that of the Soviet ruling circles." [18]

No one ever worked so hard at carrying the "hate China" gospel to the American people as did Dean Rusk, the assistant secretary of state for Far Eastern Affairs. He was totally devoted to the task—essentially a public relations one—of persuading the American people that they were seriously threatened by China, or by Russia-through-China, and that fighting this menace was America's main "commie-fighting" task. Rusk was so convinced of the "gravity of the evil" (as the Supreme Court would designate the "world Communist conspiracy" in the course of the year) that he called for the United States to smite every new Communist upsurge, no matter how remote or trivial, on the grounds that it might spread. He explained his "crime must not pay" theory in an NBC television address on January 29: "If we run away from it [the Korean fight], the aggressor will learn that there is great profit in crime, that he will not be resisted, and that his victims are weak and can be destroyed at will." [19]

Rusk was particularly fond of the Munich analogy: "We Americans have had an unforgettable lesson about what hap-

17. S.D. *Bulletin, op. cit.,* p. 205.
18. *Ibid.,* p. 167.
19. *Ibid.,* February 12, 1951, p. 263.

pens when unbridled ambition goes unchecked. We have seen the world go down the trail from Manchuria to Ethiopia to Munich to Poland and, finally, to Pearl Harbor. We must not tread this path again." He warned against allowing nations in the Far East to gain the impression "that the forces of Peiping are irresistible and that Red China's neighbors must now come to terms with communism at the cost of their freedom." [20] In a later address Rusk put to the American people the ultimate question as to the fearful consequences of abandoning Korea: "Who would be the next victim? And who next? And the next? Have we so soon forgotten Adolph Hitler . . . ? Do you remember the trail which led from Manchuria and Ethiopia to Pearl Harbor?" Not one to leave loose ends untied, Rusk answered his own question: "To abandon Korea would be to abandon the United States." [21]

The idea that backward China posed a serious threat to the United States was a proposition that did not make much sense, but it was one that the administration would have to give perfect validity in order to justify its war against puppets. Thus, Rusk and other administration vilifiers of China were always prepared, when confronted by the logical fallacy of their argument, to shift the focus of villainy to that master-puppeteer Russia whose "aggressive program," according to Rusk, had entered a "new phase," characterized by these important factors:

> First, it [the Soviet Union] has clearly shown that it is prepared to wage war by satellites so far as that becomes desirable to further its objectives—not only wars by small satellites such as the North Koreans but full-fledged war by Communist China, a major satellite. Second, the Soviet Union has shown that it is itself prepared to risk a general war and that it is pushing its program to the brink of general war.[22]

20. *Ibid.*

21. *Ibid.*, April 12, 1951, p. 655.

22. *Ibid.*, February 19, 1951, p. 295.

The American people—both the wise and the foolish—accepted such arguments with scarcely a whimper of dissent.

But there was one realm of myth that bemused even the assistant secretary of state for Far Eastern Affairs. Like other reasonable citizens, Rusk was uneasy with the "limited war" theory, but he did make a game effort to explain it in an NBC television address on April 15: "Some are saying, 'Either extend the war or get out of Korea.' They are asking us to choose which of two roads to disaster we should take." But the choice was not between alternative roads to disaster, for the second possibility he presented (get out of Korea) would have entailed no more than a return to the offshore defensive position of a year earlier. Not satisfied that he had made his point, Rusk tried another tack: "There is no more complicated problem than to bring an end to fighting which involves the world's great powers without unconditional surrender of one side or the other—an unconditional surrender that will not come except in a general war." Finally, Rusk gave it up: "It is hard to understand and hard to explain. It means a condition of half-war, half-peace." [23]

Another who did yeoman service in propagating the administration's world-view was the Republican bipartisanist and future secretary of state John Foster Dulles, who yielded to no man in the fascinated awe with which he viewed the "world Communist conspiracy" and who was second to none as an expert on the Communist art of puppetry. In one of endless speeches on the subject, he explained the worldwide ramifications of the Korean War like this:

> It is indeed ominous that the peaceful Republic of Korea should have been suddenly attacked by heavily armed forces, and that hundreds of thousands of *North Korean and Chinese Communists are being driven to slaughter in order to gain a strategic position*

23. *Ibid.*, April 23, 1951, p. 655.

which has been coveted by Russia since the days of the czars [italics added].

Bolshevik communism has . . . showed a desire to avoid the possible consequences of a breaking and entering with open violence. Even in Korea, the attackers pretend that they were engaged only in civil war and that the Chinese Communist armies came in as "volunteers." [24]

Mr. Dulles had no doubts about it; world-conquering puppets had to be stopped.

With this sort of strained logic and strident rhetoric, Mr. Acheson and his colleagues shut off all possibility of reaching an accommodation with China that might have ended the Korean War and forestalled a quarter-century of military confrontation with that power on the continent of Asia. Moreover, the secretary failed utterly to attain what was probably the major purpose of his bellicose policy, namely, to prove that the Truman Administration was exceedingly "tough on commies." His policy offered nothing but endless fighting and endless casualties on behalf of things (Korea, Formosa, Indochina) that the American people rightly suspected served no vital interest of their nation and which failed to diminish, in the slightest degree, the power of that Communist China that they were being taught to fear. Certainly this could not compete with MacArthur's "eat your cake and have it too" policy, which would have had the United States retire to strong offshore positions, thus bringing casualties down to a minimum and, at the same time, reducing China to a negligible entity through a strategy of magic—bombardment of China's coastal region by American air and naval forces and invasion of the continent by the miraculously revivified army of Chiang Kai-shek.

Adding to the administration's troubles, former President Herbert Hoover and Senator Robert A. Taft chose this time

24. *Ibid.,* February 12, 1951, p. 252.

to demand an "agonizing reappraisal" of America's entire world role. In statements issued during December 1950 and January 1951, they called upon the United States to concentrate on preserving what Hoover called the "Western Hemisphere Gibraltar of Western Civilization." The United States would hold the oceans of the world and, from offshore bases —Japan, the Philippines, and Formosa in the East; Britain in the West—it would use its air and naval forces and its great industrial power to assist the peoples of Europe and Asia in defending their own independence. Both Europe and Asia had the manpower with which to defend themselves; if they did not have the will for it, said Hoover, then it could not be done, for the United States could not create or buy spiritual force for them.

This was sensible strategy, for it would undertake nothing more than the *defense of America,* and this it proposed to do from sound, offshore positions and in league only with countries that were defensible—that is, countries with the will to defend themselves. Taft and Hoover slipped into a fatal contradiction, however, when they allowed their essentially defensive strategy to be coupled with MacArthur's dangerous proposals for attacks upon China. Such offensive operations were almost certain to lead to the endless ground war on the Asian continent that was exactly the quagmire that Taft and Hoover were seeking to avoid. At this point it is difficult to escape the conclusion that they were more concerned with a strategy for defeating Harry Truman than for defeating China.

In any case, these were strong voices added to the angry chorus of disapproval of the Truman Far Eastern policy, and that chorus was swelling daily. It was perhaps this fact that led General MacArthur to conclude that he could, with impunity, renew his attacks upon the policies of his commander-in-chief. And he now had a more compelling reason for his gross insubordination: He was not simply making global strategy at this point but trying to preserve his reputation for infallibility. Having been proven tragically wrong in his prediction that the Chinese would not intervene in Korea, he was about to be proven wrong again in his assertion that, because of the administration's prohibition of strikes "against China's continental military potential" and of its restriction upon "Chinese Nationalist military action" (use of Chiang's troops), the United Nations command would be forced to withdraw from the Korean peninsula.[25] But General Matthew Ridgway, an able officer who obeyed orders and did the best he could with what he had, was able to halt the Communist drive south of the 38th parallel and, on February 22, to launch a counter-offensive that would re-take Seoul and reclaim most of South Korea by the end of March.

It was thus no mere accident that MacArthur chose just this time—two weeks after the Ridgway offensive began and one week before the re-taking of Seoul—to renew his public debate with the President. His own dire predictions were about to be discredited and the President's restraint vindicated, and MacArthur had no intention of allowing this to happen. In statements on March 7 and March 24 he demanded that China be bombed and that Chiang's forces be unleashed, predicting a *military stalemate* if these things were not done. And then, in a letter to Congressman Joseph Martin of Massachussetts, which Martin read to the House of Representatives on April 5, MacArthur repeated his demands for the bombing of China and the unleashing of Chiang and concluded with a condemnation of the strategy of stalemate: "As you [Martin] point out, we must win. There is no substitute for victory." [26]

It should be noticed that General MacArthur was slyly

25. *Military Situation in the Far East*, p. 906.

26. Douglas MacArthur, *Reminiscences* (New York: McGraw-Hill, 1964), p. 386.

altering the terms of his dispute with the Truman Administration. In communiqués to the Joint Chiefs, he had prophesied that expulsion of U.N. forces from Korea would be the price of refusing his advice (to attack China). But those communiqués, as MacArthur doubtless hoped, would probably never see the light of day, and so it was possible to keep hidden his own silly—even panicky—predictions, while proclaiming himself the man of vision who had foretold, with astonishing prescience, a stalemated war.

The time had come for the President to act. If he would avoid war with China, he must fire MacArthur, and this he did on April 11. It might have been thought that so dramatic an act would have drawn the lines sharply between the Truman and MacArthur strategies and that the people would now be able to make a clear and intelligent choice between them. But this did not happen, for neither strategy was backed by compelling logic. It is likely that the clamorous hero's welcome given MacArthur upon his return home was more an expression of displeasure with the Truman policies than of support for MacArthur's. Disillusionment, confusion, anger, characterized the public mood, and it was clear that the whole question of the Korean War and the firing of MacArthur would be debated in an atmosphere permeated by the unrestrained rancor of a partisan political brawl.

Republicans, sensing a hot political issue, rushed to the defense of MacArthur. On the morning after the general's removal, party leaders Robert A. Taft and Kenneth Wherry of the Senate and Joseph Martin and Charles Halleck of the House met to plan their strategy. They agreed that the nation's whole military and foreign policy should be investigated "in the light of the latest tragic developments [the firing of MacArthur]," and that the general should be invited to come and present his views personally to Congress. There was even discussion of possible impeachments, and, while the culprits were not specified, the names of Truman and Acheson were bandied about off the record. As was so often the case in the Korean controversy, partisan politics made a mockery of logic and good sense. Those very Republican leaders who were so incensed that the President had not allowed MacArthur to run amuck in the Far East were the same men who had been demanding the removal of all American forces from the Asian continent and an end to American casualties.[27]

Noting this inconsistency, *The New York Times'* James Reston described it in terms of a conversation between Alice and the Mad Hatter:

> "Mr. Wherry charges the Truman Administration with appeasement," said the Mad Hatter. "So does Mr. Taft. So does Mr. Martin. They want an end to this slaughter in Korea. They want a second front in South China. They want to cut our losses and to operate in Manchuria. They want peace and unconditional surrender. And no more nonsense! What more could you ask?" "A little common sense wouldn't hurt," replied Alice.[28]

In fairness, Mr. Reston should have given the Mad Hatter's version of the President's strategy. In a radio address on April 11 he insisted that his overriding concern was to avoid war with China, and yet he clung tenaciously to his policy of ringing that country about with military force.[29] Surely this too would have brought from Alice the rejoinder, "A little common sense wouldn't hurt."

Actually, these "Alice in Wonderland" strategies had nothing at all to do with American security or with any other important American interest. And the controversy was not so much between President Truman and General MacArthur

27. *The New York Times,* April 12, 1951.

28. *Ibid.*

29. *Presidential Papers: Truman* (1950), pp. 223–227.

as between the "Trumanites" and the "McCarthyites," and
the only issue was "who is toughest on the commies?" One
writer for *The New York Times* got at least an inkling of it:

> This conflict was intensified by the long-drawn-out controversy
> over "McCarthyism"—the charge by Senator Joseph R. McCarthy
> that the Communists' gains in the Far East have resulted from
> "softness" toward communism in the Administration, particularly
> in the State Department under Secretary Acheson. "McCarthyism"
> was given impetus when it apparently paid off in Republican gains
> in last November's Congressional elections.[30]

Still, this *Times* writer saw McCarthyism as a complicating
factor and not, as it truly was, as the one and only issue.

But if press and administration could not see how completely this domestic political issue (softness on Communism)
had come to dominate Far Eastern policy, the McCarthyites
could, and they pressed matters only in these terms. On the
very day of General MacArthur's removal, Senator Jenner of
Indiana, "shouted, to the accompaniment of some applause in
the public galleries: 'I charge that this country today is in the
hands of a secret inner coterie which is directed by agents
of the Soviet Union.' "[31] Even so-called moderate Republicans
stopped just short of charges of treason, Senator Richard M.
Nixon of California demanding that the Senate censure Mr.
Truman and call upon him to restore General MacArthur to
command. "Mr. Nixon," noted *The New York Times,* "typified
the line advanced by many Republicans—that the President
had heartened and 'appeased' the world Communists by oust-
ing General MacArthur."[32]

It was entirely appropriate that Senator McCarthy himself
should have stated the matter in its simplest and crudest terms.
If the people did not fight the firing of MacArthur, said he,

30. *The New York Times, op. cit.*

31. *Ibid.*

32. *Ibid.*

"Red waters may lap at all our shores." He had no doubts that the people would indeed fight it, but he had his doubts about Democrats, warning that if they did not "help stop this trend and save the world from Communism . . . the Democratic party will label itself a party of betrayal." As for the President, McCarthy was willing to concede that he was probably not disloyal but that he should be impeached nonetheless, because "he is surrounded by the old Hiss crowd, which has hypnotic powers over him." Finally, McCarthy predicted that "the Administration apparently plans to spend just enough lives so it won't look like a sellout." [33]

There was just a grain of truth in this assertion, as was often the case with McCarthy's most sweeping charges. Although no fair-minded person would impute such bloody-minded cynicism to President Truman, it must be kept in mind how obsessed he had become with proving, through an increasingly tough foreign policy, that he was wholly dedicated to fighting Communists. Trapped by his own excessive rhetoric, he would have to go on fighting as long as it took to save from the Communist grasp all those countries to which he was now committed—South Korea, Formosa, and Indochina. Little matter how great the cost or how irrelevant to real American interests, he could make no concession that appeared to be what McCarthy called a "sellout."

The administration's obsession with the McCarthyite charge of "softness on Communism" was made very clear in the behavior of its witnesses before the Senate Armed Services and Foreign Affairs committees, which investigated the firing of MacArthur and the whole Far Eastern situation. These spokesmen were more concerned to show themselves eager opponents of Communism than to prove that fighting for the defense of South Korea was vital to American interests.

33. *Ibid.*

Fighting Communists had become America's main business, and so it mattered little who the Communists were or where.

Quite as devoted to this point of view as any civilian were the nation's military leaders, including such distinguished officers as Secretary of Defense George Marshall, who had returned to the cabinet in September 1950, chairman of the Joint Chiefs of Staff Omar Bradley, and the chiefs of Army, Navy, and Air Force, respectively, Joseph Lawton Collins, Forrest Sherman, and Hoyt Vandenberg. These men all took care to parade their anti-Communist orthodoxy before the senators, even to the point of foolishness. It was General Marshall himself who coined the mischievous little phrase of warning to China, "You can't shoot your way into the United Nations." And General Bradley, while never willing to concede that Korea was vital to American security or that it was a good place to fight a war, accepted the intervention there on the vague moral grounds that one could not go on forever appeasing aggressors.

None of these military men dared get very far out of step with General MacArthur.[34] To do so would have laid them open to the "commie smear," and they had seen how much damage this could do to the reputation of even so great a soldier as George Marshall. Thus, they made no strong case against MacArthur's conduct in the Far East but tended, rather, to uphold most of the things he had done. It was easy enough to acquit him of insubordination, since they had not usually given him direct orders but had "advised" or "sug-

34. Columnist Drew Pearson, having witnessed the wild ovation given MacArthur upon his arrival in Washington after his dismissal, commented in his diary for April 19: "The most ironic spectacle was a group of brass hats, Marshall, Bradley, et al.—who had recommended MacArthur's dismissal—at the airport at one o'clock in the morning jostling each other in an effort to shake hands first. When did a man who was fired ever receive an ovation like this?" Drew Pearson, *Diaries, 1949–1959*, ed. by Tyler Abell (New York: Holt, Rinehart and Winston, 1974), p. 155.

gested." As to the possibility of bad judgment on the part of MacArthur, well, one did not second-guess commanders in the field thousands of miles from home.

The man on the spot in these hearings was Secretary of State Dean Acheson. It was he who must carry the President's cause, which was primarily the task of proving that the administration was more dedicated than Senator Joseph McCarthy to fighting Communists. One might have thought that the Korean intervention had proved this, beyond all possibility of doubt, but General MacArthur had gone the administration one better by his insistence that "there is no substitute for victory." Thus it was Acheson's galling duty to try to convince the senators that the administration had the greatest respect and admiration for General MacArthur and that, while not willing to bomb China as the general demanded, it hated the Chinese Communists with as pure a virulence as he, that it was determined to harass them in every way possible, and that it always had felt this way.

It should be remembered that Dean Acheson, a man strongly committed to the practice of *Realpolitik,* had always believed that to give ideology prominence over national interests in the Russo-American conflict was to "put the cart before the horse." He had been appalled by the single-minded anti-Communism of the American people in their interpretation of the Marshall Plan and disgusted by the Senate's ritual of confirmation, which had required him to show evidence of anti-Communist fanaticism as a test of fitness for the secretaryship of state. And he had always been strongly opposed to the commitment of American power to the continent of Asia and to intervention in China's civil war.

But McCarthyism had worked a marvelous transformation in the thinking of the secretary of state. It was McCarthyism that had forced him to prostrate himself before a Senate committee to plead his innocence of treason. It was McCar-

thyism that had forced him to constantly defend the State
Department against charges of disloyalty, while throwing individual department employees to the McCarthyite wolves. It
was McCarthyism that had led him to conclude that it was
proper to "put the cart before the horse" and to expend more
energy fighting Communists than in looking after the security
and well-being of America. And it was McCarthyism that
would set the terms of his confrontation with the senators at
the MacArthur hearings, where Acheson not only tried to
set the administration right with General MacArthur but even
more so with Senator McCarthy by proving that the Truman
Administration had never really intended to disengage itself
from the continent of Asia, or to avoid military involvement
there, or to normalize relations with Communist China.

Acheson insisted that the administration opposed the recognition of China and that there never had been a time when it
had given serious thought to such action. But the secretary
was not being entirely candid. Certainly that option had been
under consideration when the State Department's Round
Table on China policy was told by Far Eastern expert Walton
Butterworth in October of 1949 that the United States "will
keep the traditional service [consulates] at Peking, Tientsin,
and Shanghai, Nanking and Hong Kong, and we have no intention of closing them." [35] This amounted to *de facto* recognition. Moreover, the China experts at that famous Round
Table, upon being asked to discuss the question of recognition,
expressed a strong consensus in favor of an early normalization of relations with China.[36] .

When the subject was raised of the administration's view on
the admission of Communist China to the United Nations,

35. *Institute of Pacific Relations*, p. 1565.
36. *Ibid.*, pp. 1558–1570.

Acheson was probably much relieved that no one recalled his public statement of March 1950 in which he had stated that, while the United States would not vote for the seating of China, *it would not oppose it.* Thus he was in a position to boast of the fact that of the seventy-seven times the question of that government's admission to the forty-six different United Nations agencies had come up, the United States had defeated it seventy-six times. It was defeated on the seventy-seventh attempt without American intervention. By way of summarizing his position and giving it the emotional impact that the McCarthyite mood required, he quoted General Marshall's proud moral boast, "We cannot allow governments that want to get in the United Nations to shoot their way in." [37]

On the question of why the administration should have reversed itself on the Formosa question and rushed back to the defense of that island at the time of its intervention in Korea, Mr. Acheson found himself on a hook not easily escaped. When pressed very hard by Senator Knowland as to why Formosa should have been written off as of no strategic importance, Acheson insisted that he had never regarded it as of no importance: "I never had the slightest doubt about the fact that it was of strategic importance and that our Chiefs of Staff thought so, and that means should be taken . . . to prevent it from falling into hostile hands." Why then, Knowland wondered, had a State Department advisory memorandum of December 23, 1949, instructed America's diplomatic officials around the world to try to correct the "mistaken popular conception of its strategic importance to United States defense in the Pacific." The secretary answered this by explaining that the memorandum was simply an information

37. *Military Situation in the Far East,* p. 1728.

paper, instructing officials to do all they could to minimize the effect of Formosa's fall.[38]

Senator Knowland did not get the opportunity to complete his questioning, and so some loose ends were left hanging. For example, if Formosa did have strategic value for the United States, why then had it been written off, not only in the State Department's information paper of December 1949 but in the administration's officially announced policy of January 5, 1950. In a friendly exchange with Senator John Sparkman of Alabama, Acheson offered the lame explanation that Formosa had been written off in 1950 for the simple reason that the United States had not been able to defend it.[39] But, if this were true, how had it suddenly become possible to defend the island less than six months later? The truth is that the administration was now defending Formosa and heatedly denying that it had ever intentionally written off the island for the simple reason that America's supreme "commie-fighters" Joseph McCarthy and General Douglas MacArthur had decreed it to be the rankest heresy to question either the strategic value of that island or the greatness and goodness of its ruler.

Then there was the question of why the United States had violated its own offshore perimeter of defense by rushing back to the Asian continent to defend South Korea. Senator Styles Bridges of New Hampshire tried to corner Acheson on this point but succeeded no better than others who tried it. Bridges only wanted the secretary to admit that, in drawing the offshore perimeter, he had excluded Korea from the area that the United States would defend with military force. Acheson could not deny this obvious fact, but he found a way

38. *Ibid.,* pp. 1804–1805.
39. *Ibid.,* p. 1810.

to explain the Korean intervention without admitting that the administration had reversed its policy, which could not be admitted under any circumstances. He reminded the senator that, when he drew the offshore perimeter in his National Press Club speech on January 12, 1950, he had told those nations outside the perimeter that, for their own defense, they should look mainly to themselves and then to that "no weak reed" the United Nations.[40] Apparently then, the vague, meaningless "no weak reed" statement had actually been the very heart and soul of America's Far Eastern policy, while the strong, clear non-involvement statements of January 5 and 12 had been no more than empty generalities.

The ultimate humiliation for Secretary Acheson came in connection with a speech by Assistant Secretary of State for Far Eastern Affairs Dean Rusk. On May 18, just two weeks before Acheson was to take the stand at the MacArthur hearings, Rusk spoke at the China Institute dinner in New York City and delivered himself of an emotional diatribe that Senator Joseph McCarthy would have been proud to deliver. Communist China was disposed of in this manner:

> China has been driven by foreign masters into an adventure of foreign aggression which cuts across the most fundamental national interests of the Chinese people. This action stands condemned by the great world community in which the Chinese people have always aspired to play a worthy role. . . . We do not recognize the authorities in Peiping for what they pretend to be. The Peiping regime may be a colonial Russian government—a Slavic Manchukuo on a larger scale. It is not the Government of China. It does not pass the first test. *It is not Chinese.* [Italics added.] [41]

The assistant secretary was convinced that China would again be free, and freedom meant domination by the Chiang regime,

40. *Ibid.,* pp. 1740–1741.
41. *Ibid.,* Appendix J., p. 3191.

for, said Rusk, "We believe it more authentically represents the views of the great body of the people of China. . . ." [42] He then concluded with these alarming words, "If the Chinese people decide for freedom, they shall find friends among all the peoples of the earth who have known and love freedom."[43]

This stopped just short of the MacArthur plan for attacks upon China in league with Chiang Kai-shek. When asked by Senator Bridges, two weeks later, if this did not signal a change in administration policy toward Chiang and Formosa, Acheson replied that all the statements of policy contained in the speech "have been followed for a long time and are still being followed and we will still continue to follow them." [44] This must have been a moment almost too painful for Acheson to endure. He had been forced to press Chiang Kai-shek to his bosom once again and to reaffirm a complete solidarity of interest between the United States and the "incompetent bunglers of the Kuomintang."

The incredible contradictions in the administration position have never been satisfactorily explained, and the explanations offered raise more questions than they answer. If the administration, when drawing its offshore defense perimeter in the Pacific, had deliberately put a breach in it, through which the United States could rush back to the Asian continent (behind that "no weak reed" the United Nations), why had it bothered to draw the line in the first place? And if the Administration always had been as strongly committed to the Chiang regime and the defense of Formosa as was indicated in Acheson's endorsement of the Rusk speech, why had it stated so clearly and emphatically on January 5, 1950, that it would not defend Formosa? Finally, if the Korean War was fought largely as an indication to Europeans of American steadfastness, why

42. *Ibid.,* p. 3192.
43. *Ibid.*
44. *Ibid.,* p. 1739.

was the administration so contemptuous of European fears that their own security was endangered by an overcommitment of American power to the Far East?

If one seeks clarification in Acheson's memoirs, the mystery is only deepened, for Acheson, who had no love for cold war revisionists, was one of the first of them and one of the cleverest. In the face of the McCarthy onslaught, between February 9 and June 26, 1950, he changed his policy from one of stalwart non-interventionism in Asia to one of extreme China-harassment and then worked hard at revising interpretations to make it appear that he had never held any view but the latter. But when Acheson was preparing his memoirs in the late 1960s, the policy of intervention, whether in Korea, Formosa, or Indochina, had been shown up for the monstrous error it had been. Thus, in the memoirs, one finds Mr. Acheson busily revising interpretations once again, trying to give the impression that he had never pursued a policy of harassment of China and, indeed, that he had never departed from his offshore position in any significant way.

In discussing Korea in his memoirs, Acheson clung to the view that the intervention there had been no departure from the offshore line but, rather, a selfless, idealistic action, above and beyond the call of America's defense needs, taken on behalf of the ideal of world law under United Nations auspices. The memoirs dealt with the Formosa question by simply ignoring it. Although one finds a passing mention of the fact that the Seventh Fleet had been sent to the Formosa Strait at the time of the Korean intervention, Acheson did not even take up the question of the renewed and enlarged—and permanent, as it would prove to be—commitment to Chiang Kai-shek. One would get the impression that no such action had ever been taken or that, if it had, it had been done without the knowledge of the secretary of state. The Indochina matter was dealt with in a late chapter of the memoirs, entirely apart from discussions of the dramatic policy reversals of 1950. It is seen in the context of European policy, France apparently having been bribed to participate in its own defense in Europe by promises of American assistance to its defense of Indochina. Or, as Acheson explained it in an interview of later years, "The French blackmailed us." [45]

President Truman had no such difficulties as Acheson in harmonizing his true feelings with his own administration's dizzying policy shifts. More the anti-Communist ideologue than Acheson, he probably found it as easy to project China into the "world Communist conspiracy" as it had been to transform the power struggle with Russia into an ideological-military crusade against Communism. In any case, from the moment when he made his impulsive decision to "stop the sons-of-bitches" in Korea, he apparently never took a backward glance or indulged in the vain and morally debilitating game of second-guessing himself. He moved forward in the firm conviction that he was right, whether he was preserving the United Nations, forestalling a "second Munich," symbolizing American resolution for Europeans, or "stopping the Russians."

Still, there were times, particularly after he left the Presidency, when the matter-of-fact Harry Truman must have found it very difficult to keep himself convinced that he had always consistently followed the policy in which he truly believed. At the age of seventy-seven, he gave this very interesting assessment of Chiang Kai-shek and his American friends:

> They [the Asialationists] wanted me to send in about five million Americans to rescue him [Chiang], but I wouldn't do it. There wasn't *anything* that could be done to save him and he was as

45. Quoted in Foster Rhea Dulles, *American Foreign Policy Toward Communist China, 1949–1969* (New York: Thomas Y. Crowell, 1972), p. 125. See also Acheson, *op. cit.*, particularly Chapter 70.

corrupt as they come. I wasn't going to waste one single American life to save him, and I didn't care what they said. They hooted and hollered and carried on and said I was soft on Communism and I don't know what all. But I never gave in on that, and I never changed my mind about Chiang and his gang. Every damn one of them ought to be in jail, and I'd like to live to see the day they are.[46]

These were undoubtedly the true and honest convictions of Harry Truman, and, for the most part, quite accurate.

But Mr. Truman's recollections in his declining years are far more interesting for what he failed to recall. He remembered how "They hooted and hollered and carried on and said I was soft on Communism and I don't know what all," and he recalled quite well the policy he had pursued up to June 1950: "I wasn't going to waste one single American life to save him [Chiang], and I didn't care what they said." But those painful policy reversals of 1950 were not remembered accurately, and Mr. Truman was quite in error when he asserted "I never gave in on that. . . ." The fact is that he had given in on that and had indeed gone to the rescue of "Chiang and his gang" when, on June 27, 1950, he sent the Seventh Fleet to the Formosa Strait. Of course, Mr. Truman continued to say some rather hard things about Chiang Kai-shek in 1951 and to insist, quite correctly, that it had been impossible to save Chiang on the mainland of Asia. But saving mainland China for Chiang or saving Formosa for Chiang came to pretty much the same thing. Either course meant saving the "Chiang gang," without thereby serving an American interest, and there is little doubt that the "hooting and hollering" had much to do with this decision.

46. Quoted in Merle Miller, *Plain Speaking: An Oral Biography of Harry S. Truman* (New York: Berkeley, distributed by G. P. Putnam's Sons, 1974), p. 283.

Certainly the "hooting and hollering" go far to explain the secretary of state's attempts to explain away the writing-off of Formosa in January 1950. It explains why Acheson and his colleagues labored so desperately to rationalize away all foreign policy decisions of the past that were displeasing to the McCarthyites. They knew that if they failed to sustain in the public mind the conviction of an administration totally dedicated to fighting Communists, the brand of treason being applied to them would be indelibly fixed. And, since McCarthy had preempted for himself the role of chief "commie-fighter" at home, they would have to win for the administration the role of chief "commie-fighter" abroad. That line had been laid down by the President in the spring of 1950, even before the eruption of the Korean War: "We know that the greatest threat to this country does not come from the Communists in this country, where they are a noisy but small and universally despised group. The *greatest threat comes from Communist imperialism abroad. . . .*" (Italics added).[47] It was imperative that the American people be convinced that they were being saved from this threat by the Truman Administration.

The activities of Acheson and others in this regard have been noted, and even General Marshall joined in the endeavor. He would not go along with the MacArthur plan for attacking China, and he was not willing to see wars on the periphery of China as more than delaying actions: "Our efforts in Korea have given us some sorely needed time and impetus to accelerate the building of our defenses and those of our allies against the threatened onslaught of Soviet imperialism."[48] Still, Marshall had accepted the Truman Administration's ideologized foreign policy with all its sweeping

---

47. See p. 172.
48. *Military Situation in the Far East,* p. 325.

assumptions and its Olympian moral judgments. At the Mac-
Arthur hearings he presented the image of one who, like
Truman and Acheson, would never compromise with evil or
negotiate with sinners, expressing confidence that the United
States will always oppose "any settlement of the Korean conflict which would reward the aggressor in any manner whatsoever, and it will oppose the attempt of any nation or regime
to shoot its way into the United Nations." [49]

But no matter how hard and fast the Truman people talked
or how loud and often they protested their violent hatred of
"the commies," they could not escape the trap that, like a
gigantic pincers, was closing upon them. Just as Senator Mc-
Carthy had outflanked them on the issue of "Communism
within," General MacArthur had outflanked them on the issue
of "Communism without" in his demand for victory in Asia.
Perceiving, with the instincts of a gutter fighter, that the administration's only avenue of escape had been cut off, Mc-
Carthy rushed to co-opt the MacArthur position. He would
now assert that the administration was as soft on Communism
abroad as at home.

It was thus no mere coincidence that McCarthy made his
most damning charges against the Truman Administration
within a month of the adjournment of the MacArthur hearings. He asserted it as fact that America had been brought
from the pinnacle of power at the end of World War II to the
very brink of disaster as the result of the sinister machinations
of key figures in the American government:

> How can we account for our present situation where we believe that
> men high in the Government are concerting to deliver us to disaster.
> This must be the product of a great conspiracy, a conspiracy on a
> scale so immense as to dwarf any previous such venture in the
> history of man. A conspiracy of infamy so black, when it is

49. *Ibid.*, p. 323.

finally exposed, its principals shall be forever deserving of the maledictions of all honest men.[50]

In a 60,000-word diatribe delivered to the Senate on June 14, 1951, McCarthy spelled out the details of this alleged conspiracy.

But who were the guilty parties? As could have been expected, Dean Acheson and Alger Hiss were assigned important roles in the gigantic plot. But these men had been relatively minor figures in the government during most of the period of the plot's unfolding. To make the conspiracy theory stick, McCarthy needed to find a key figure who had been high in administration councils during and immediately after World War II, one already weakened in public confidence by repeated insinuations of disloyalty. General Marshall was perfectly cast for the role. He had participated in important policy decisions during and after the war; he had already been under heavy attack and had no powerful political base from which to fight back; moreover, he was too much the high-minded gentleman to engage in a gutter brawl with the likes of Joe McCarthy. What was most frightening about all this was that McCarthy could now, with perfect impunity, deliver the fatal blow: "It is when we return to an examination of General Marshall's record since the spring of 1942 that we approach an explanation of the carefully planned retreat from victory." [51]

It was almost beyond belief that such outrageous things could be said, let alone believed. The reputation of one of America's greatest and most selfless public servants had been irreparably damaged, and there was no way that the administration could effectively refute the charges. For a long time now it had been trying to obscure the fact that Marshall had

50. *Congressional Record*, XCVII, 82nd Cong., 1st Sess. (1951), p. 6602.
51. *Ibid.*

once attempted, in entire good faith, to mediate between the Communists of China and Chiang Kai-shek in a desperate effort to save the latter, and failing in that, had wisely recommended that the United States draw back from the Asian continent. But the administration, no longer willing to admit that it had ever attempted to disengage itself from the Asian continent, could only have been embarrassed by the continued presence in its ranks of a man who had been so much associated with a policy of disengagement and too little associated with the senseless harassment of China. Thus, when the ailing general was forced to leave his post as secretary of defense in September, the administration was probably not sorry to see him go, although it was indeed a sad moment for America. The departure of this great man perfectly symbolized the victory of McCarthyite fanaticism over calm, reasoned judgment in the conduct of the nation's Far Eastern policy.

EPILOGUE

Harassment of China Institutionalized
(1951–1971)

Senator Joseph McCarthy's victory was no small or minor aberration. He had swept all before him and set the terms of America's Far Eastern policy for the next quarter century. No important political leader, including the handful who dared fight him on the domestic front, had the courage to challenge his anti-Communist dispensation in foreign policy. It was the fear of McCarthy—and only this—that explains the Senate's refusal in October to confirm Philip Jessup as a delegate to the United Nations, for here was a veteran diplomat who had been repeatedly cleared for the most sensitive work at the highest echelons of the State Department. And it was the same terrible dread of the McCarthy wrath that led the executive branch to conduct a campaign—participated in by both the Truman and Eisenhower administrations—to hound out of the State Department the nation's ablest China specialists. Among the victims were those extraordinarily knowledgeable and gifted China experts John Carter Vincent, John Paton Davies, Edmund Clubb, and John Stewart Service, of whom it was said, in the final disposition of their cases, that they lacked "judgment, discretion and reliability." What this meant, if indeed it meant anything at all, was that these men had been more concerned with the vital interests of the United States than with "fighting commies," and for that, Senator McCarthy had put the kiss of death on them: they were "soft on Communism."

The American press, like the politicians, crumpled up before McCarthy. There were, of course, liberal journals like *The Nation* and the *New Republic* and a few liberal newspapers that deplored McCarthy's methods and challenged the scope of his operations. There were even a few conservative publications—including at least two who out-McCarthyed McCarthy in foreign affairs, *The New York Times* and Henry Luce's Chiang-adoring *Life* and *Time*—that found the courage to engage in this exercise in respectability. But no publication of consequence and no public figure of note challenged McCarthy's purpose or dared suggest that the nation abandon "commie-fighting" adventures abroad. Even that determined little band of liberals, the Americans for Democratic Action, came up with their own comprehensive program of "commie-fighting" in Asia. As reported by the liberal *New Republic*, they praised the United Nations' resistance to "communist aggression in Korea," called for aid to Chiang Kai-shek, and opposed the admission of China to the U.N., or recognition by the United States, until China subscribed to U.N. principles.[1]

America's liberals did try to keep at least one foot planted on solid ground through their strong opposition to General MacArthur's call for air and naval attacks upon China, just as in future years they would quibble with conservatives over whether or not the defense of the islands of Quemoy and Matsu, within spitting distance of the China mainland, was essential to the defense of Formosa (presidential election of 1960, for example) and as to whether or not the defense of South Vietnam required the bombing of North Vietnam and,

1. *New Republic,* March 5, 1951.

if so, how near to the China border. Conservatives, meanwhile, would go on muttering angrily about "no-win wars" and
"privileged sanctuaries" and even demanding that the American Air Force "nuke 'em" or "bomb them back to the stone
age." But even conservatives, generally speaking, were not
prepared to recommend the one course of action that might
have brought them the victory they craved—that is, all-out war
against China.

For the conservative catchphrase "no-win war," the liberals
substituted the more sophisticated "limited war." With this
obscurantist theory, they undertook to prove that the United
States could provide perfect security for itself and the so-called
free world, at the same time avoiding a nuclear showdown
among the great powers, by fighting the all-conquering puppets of Russia and/or China one at a time, presumably *ad
infinitum*. America's tough—but limited—liberal warriors never
explained how they would hold those tenuous beachheads
around China's periphery by "limited war" if the time ever
came when a defense against China was actually needed—
that is, when China became a nuclear power.

They did not have to explain, because the question was not
generally asked, as, in fact, very few embarrassing questions
were asked of "commie-fighters" during those years. This was
fortunate for them, for if that pertinent question had been
asked, these "limited warriors" might have been forced to
explain how it was that they had suddenly discovered that it
was necessary to defend remote, inconsequential little Asian
lands only after Senator Joseph McCarthy had begun to brand
them (the liberals) as "soft on Communism."

Since the only important question for the United States—
whether or not it should be involved on the continent of Asia
at all—could not even be discussed, the debate over Far Eastern policy always settled down to a squabble between Tweedle-
dee and Tweedledum: Should American involvement around

the periphery of China be somewhat more or somewhat less? That this would be the nature of things for some time to come, and that America's Far Eastern policy would be characterized by neither courage nor vision, was clearly presaged in the presidential election campaign of 1952. Republican Dwight Eisenhower and Democrat Adlai Stevenson both committed themselves to peace-making in Korea but quibbled over how difficult the task would be and who was best equipped to accomplish it. Eisenhower seemed to think he would have no great difficulty arranging peace in Korea. Besides, said he, in one of his grandest non sequiturs, "I will go to Korea." Candidate Stevenson dared not try to top that. Rather, said he, he would "talk sense to the American people": peace-making would be a slow and tedious process of negotiation, accompanied by a slow and tedious war—"limited," of course. Neither candidate indicated that he would even consider withdrawing from positions that did not, in any way, strengthen America's defenses, advance American economic interests, or serve the cause of American democracy. Both undoubtedly knew these things, but they also knew that to back away from a war against "the commies"—little matter how senseless—would have been displeasing to Senator McCarthy.

"For two decades into the future . . ." said George F. Kennan, "there would not be a President who would not stand in a certain terror of the anti-Communist right wing of the political spectrum and would not temper his actions with a view to placating it and averting its possible hostility." [2] The craven course that the Eisenhower Administration would pursue in foreign policy was clearly revealed when, during the presidential election campaign of 1952, the great hero of World War II made his obeisance to Senator McCarthy. The general's long-expected defense of his old friend and bene-

2. George F. Kennan, *Memoirs, 1925–1950,* II (Boston: Little, Brown, 1967), pp. 227–228.

factor George Marshall against McCarthy's vicious attacks turned out to be so tame as to be virtually meaningless, whereas his surrender to McCarthy was dramatic and abject. Not only was the senator extended the honor of riding across Wisconsin on the Eisenhower campaign train, he was also accorded the enormous personal satisfaction of hearing the Eisenhower headquarters announce its complete agreement with him on getting subversives out of government. As McCarthy gleefully noted, he and the general agreed on the important issues—like "fighting commies."

There was a time in 1954 when it appeared that Eisenhower might actually abandon the "China harassment" policy. He made the necessary concessions (and possibly an indirect threat to use "the bomb") to get peace in Korea, and when France's hold on Indochina (the West's beachhead on China's southern flank) was seriously threatened, he refused to go to the rescue. He quickly repented of this aberration, however, and before the year was out was pledging renewed support to South Vietnam, after France salvaged at the conference table in Geneva this non-Communist stronghold that it had not been able to secure on the battlefield. He then gave his Communist-obsessed Secretary of State John Foster Dulles almost unlimited authority to commit the United States to "commie-fighting" in Southeast Asia. In the Southeast Asia Treaty, in protocols to that treaty, and in the Formosa Resolution, Dulles broadened this American commitment during the next two years to include the possibility of direct American intervention as well as arms assistance, and he extended it beyond Formosa and Vietnam to include Laos, Cambodia, Thailand, Pakistan, and the Philippines.

With the elevation to the presidency of John Fitzgerald Kennedy in 1960 there was opened up again the possibility of a return to sanity in America's Far Eastern policy. Here was a young politician said to be of a new age and a new generation, one renowned for having chronicled great acts of political courage. It turned out, however, that John Kennedy was a politician who found it much easier to write of an act of political courage than to perform one. "I can't afford a 1954 kind of defeat now [in Vietnam]," he told White House aides.[3] The reason, as summarized by David Halberstam, was this: "He was afraid of being charged with losing a country and deserting a brave ally, and thus of the domestic implications of not having given greater aid, of not having tried." [4] And so the line had to be held everywhere and the harassment of China continued, even in the matter of China's seat in the United Nations. "You have the hardest thing in the world to sell," he told U.N. Ambassador Adlai Stevenson, "it really doesn't make any sense—the idea that Taiwan represents China. But, if we lose this fight, if Red China comes into the U.N. during our first year . . . they'll run us both out." [5]

Lyndon Johnson had no more taste than Kennedy for being "run out" of the presidency, which he inherited from the latter in 1963. After he won his own popular mandate to the office the next year, he made it clear that he too would hold South Vietnam at all costs, although he had led many people to believe during the campaign that he would not "send American boys to fight wars that should be fought by Asian boys." Sensitive to charges that he had misled the people, Johnson insisted that the American people had known perfectly well that he was not going to desert those thousands of Americans in Asia: "They were there for a purpose, to defend what four

3. David Halberstam, *The Best and the Brightest* (New York: Random House, 1972), p. 149.

4. *Ibid.*, p. 175.

5. Arthur M. Schlesinger, Jr., *A Thousand Days, John F. Kennedy in the White House* (Boston: Houghton Mifflin, 1965), p. 483.

American Presidents and the Congress of the United States had said were vital American and world interests." [6]

Johnson was not able to explain any better than the four Presidents who preceded him what those "vital American and world interests" were, but, rather, talked vague, idealistic nonsense about making it clear "that those who were ready to fight for their own freedom would find us ready at their side if they wanted us and needed us." It is not possible to believe that the tough political realist Lyndon Johnson was prepared to spend a hundred billion dollars and more than 40,000 American lives on such moral abstractions. Probably he was much nearer the point when he said: "They [the American people] knew Lyndon Johnson was not going to pull up stakes and run." [7] This then was what it was all about: Lyndon Johnson would not, as the popular parlance had it, "cut and run," especially not from Communists. He had the most vivid recollections of how the losing of China had been the undoing of Harry Truman: "A divisive debate about 'who lost Vietnam' would be, in my judgment, even more destructive to our national life than the argument over China had been." [8] "Well," Lyndon Johnson confided to intimates, "he did not want the blame for losing Vietnam, it might mean the loss of other things he wanted." [9]

The greatest irony of the whole Asian adventure is that Richard Milhouse Nixon, the man who had probably gotten the most political mileage out of "commie-fighting" and who had done as much as anyone to drive America toward its "China-harassment" policy, should have been the one to re-

6. Lyndon Baines Johnson, *The Vantage Point: Perspectives of the Presidency, 1963–1969* (New York: Holt, Rinehart and Winston, 1971), p. 68.

7. *Ibid.*

8. *Ibid.*, p. 152.

9. Halberstam, *op. cit.*, p. 425.

verse course and to begin to liquidate that foolish and tragic policy. When Nixon assumed the presidency in 1969, it had become quite clear that the American people would no longer support endless military adventures around the periphery of China. Indeed, they had never given more than grudging support to a policy that did not, in a way they could clearly understand, serve a vital national interest.

Consequently, after a last, costly attempt to hold South Vietnam, President Nixon perceived that he had no choice but to "lower the nation's profile in Asia," a policy that he began to implement by reducing the American commitment to Korea and Formosa, disengaging American troops from the fighting in South Vietnam, and beginning the process of normalizing relations with China. When the process of disengagement has been completed with the liquidation of the remaining commitments to Korea and Formosa, the United States will have returned to precisely that offshore position that it occupied from 1947 through the middle of 1950 and that, in policy statements of January 5 and January 12, 1950, had been affirmed as official and irrevocable policy.

At a cost of hundreds of billions of dollars, more than 100,000 lives, and a fearful rending of the body politic, this "China harassment" policy was doggedly pursued for a twenty-year period before the anti-Communist hysteria had subsided to the point where the sheer madness of it could, at last, be revealed and, as noted, a reversal of course be undertaken. The real tragedy of it is that the wisdom of hindsight, bought at such a terrible price, was totally unnecessary, for Harry Truman and his secretaries of state Marshall and Acheson had known from the beginning, as their numerous policy statements indicate, that the United States should never, under any circumstances, involve itself militarily on the continent of Asia. But in the end, they did not have the courage of their convictions. The Truman Administration and its four successors ran madly in pursuit of Communists around the periphery of China for no other reason than to prove that they had attained the level of anti-Communist orthodoxy demanded by "external McCarthyism." None of them ever asked, until forced by the people to do so, if an important American interest was at stake. The only question asked was concerned with domestic politics, and always implicit in the question was the answer, as Daniel Ellsberg of *Pentagon Papers* fame so cogently phrased it, "This is not the year to lose Asia to the Communists."

INDEX

ABOUT THE AUTHOR

Lewis McCarroll Purifoy is chairman of the department of history at Emory & Henry College in Virginia. He studied at Maryville College in Tennessee (B.A.), the University of Tennessee (M.A.), and the University of North Carolina (Ph.D). Under a Ford Foundation grant, Professor Purifoy studied the history of modern China in 1967–1968 at the University of North Carolina–Duke University.